AF598781

White!
Light!
Bright!

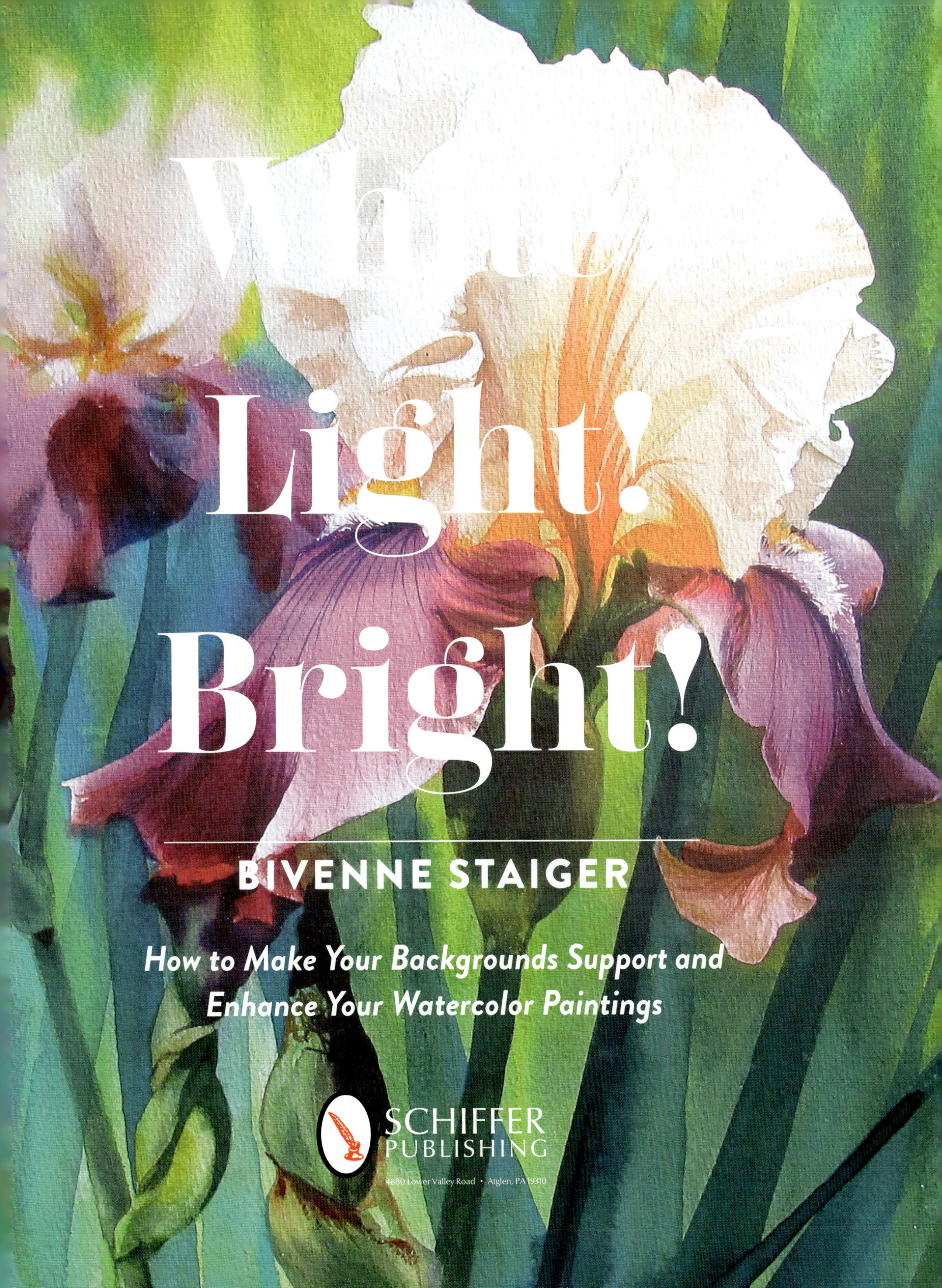

White Light! Bright!

BIVENNE STAIGER

How to Make Your Backgrounds Support and Enhance Your Watercolor Paintings

SCHIFFER PUBLISHING
4880 Lower Valley Road • Atglen, PA 19310

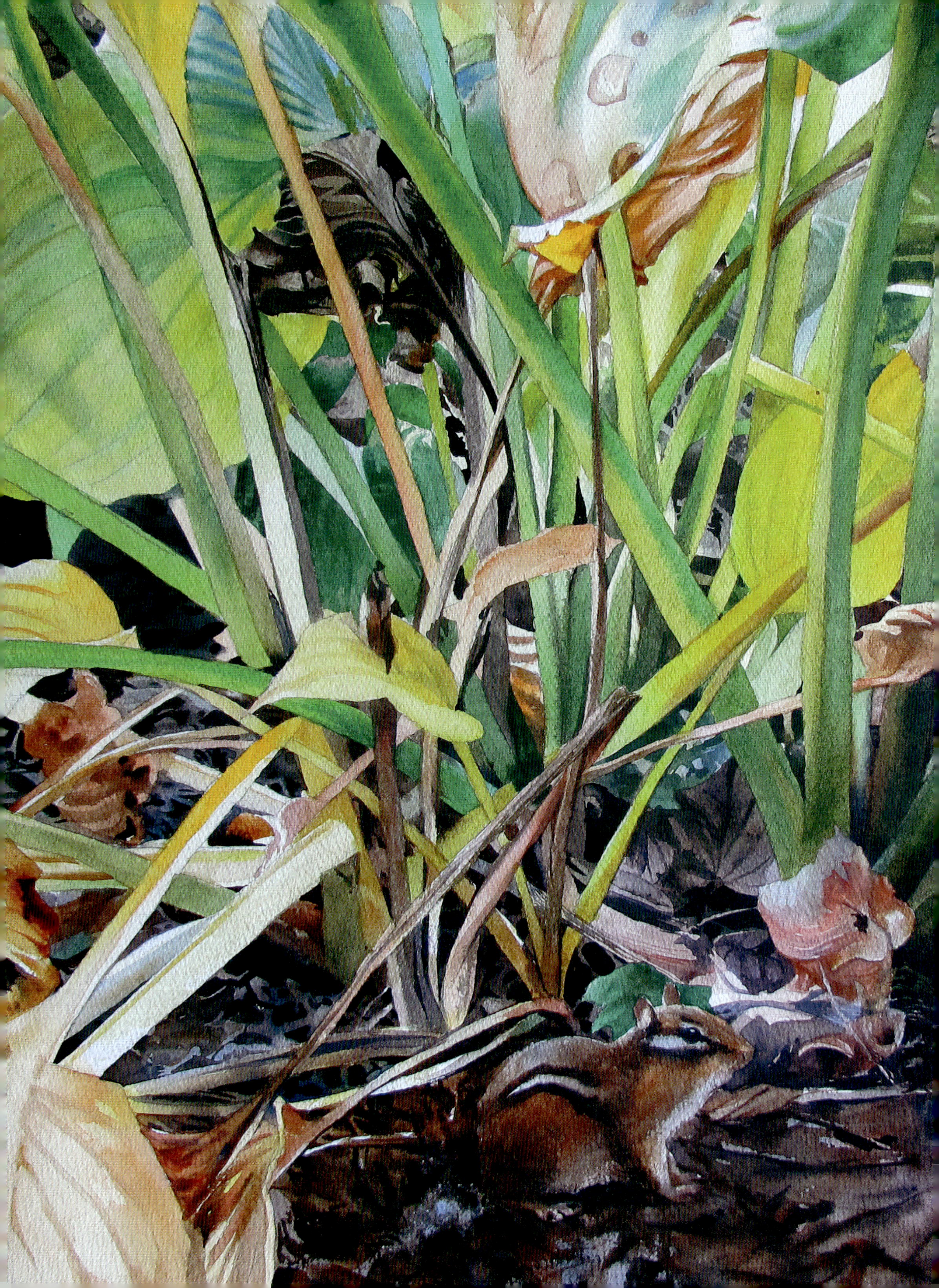

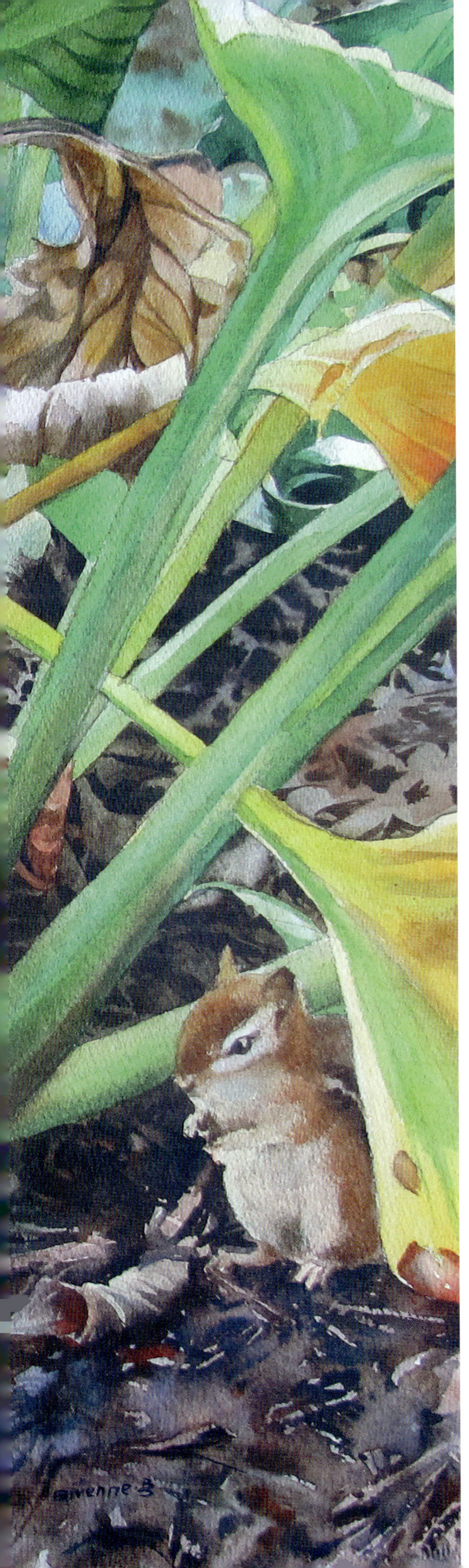

Other Schiffer Books on Related Subjects:

Painting the Elements: Air Water Earth Fire, Parramon, ISBN 978-0-7643-5953-8

Fire and Light: A Method of Painting for Artists Who Love Color, Julie H. Hanson, ISBN 978-0-7643-5217-1

Watercolor the Easy Way: Step-by-Step Tutorials for 50 Beautiful Motifs Including Plants, Flowers, Animals & More, Sara Berrenson, ISBN 978-0-7643-5982-8

Library of Congress Control Number: 2021931775

Cover design by Molly Shields
Design by Ashley Millhouse
Front cover: *Iris Spring*, 15" x 22"
Copyright page: *Hosta la Vista!*, 22" x 30"
Acknowledgements page: *Nuthatch in Spring*, 15" x 22"
Contents page: *Those Eyes!*, 11" x 15"
Type set in Carina Pro/Demos Next

ISBN: 978-0-7643-6266-8
Printed in India

Published by Schiffer Publishing, Ltd.
4880 Lower Valley Road
Atglen, PA 19310
Phone: (610) 593-1777; Fax: (610) 593-2002
E-mail: Info@schifferbooks.com
Web: www.schifferbooks.com

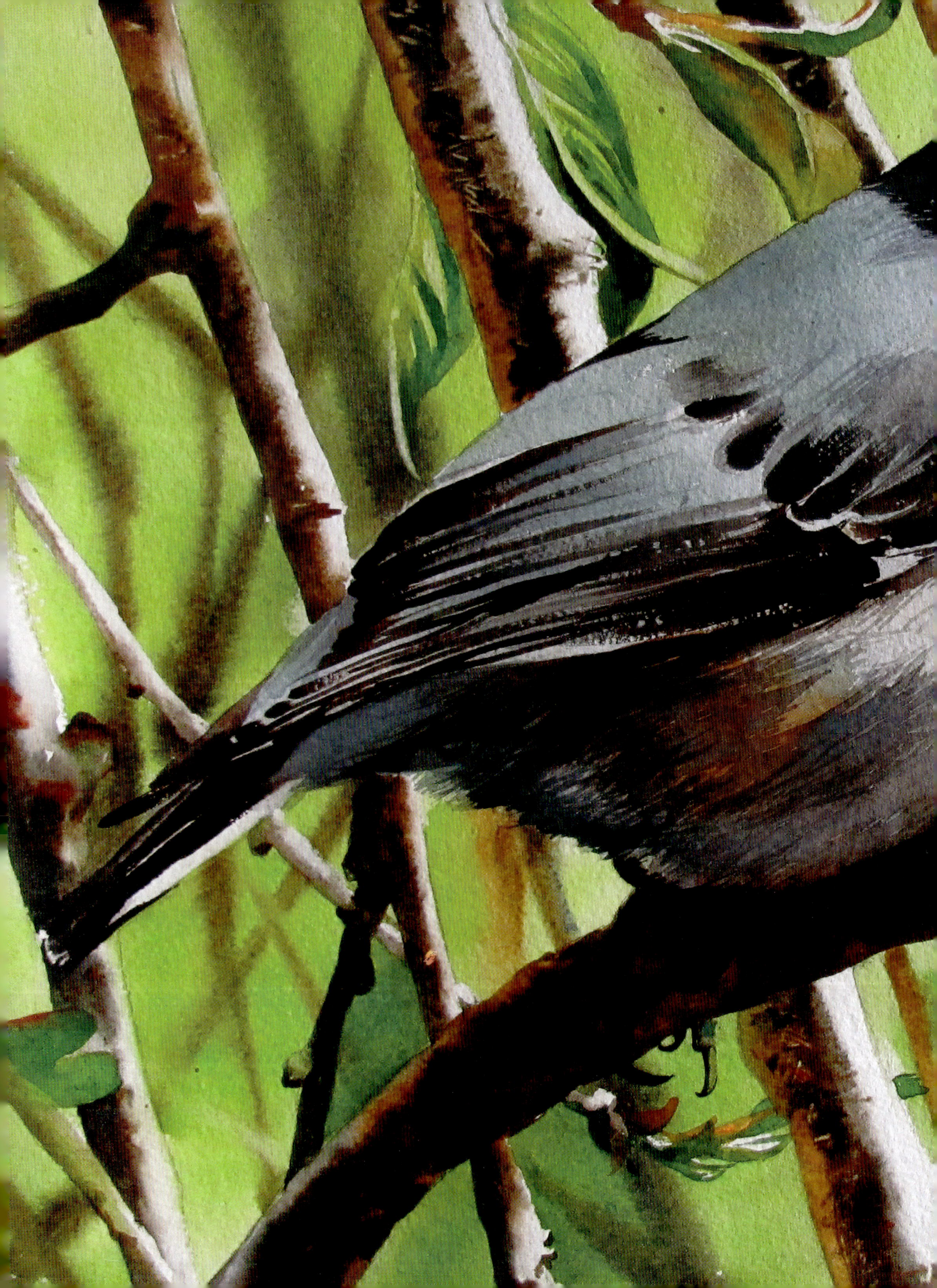

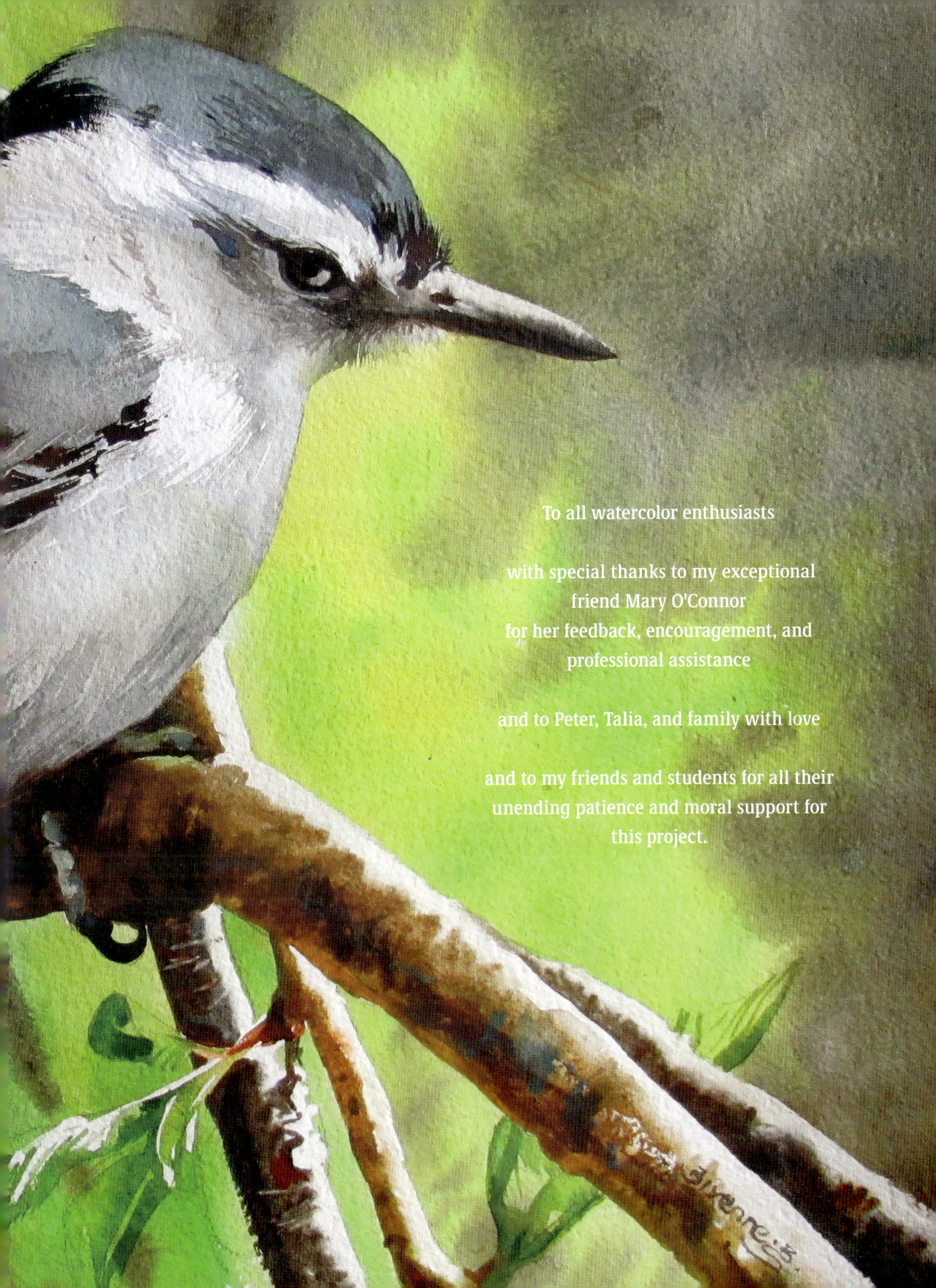

To all watercolor enthusiasts

with special thanks to my exceptional friend Mary O'Connor for her feedback, encouragement, and professional assistance

and to Peter, Talia, and family with love

and to my friends and students for all their unending patience and moral support for this project.

Contents

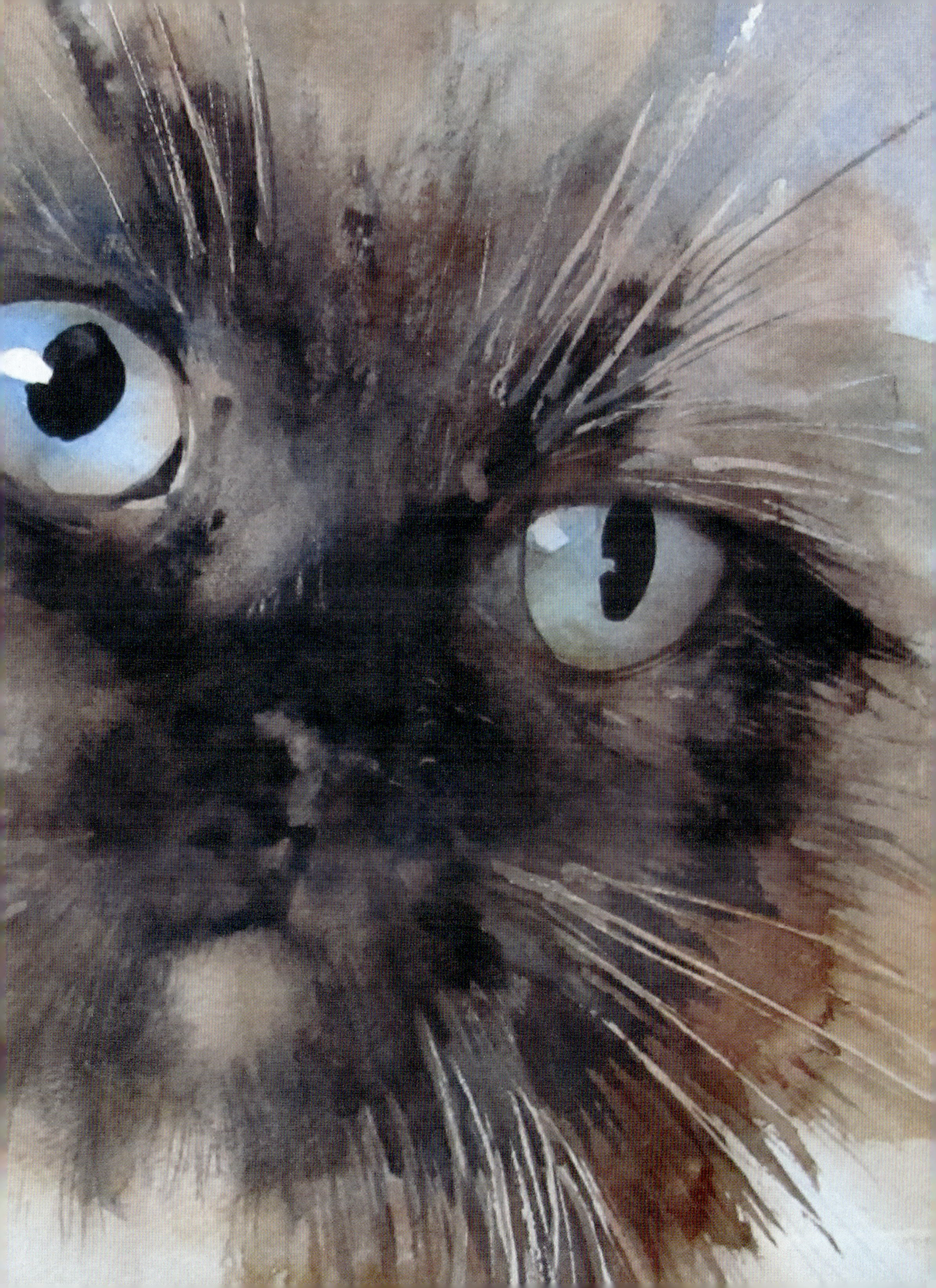

Foreword

When I was an art student majoring in painting at the Washington University School of Art, I attended a studio presentation by a graduate student who discussed his painting style and technique. Much to my dismay, this instructor stated that after graduation from college, it would take each of us perhaps ten years of work before we were able to create a distinctive style of painting in which we were proficient.

Now, forty-plus years after receiving my bachelor's degree in fine arts, I realize the wisdom in that statement, and I understand the many hours of practice that perfecting one's art and technique require. In the following volume, Bivenne Harvey Staiger lays out a clear strategy to assist the artist in defining the subject matter of a painting. With specific techniques, utilizing a careful analysis of color value and planning, she demonstrates how to set apart the primary subject of the painting.

All painting media have specific strengths and weaknesses. In watercolor, perhaps the most characteristic quality of the medium is the manner in which a fluid wash settles into the paper, leaving a distinct but subtle pattern. Some pigments that are very finely ground will create a wash that is smooth and clean, while other pigments will deposit tiny grains of material that settle into the valleys of the paper's texture, thereby creating a characteristic design that only watercolor on paper can create. In addition, the watercolor medium naturally creates a distinct, crisp edge. Oftentimes there is a slightly darker gradation at the edge of a wash. A final unique quality of watercolor is the fluid blending of colors when the wet in wet technique is employed. Utilizing these qualities to one's advantage is the mark of a successful watercolorist. The paintings within this volume illustrate these techniques. Bivenne presents a method of creating a painting so that the finished image will retain passages of white paper for the highlights, will include crisply painted middle tones applied with washes in one pass, then left to dry, and will be completed with darker passages, which set off the midtones and highlights.

One of the first compositional directives beginning students learn in laying out a design for a painting is called the law of thirds. Though perhaps labeled with different words by different artists, this rule refers to the process of dividing an image into a grid of thirds, both vertically and horizontally. When positioning the subject of the painting, one tries to place the subject approximately one-third of the distance from the edge of the image, or, said in another way, the artist tries to avoid plunking their subject matter smack dab in the middle of the painting, which would create a static design, limiting the pathways for the eye to travel in and around the image. While there can be many subtle variations to this rule, and even contradictions that may be quite successful, this is a common painting design formula. In similar fashion, this rule can be applied to the light and dark values of a painting as well. If an entire image is created with a narrow range of values, or a range of values created in a random pattern, the artist loses the chance to use the value composition of the painting to highlight and clarify the subject matter.

Planning the compositional elements of a painting to transition from white, light, and bright color to midvalues and finally to darks enables the artist to envision in their mind's eye, prior to putting the brush on paper, the final image of the painting. Planning a painting in one's imagination can be greatly facilitated with additional studies and sketches. In fact, for many artists their most accomplished works are based on numerous preparatory studies and sketches to plan a method of attack. This is most efficacious with watercolor, since the requirement to lay down a watercolor wash in certain areas once, and only once, thereby creating a crisp, clean passage of color, with no reworking, showcases the watercolor medium at its best. In this manner, the actual painting of a work becomes somewhat of a performance piece, which can be done only once. Yes, there will be future performances, but for this passage in this painting, you have only one shot.

The imagery from nature shown in Bivenne's work is favored by many artists, since most of us have ready access to the great outdoors. Many of us enthusiastically pursue our outdoor activities both for recreation and rejuvenation. On a grander scale, communing with nature, being in the out-of-doors, and then trying to capture some of that experience by re-creating a visual image of the scene is part of a long tradition of creative artistic expression, all the way from the primitive Lascaux cave paintings to the grand Hudson River landscapes. Our own painting, which documents and celebrates those animals, plants, and landscapes that we find dear to our hearts, enables us to pursue two creative endeavors at the same time: a love of nature and a pursuit of artistic creation.

As Walt Whitman said, "This is what you shall do; Love the earth and sun and the animals." For many of us of the artistic ilk, as part of our love of nature we try to recreate it in our art. Learning techniques that will facilitate that expression is to every artist's benefit.

—John Atwater, AWS
President, Connecticut Watercolor Society

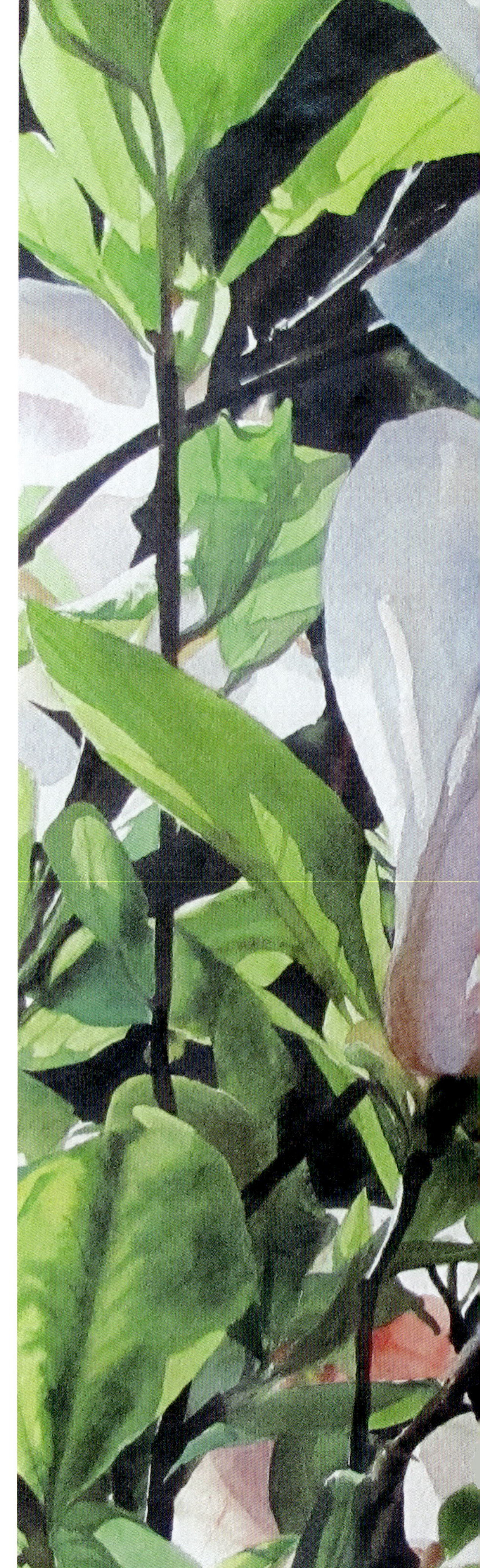

Among the Magnolias, 22" × 30"

Introduction

White! Light! Bright! is written with a twofold purpose. On the one hand, as its title suggests, it is meant to share with others the joy I personally get from painting in watercolor—to help others catch the energizing spark found in the contrast of light and dark and the magic of bright, colorful washes. These are perhaps the most frequently expressed wishes of watercolor painters.

There is, however, a second, and possibly more important, goal, as is reflected in the book's subtitle, "How to Make Your Backgrounds Support and Enhance Your Watercolor Paintings." Throughout my years of experience, I have all too often observed the frustration and disappointment of many watercolorists who have difficulty connecting their painting's background with their primary subject matter in a manner that supports, complements, enhances, and leads to distinctive work.

Backgrounds are as critical a painting element as any primary subject shape. It is the ability to incorporate them together that is the crux to a painting's success. That is the goal of this book—to unravel the secrets of watercolor through a focus on the importance of planning well and painting in a specific, three-step

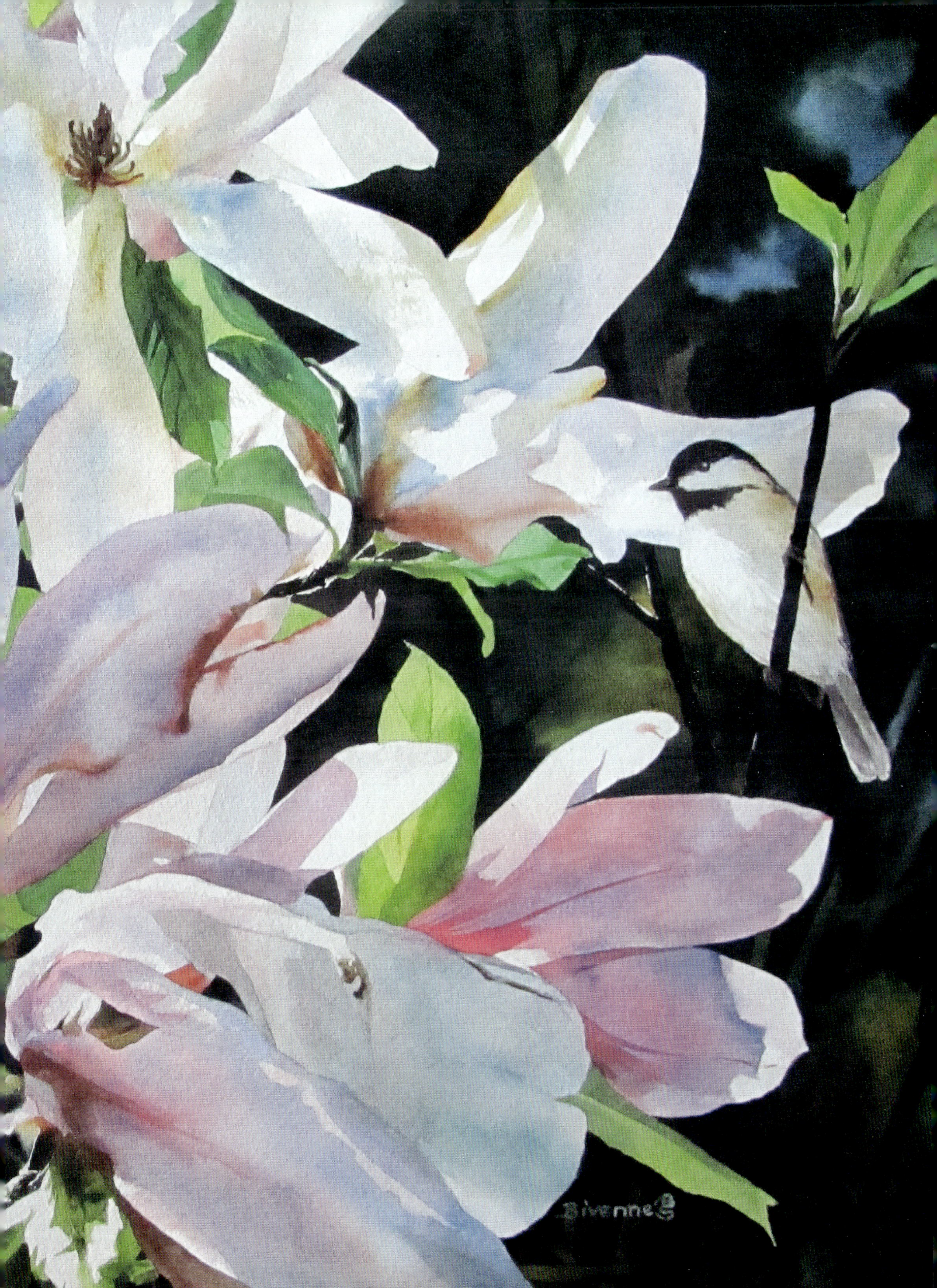

sequence that maximizes painting efficiency, success, and confidence.

I've therefore organized this book into two parts: one for planning a subject with its background, and the other for painting the two together.

The first section offers tips to focus on your motif's essential elements so that you don't have to draw and paint everything you observe. Rather, it shows you how to decide what it is about your subject—its shape or color, the lighting and shadows, patterns, or something else—and its surroundings that not only move you (and hopefully the viewer when you've completed the painting) but also will contribute to a great painting. Only you as artist can make these decisions and change elements, but Part 1 lays out how to home in on the most critical and weed others out. Planning is as important in watercolor as painting intuitively.

The second section covers the three painting stages, which are broken into individual chapters. Each acts as a foundation for the next by saving white shapes, painting bright and colorful washes, adding midvalue shapes and shadows, and finally adding dark shapes to tie every element together. This method is a result of years of my own painting experience, of overcoming the challenges every watercolorist faces at first, and which I have found makes watercolor painting very easy. I hope you will enjoy following along with me as we see how and in what order parts of a painting are brought to life.

What is painting?

Painting is in many ways an intuitive process of grouping shapes, colors, and other elements onto a flat surface of fixed dimensions. It's also an embodiment of creativity, a manifestation of a concept derived from what an artist observes or imagines.

The painting elements that visual artists use are color, value, line and direction, shape, form, space, texture, and size. These allow for freedom of expression and convey the artist's unique style. An artist might use just a few or all elements in any one painting.

Nevertheless, concepts are not always easy to explain, communicate, or render because they are essentially theoretical before they become physical works of art, and what we see and interpret is ultimately subjective. Beauty, after all, is in the eye of the beholder.

Yet, there are many aspects to painting that are not necessarily intuitive. Techniques can be learned and successful designs implemented for maximum visual effect. The ultimate goal for most artists is to capture the viewer's attention and to keep it there.

What is design?

A good design provides a pleasing structure for painting elements. Called a *composition*, this takes planning, which is made easier by using a long-established set of design principles. While some artists choose to break some or not use all, the principles of variation, contrast, harmony, emphasis, dominance, balance, variety, repetition, pattern, rhythm, proportion, and unity are not arbitrary or illogical and have proven to contribute to wonderful paintings that stand the test of time.

Often the most amazing works of art are a result of both the artist's intuition and good planning.

Representational paintings of a particular subject usually necessitate a planned arrangement of background elements that support, enhance, and don't distract from it (sometimes artists use the element of space for a blank background). Watercolorists and other visual artists most especially use color, value, and shape to represent and support their motif; other elements such as line and space are also utilized. The placement of each element in a painting affects the strength of the design.

Why is a plan for painting subject and background together essential?

Though a design plan involving subject and background applies to painting in any medium, it is particularly important to watercolor because watercolor paintings are created in stages from light to dark value, from white and brightly colored elements to dark and dull ones, and from loose, indistinct shapes to defined, identifiable details. These stages break down the painting's many potential components into three major values: white and pale, midvalue, and dark. Value is thus a key element.

A white, brightly colored, or pale value shape in a space already coated with dull or dark paint is difficult (though generally not impossible) to recover in watercolor. Therefore, since both subject and background entities can vary greatly in value, color, and shape complexity, it is essential in watercolor to plan the placement *and* timing of painting the value range with those of other painting elements so that subject and background spaces are painted simultaneously in value sequence.

Timing also affects washes and shape edges, which comprise lines. Paint applied quickly on wet paper leaves a very different edge from one painted slowly on dry paper. So a good design plan helps make painting easier and more efficient.

This book therefore guides you through the steps not only to identify the lightest, medium, and darkest values in a subject and its background, but also to efficiently paint both spaces together in the proper value sequence. Lightest values, brightest colors, and softest edges are usually painted first.

Identifying important parts of your subject and planning early how you'll emphasize them against background elements determine the timing for painting each. Maybe a key part of the subject will be painted first, if it's pale or brightly colored—or last, long after the background is complete, if it's dark, for instance (this assumes that you'll use color or value contrast as a way to emphasize something, as I often do in my work).

Similarly, planning secondary elements of the subject and background involves making decisions on whether you'll eliminate all, most, or a few, and whether and how those you are including should be reduced or emphasized using value, color, line, shape, size, or other visual cues.

Taking your idea and putting it into a physical representational painting is really a matter of *seeing*. Plan to eliminate nonessentials that distract, but include only those background elements that best support your subject. Observe stark contrasts and obvious similarities in subject and background shapes, colors, values, patterns, lines, and textures. Even if you're unaware of them, you'll incorporate subtleties in their integral elements with your sense of intuition as you paint.

Planning and painting a subject with its background is thus essential to painting quickly at times in watercolor, facilitating the process and making it much more fun!

Challenges with this medium can be overcome by practicing (more) with manipulating and controlling water in brush *and* on paper; understanding paint idiosyncrasies and value, color, and negative space painting; planning a composition that includes the background; and painting from light to dark.

I know this because I myself went through that learning curve.

For this reason, I hope to erase or at least minimize any belief that painting in watercolor is difficult, no matter where you are on your painting journey. Though I use many wildlife and especially bird and a few pet and flower motifs here, my methods of watercolor painting apply to almost any up-close subject.

It's as simple as that!

Color and value are my favorite elements because extreme value contrast empowers color. Bright watercolor paint seeping across wet paper is to me like a bird bursting into flight. Light passes through transparent paint as it does through stained glass, energizing color especially when it's juxtaposed by saturated darks.

These and other qualities therefore make watercolor unlike any other medium. With practice and despite all the planning involved, there is ample opportunity for much expression, creativity, and freedom, starting with the painting elements *you* decide to use.

You will learn how to

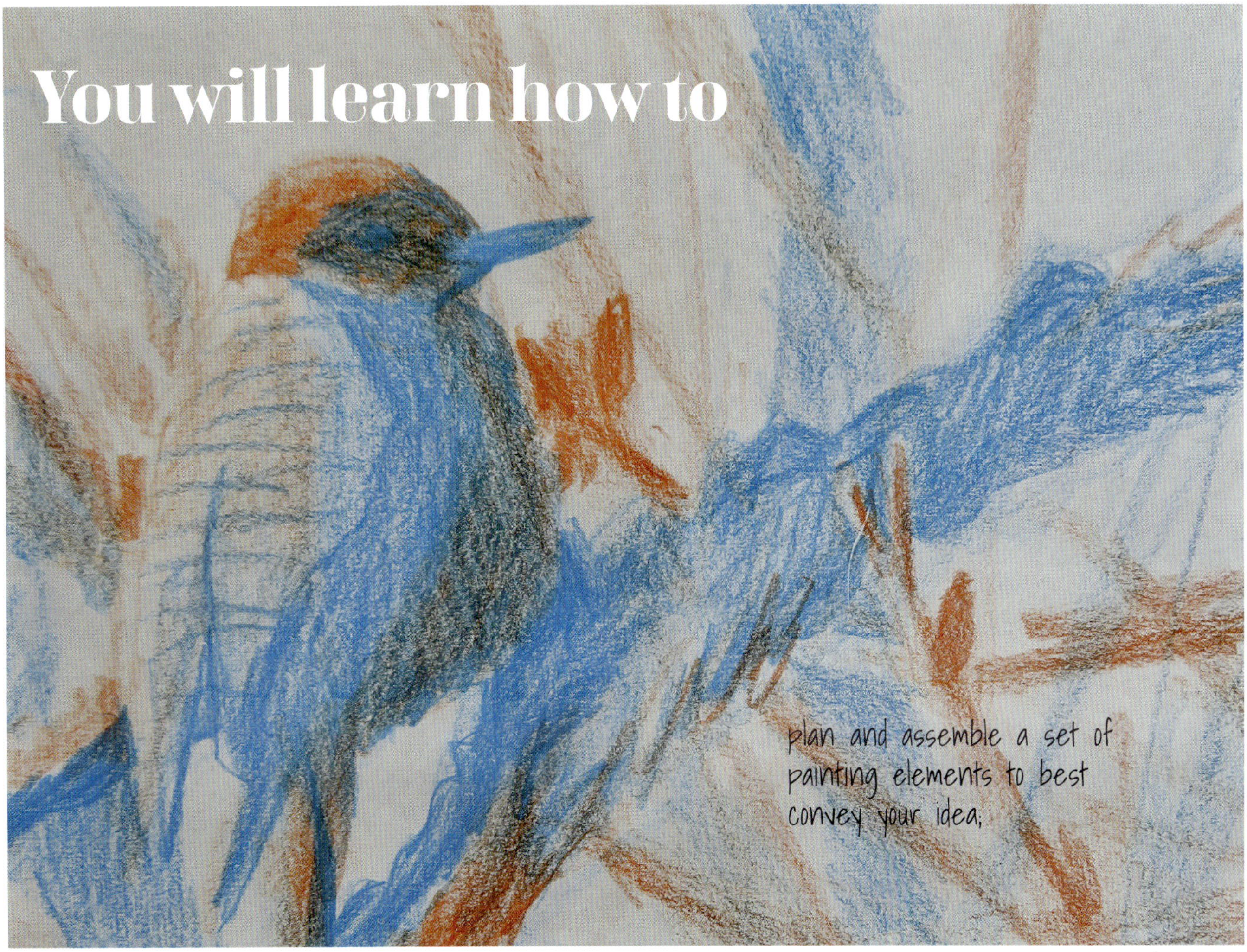

plan and assemble a set of painting elements to best convey your idea;

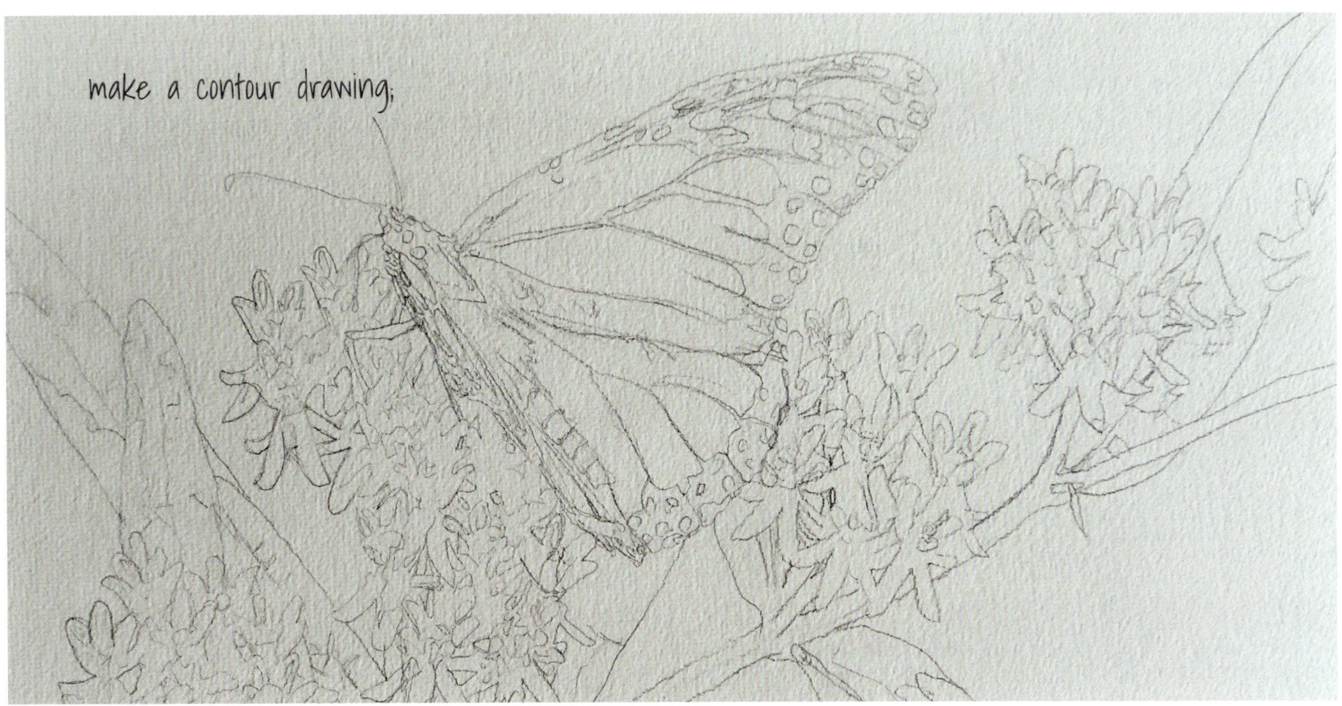

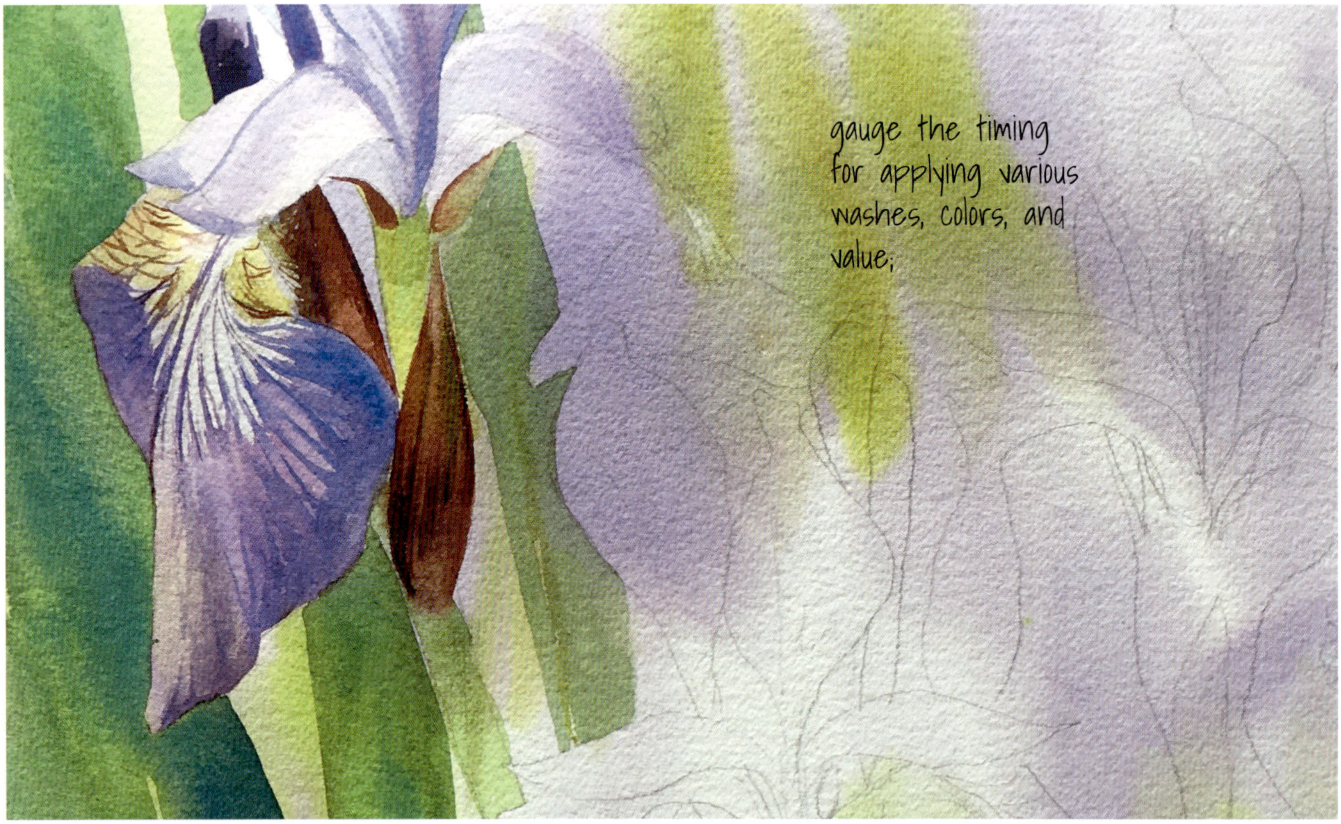

gauge the timing for applying various washes, colors, and value;

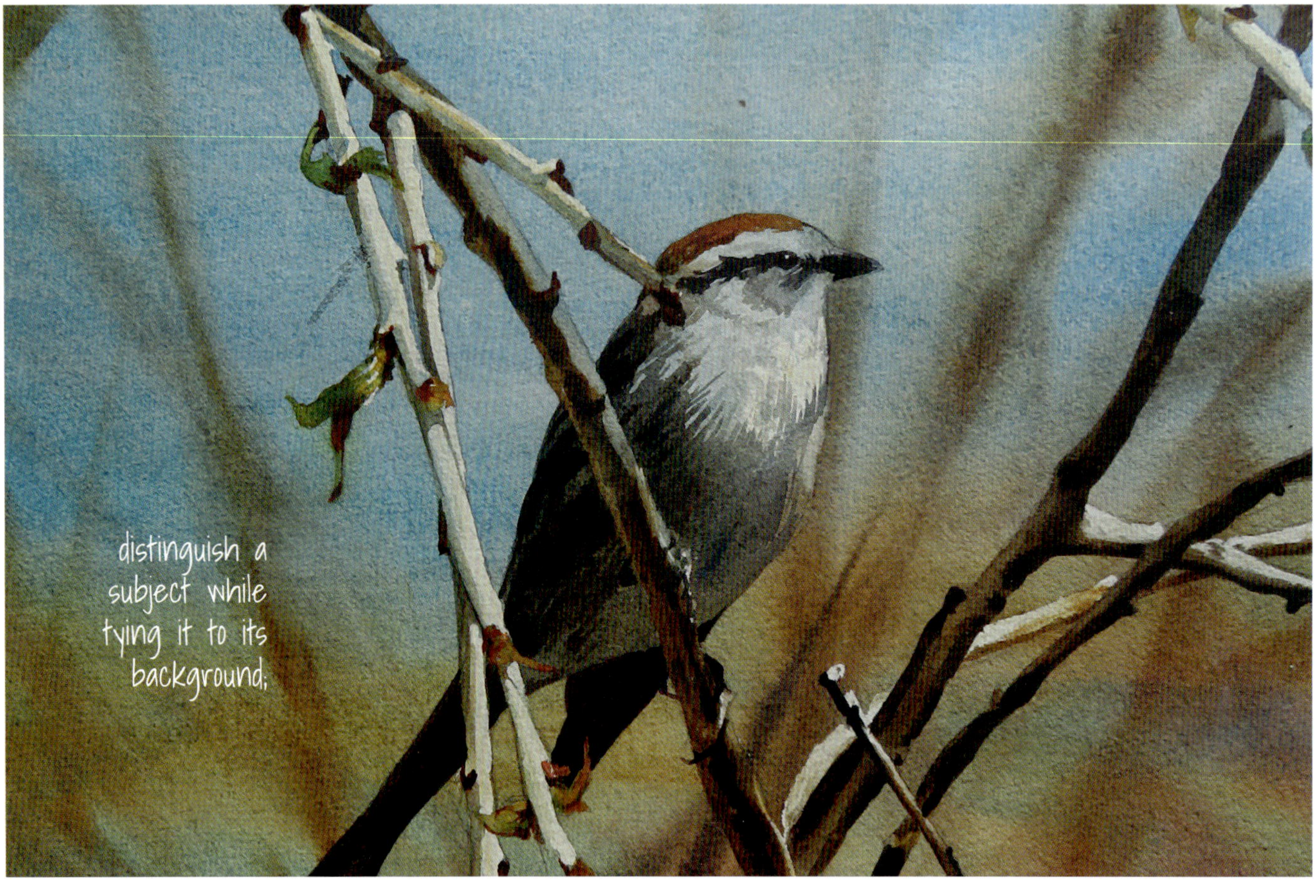

distinguish a subject while tying it to its background;

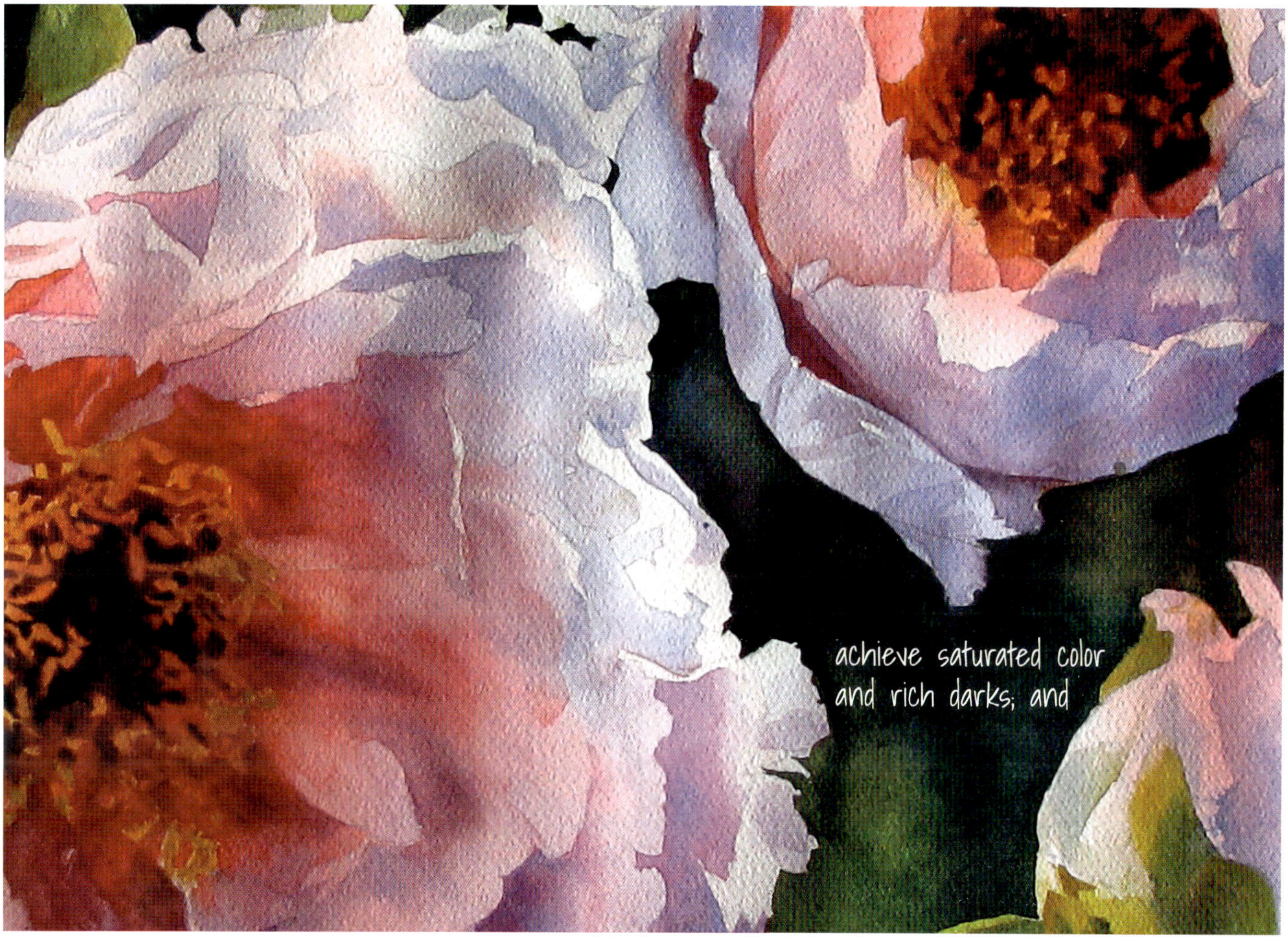

achieve saturated color
and rich darks; and

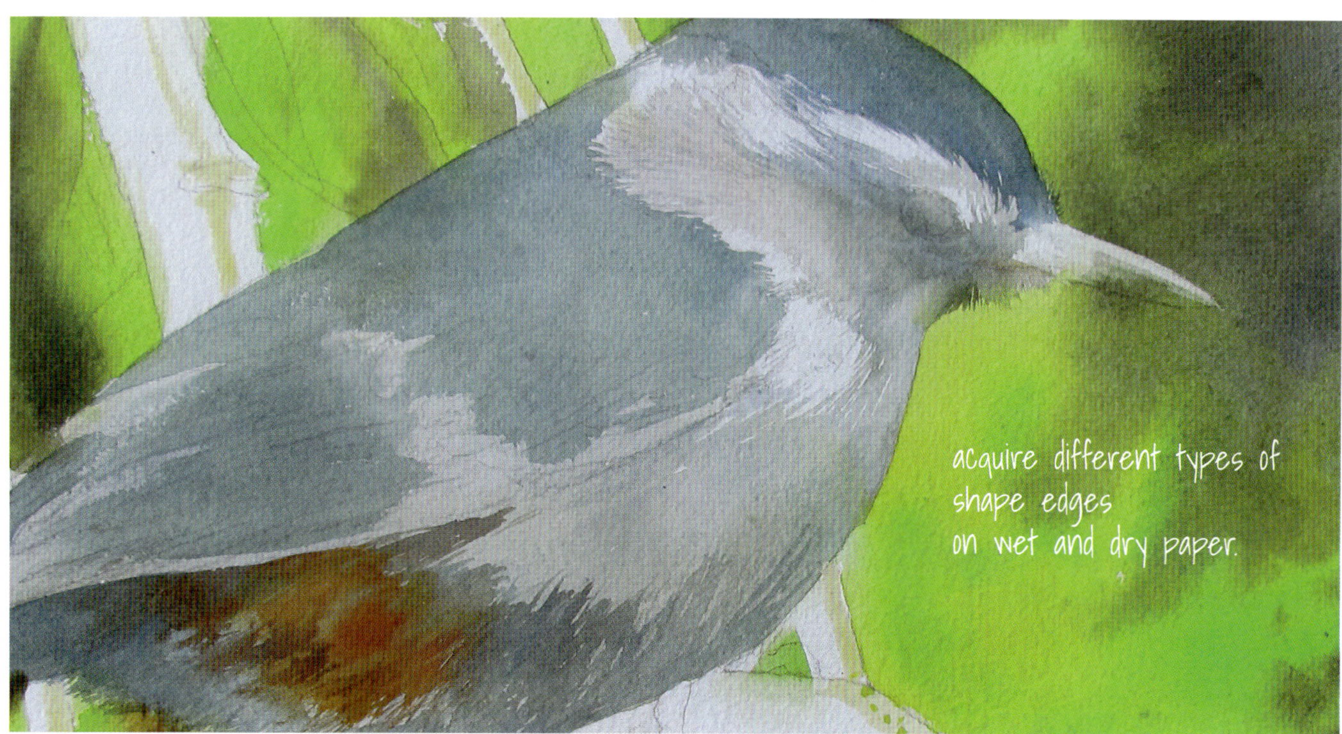

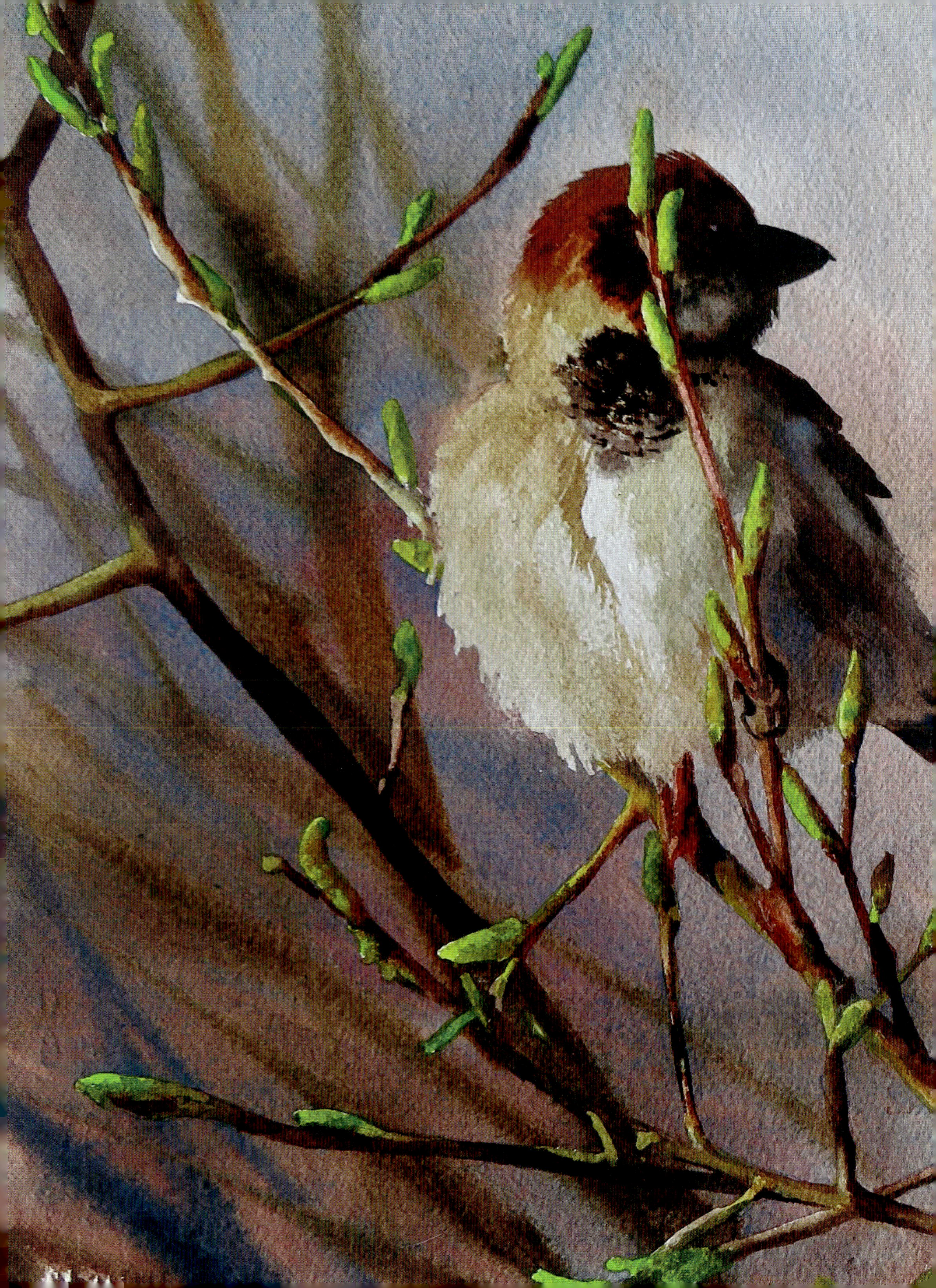

PART 1: Planning

Planning and creating a good design provides a structure for painting and is essential to watercolor. It means strategically arranging painting elements such as shapes, colors, and value, and then producing a contour drawing based on it. Preparing to paint quickly for certain effects and more slowly and carefully for others is all part of planning, too, because, as you will soon see, when as much as possible is planned ahead, it makes painting in watercolor easy and exciting.

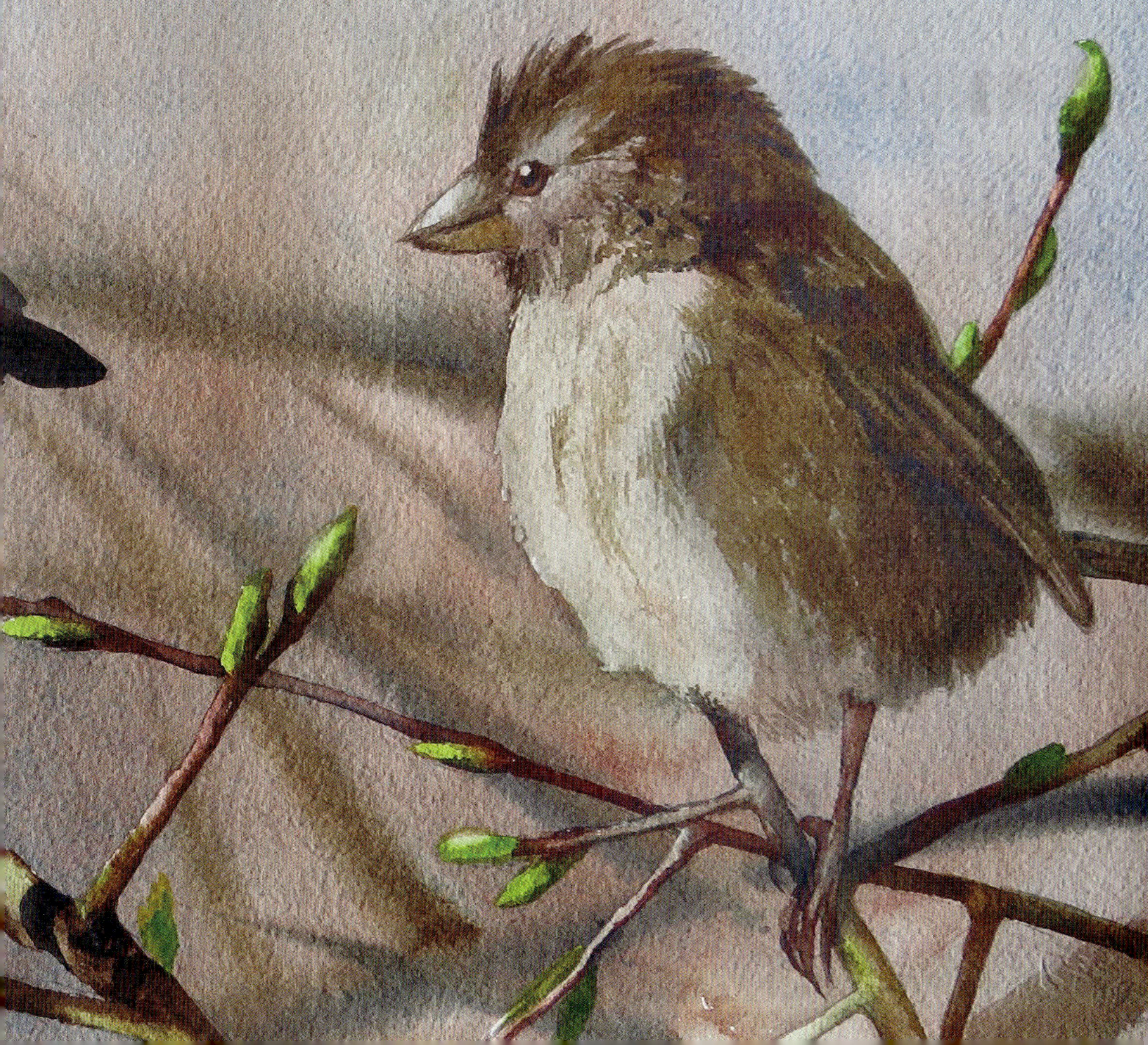

1 Designing a Subject with Its Background

Take your time to plan a proper composition.

Since brush and paper begin to dry whether or not you are ready for a particular wash, being unprepared or without a plan leaves little or no time to think through an unresolved design problem, refill an empty well with paint, thoroughly load a brush, prepare the paper, or even to control bleeding paint. Having all of this resolved beforehand is therefore extremely helpful. Those are the easy watercolor plans.

More challenging and perhaps daunting at first is composing and drawing a subject with background elements that support and don't distract from it. This is easily achievable and is worth the time and effort and, with practice, can quickly feel intuitive. Planning and drawing actually make *painting* easier!

I begin a watercolor painting with a contour drawing of pertinent shapes that include key details and light and shadow shapes. Then I paint in three major value stages, which are covered here in separate chapters.

All objects in a representational painting and *every dab of paint*, even empty spaces, are actually *shapes* of color and value and affect all parts of a painting.

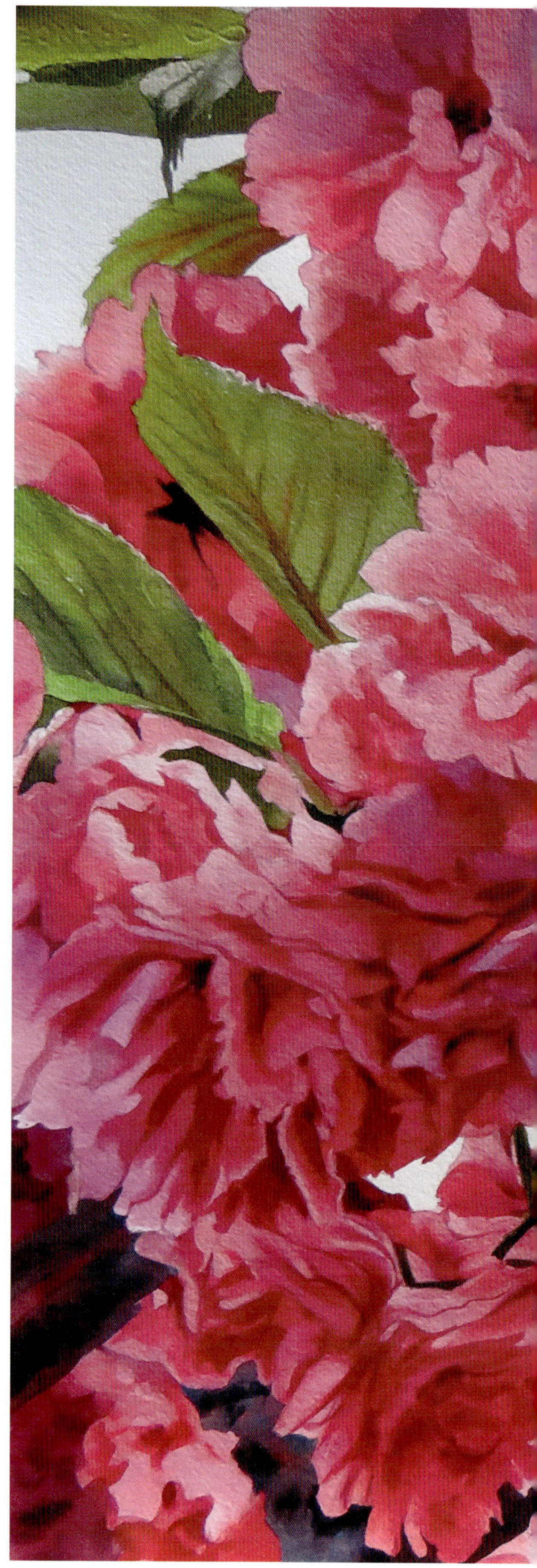

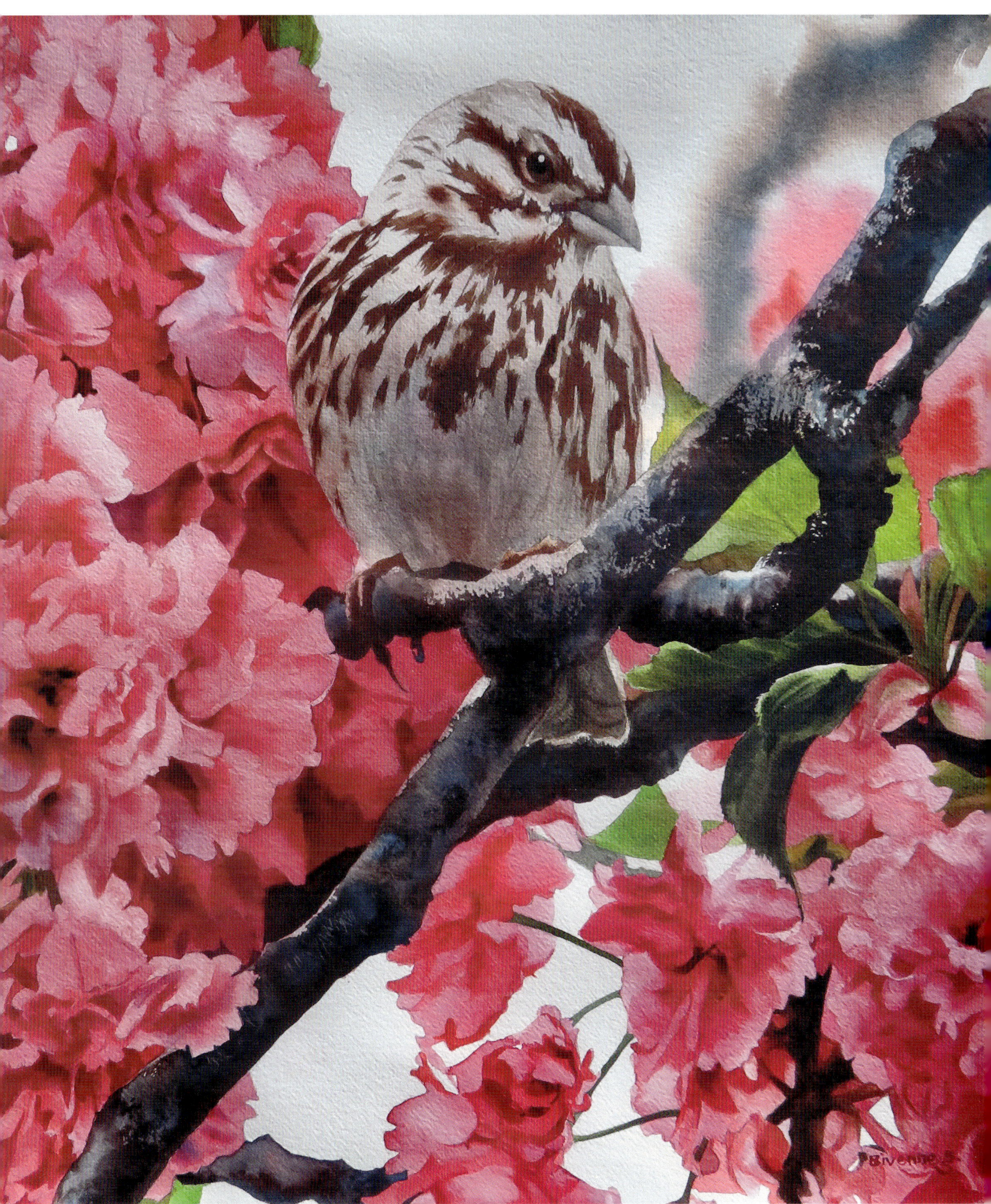

Song Sparrow in the Cherry Tree, 22" × 30"

Therefore, decisions matter about which elements to use, where they're placed, and which will dominate.

Shape, value, color, form, size, space, texture, line, and direction are painting elements. Artists use as many or as few as they wish in any one painting. I usually use the first three in subject and background spaces and to create the fourth. Size and texture establish details, and the others are often used in backgrounds.

One or more elements might emphasize critical parts such as a subject's face, and others could minimize certain background entities that are less important. Contrasting elements draw attention, while harmonizing ones reduce impact.

Artists use a variety of elements and vary them to achieve design principles such as emphasis, harmony, contrast, and rhythm. Determining which elements in both subject and background would best achieve most or all principles requires careful thought, though intuition and creativity are often used with the plan.

Variation, contrast, harmony, emphasis, dominance, balance, variety, repetition, pattern, rhythm, proportion, and unity are composition principles that provide a structure for painting elements. Try to incorporate as many as possible in every painting.

Artists love to portray light in their representational paintings, because with shadow, light not only creates form (another element) but also enhances and energizes object shapes, colors, values, and textures through contrast.

Since a midvalue range dominates most of what we see, strong light and shadow contrast creates interest. Light and shadow shapes generate paths for the eye to follow on objects and across background space shapes and help bring attention to key areas of interest through value differences. Even an illuminated colorless object seems more dramatic when rich shadow frames or surrounds it, like an actor spotlighted on a dark stage.

Once you decide on a subject, consider its qualities that influence the element(s) you'll use in your painting. Do any of them repeat in the background? How do the subject's elements appear against the background, and vice versa? Do key elements in either space emphasize the focal area, or do they compete with it?

In representational painting, any distraction from the subject or its disassociation from the background is a potential problem, like elements in both spaces that don't relate in some way with each other. Just as you should be aware of distracting background elements when photographing a person, for example, the same applies to painting. You probably wouldn't be happy if a trash can somehow ended up in the background of your baby's portrait.

Distracting elements don't just apply to identifiable object shapes. Any element such as a subject's pattern, texture, or lines might also distract if there's no relationship to the painting's other parts. Unlike a photographer, you as the artist can choose which of these and possibly other elements to include, alter, or eliminate.

This choice is a good thing, because it means you can change elements to use a key composition principle in painting: variation. If differences and similarities are not obvious as you observe them, use your imagination, your intuition, to vary them.

As you plan, ask yourself: Should some elements be added (and if so, where) to the subject or to the background? Should any be moved or removed? Can one or more of the subject's characteristics be made *more* interesting with a change in color, value, or some other element? If not, consider adding more impact to the *background* with similar or different elements.

You might plan to vary both. Being open minded about altering elements in your motif or to its background (or both) while you plan *and* paint is critical to a successful design.

For instance, consider as a subject a female house sparrow, a drab bird with an ordinary shape and a patterned back.

An outstretched wing would alter and make more compelling its otherwise unimpressive and predictable *shape*.

Changing the *value* of the bird's plumage to either very light or very dark against the opposite value in its background would give its mundane color greater impact. This was done to emphasize the male (*at left*) in *English Sparrows*. Or contrast its dull hue with a very colorful background, either very light or very dark in value. You see, there are many options for changing elements to improve the impact of your motif.

The complex feather *pattern* on this bird's back might necessitate simplifying pattern elements behind it so that interest remains on the bird. You could vary or even eliminate the number, color, value, texture, direction, and other qualities of branch *line* elements and simplify other habitat object *pattern* elements. Try varying each element separately to see its effect on your subject. Or place the bird against open-sky *space*.

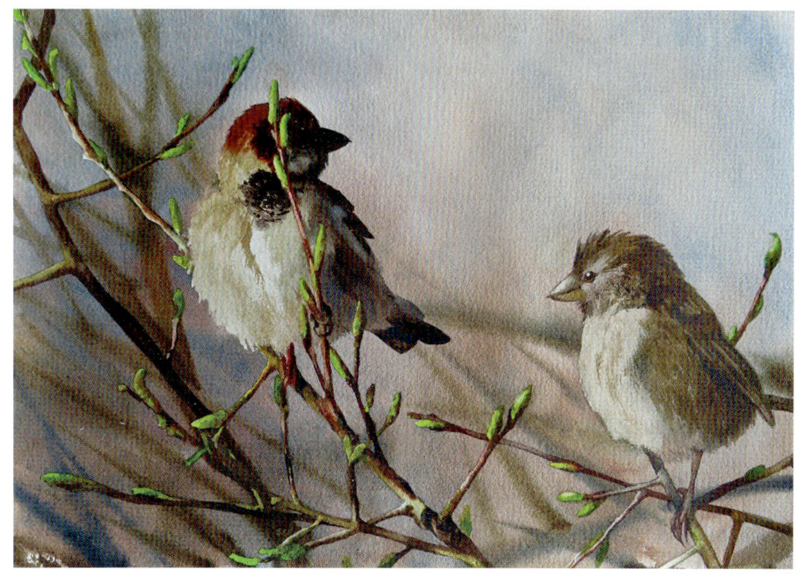

English Sparrows, 15" × 22"

These are examples of variation in subject and background elements that affect the impact, and ultimately the success, of a composition. Therefore, plan them together.

So how are they *painted* together? This will be covered later, in the chapters discussing the painting stages, but properly composing key parts in synchrony with background elements makes painting much easier!

SUBJECT PLACEMENT

The first thing that creates interest in your painting is the proper placement of your subject in the composition space. Use paper of unequal dimensions, such as a rectangle rather than a square, and imagine dividing that space into thirds both horizontally and vertically. These divisions, also known as the Rule of Thirds or Golden Rule/Ratio/Rectangle, form an imaginary interior rectangle, the corners of which are called *power points*.

Place your subject or a key part of it at or close to one power point. This keeps that focal point away from the center, which is key. Place important secondary object (or background) shapes that visually support the subject at the power point diagonally opposite, if possible.

For instance, place a person's eyes or face (primary focus) at the upper-left power point, and hands (of secondary importance) at the lower right. Or put a bird at one power point and an apple (varying a shape element) on its perching branch diagonally opposite at a different power point. Position a face in profile at a power point that leaves greater space in front of it: one looking to the right would traditionally be placed at a power point on the left.

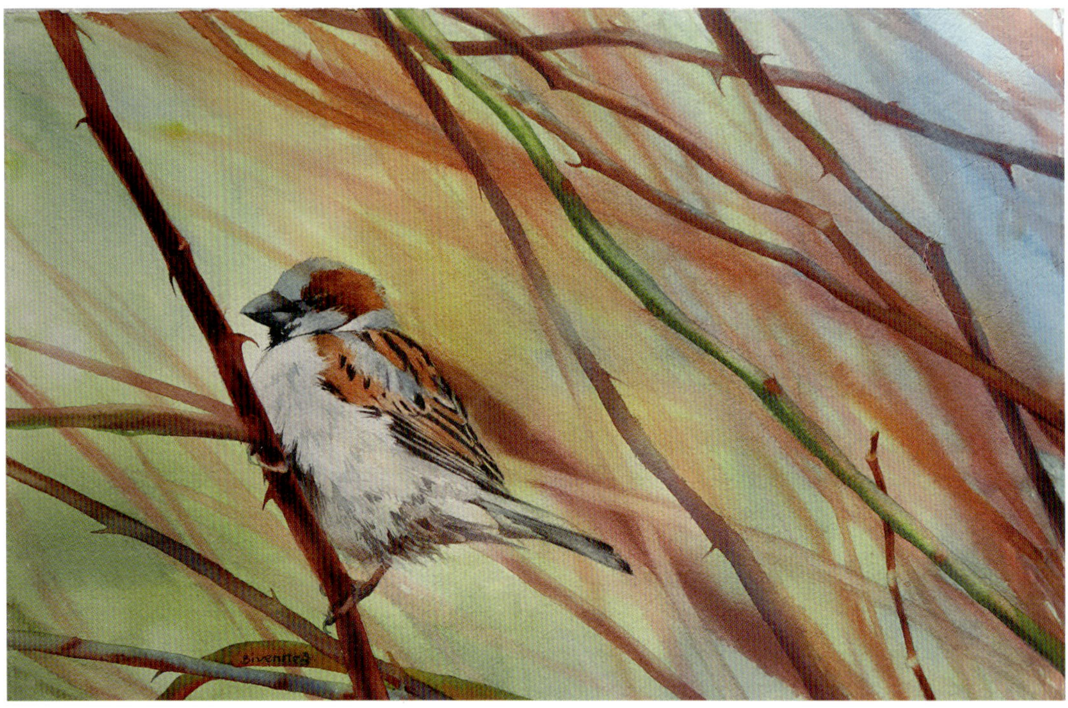

Though more space placed in front of a profiled face is optimal, I decided more clearance behind this bird would suggest that it's ready to fly off. Diagonal background and focal rosebush stem shapes guide the eye toward the bird and help convey this dynamic.

Sparrow on Wild Rose, 15" × 22"

CONNECTING SUBJECT TO BACKGROUND ELEMENTS

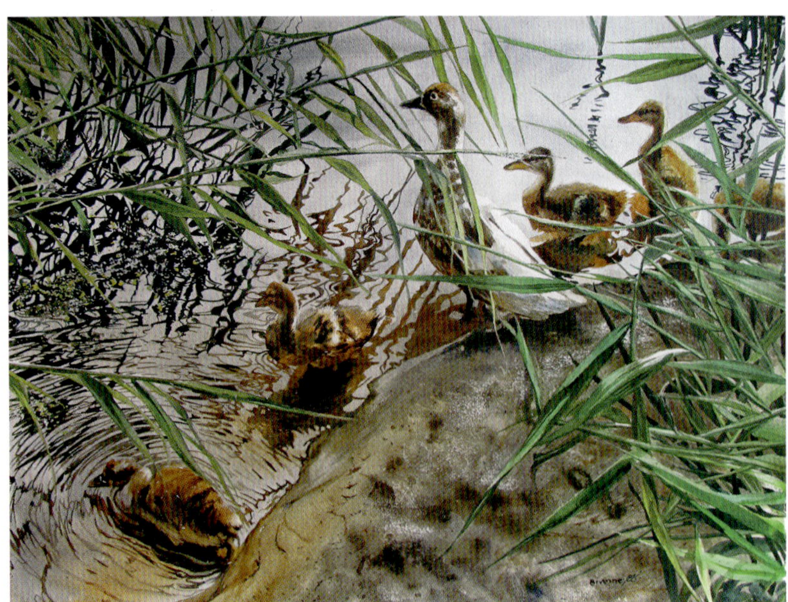

Dutch Ducks, 22" × 30"

Shape, value, and pattern elements contrast sharply in this painting, yet the warm golden color unifies the ducks with the background. Open-space shapes in the water and mud allow places for the eye to rest. Directional lines of reeds, reflections, and water's edge guide the eye to the birds.

Now observe elements that your subject and background elements have in common, such as color. Similarities, using the principle of harmony, connect the two spaces. Along with the aforementioned variation and contrast, harmony is a key principle used to more subtly connect disparate or contrasting elements.

Think of your subject and background at this point as two major separate and distinct *shape* elements. Take special note of elements that can tie the two spaces together, and those that contrast, directing attention away from or bringing scrutiny to the subject—or both.

Shared similarities are critical in integrating or harmonizing the two, but only a few need to relate in any one painting. The value of each and any shared color will determine when and which part to paint first and which to paint last. This is key. In my paintings, color, shape, line, and value incorporate my favorite design principles of contrast, variation, and harmony.

Color harmony can be established right from

the start by painting similar hues in pale or bright washes across subject and background shape edges, such as letting a yellow flower's color bleed into its green foliage background. This is discussed in chapter 3.

Similarities and differences in other elements such as shapes or line direction can also be used to harmonize or contrast subject and background. Harmonizing elements help guide the eye around the painting, while contrast draws and holds attention. Plan them together so they can be varied as necessary. The possibilities to vary elements in these two major spaces are practically endless, and all elements in both spaces affect the impact of the other; therefore they're inseparable. Choose your elements carefully and plan them simultaneously, because how they're used *and* when they're painted can make or break a painting.

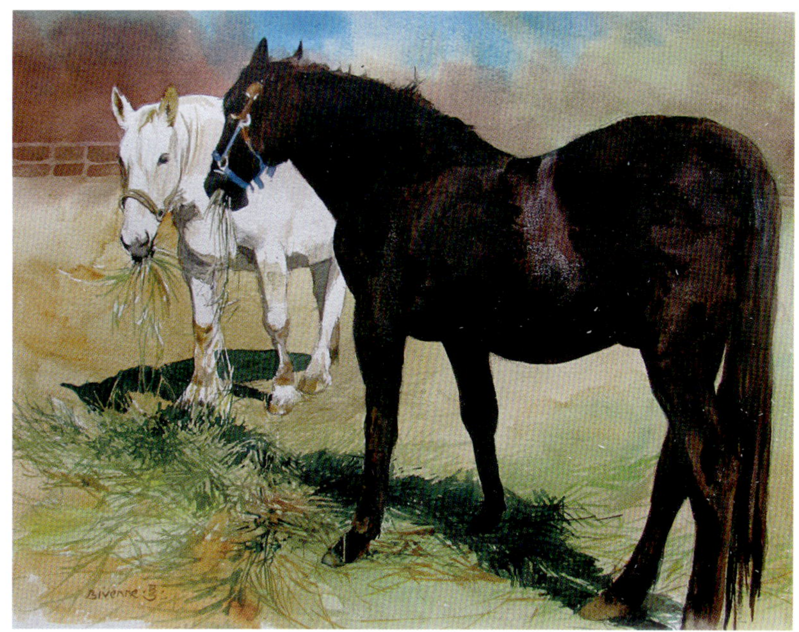

Black Beauty, 11" × 15"

GENERAL GUIDELINES TO INCREASE IMPACT

Give a very dark subject a compelling, recognizable shape (or silhouette) and then contrast it with a background light or bright. The more intriguing its dark silhouette, the less complex its background

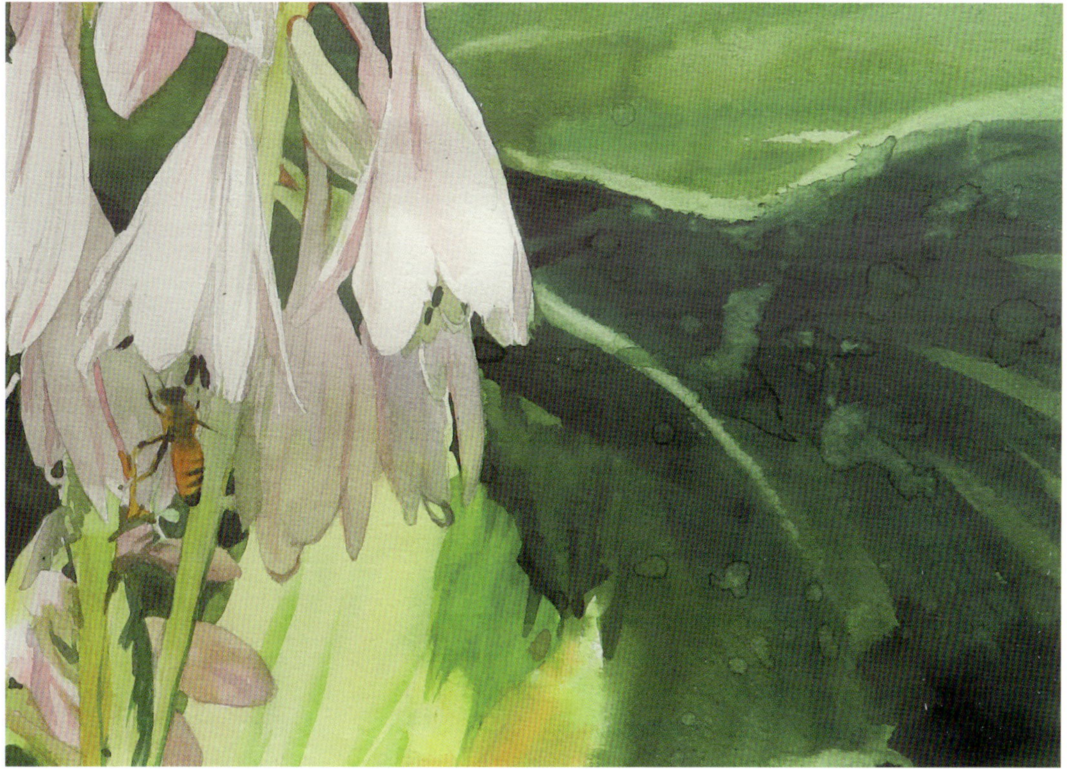

Honey Bee and Hosta, 11" × 15"

Varying in color temperature, line, and value, the large, simplified background leaves create bold, almost abstract shapes, a perfect foil to the complex, delicate flowers. Subtle leaf lines guide the eye around and to the flowers. The honeybee is at a power point.

To show how creatures are often imperceptible in their habitat, I let the multiple flowers compete with the birds for attention (similar size and shapes). Yet, branches crisscrossing the space lead the eye around the painting and to them; the birds are also at power points.

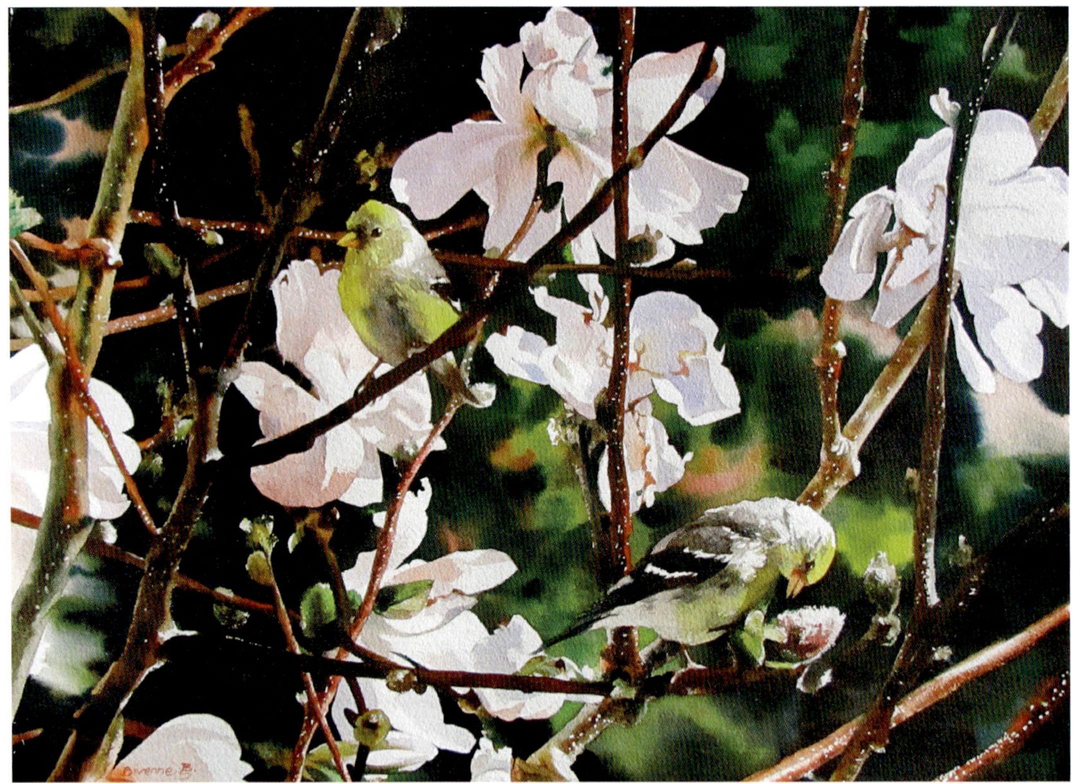

Goldfinches in the Magnolia, 22" × 30"

Large snow shapes around the bird break up the busy plumage and grass patterns. Similar lines and colors plus (triangular) shape repetition connect subject to background and guide the eye around and back to the bird subject.

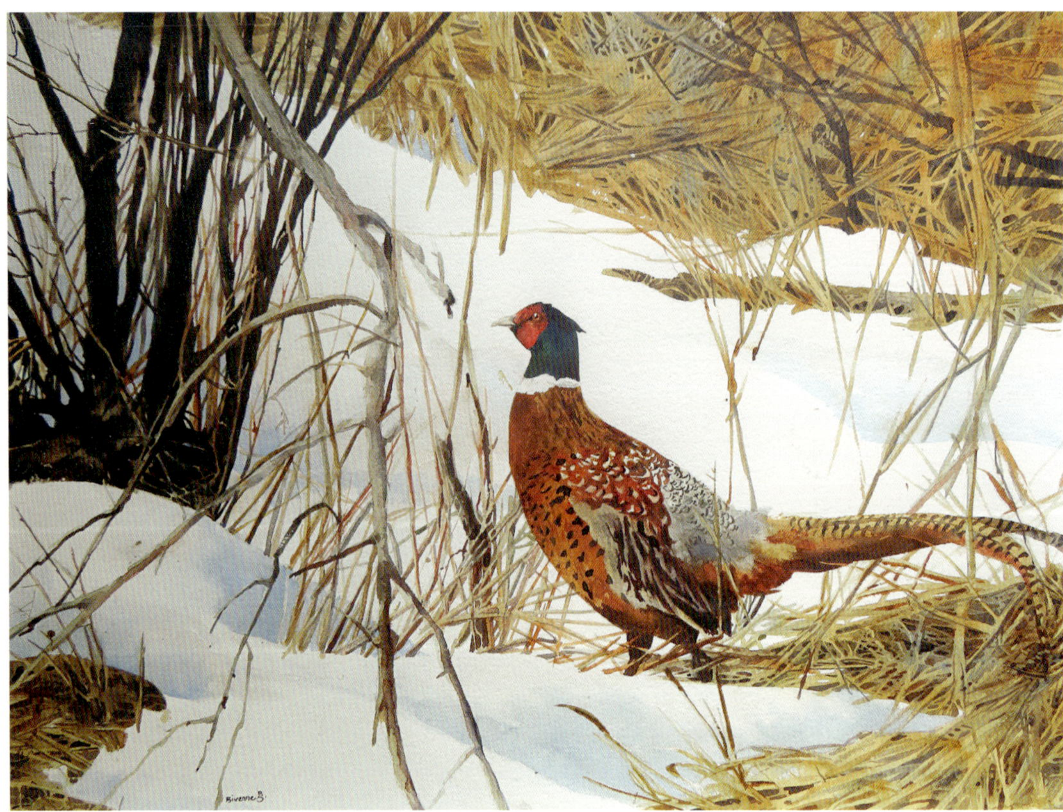

Struttin' His Stuff, 22" × 30"

patterns or shapes need be.

If both subject and background are equally elaborate in silhouette, pattern, texture, or color, simplify or vary qualities in one or the other to contrast them more, so the two don't compete for attention, as seen in *Hydrangea Shadows* (page 116).

Add a dark or colorful background to a light-value or white subject. One particularly large or simple in shape and texture might also benefit from a complex background with a variety of supporting elements, as in *Snowy Egret in the Reeds* (page 39).

Conversely, since a small subject might easily be unnoticeable against a complex background, consider various options: enlarge it in the composition space, greatly increase its quantity if possible, tone down or simplify competing background elements, increase background value or color contrast, or use harmonious lines and other composition tricks to guide the eye toward it (or use a combination of these).

Plan a simple, plain, open-space background or one of contrasting color or value (or both) around a highly patterned subject.

Design a very dark or very light background, either complex or simple, to emphasize a brightly colored subject, such as a male cardinal against gray or green brambles or bright snow, or a red flower against dark-green foliage.

With multiple subject shapes, let one element, such as size, color, number, value, or shape, dominate the others. Dominance is a design principle that helps convey what's most important in your painting. More than one element can dominate, but balance them asymmetrically if possible. Flower color and size dominate the other elements in *Titmouse in the Magnolia* (page 30); yet, attention is on the bird because it's placed within the golden rectangle and contrasts with the other elements. The bird also asymmetrically balances the visual weight of the flower and suggests a sense of scale.

In all cases, whatever elements you use to convey importance should both contrast *and* harmonize in some way with other elements in the background. It could simply contrast in value and harmonize in color. But there are countless other options to achieve this, and it's up to you!

Let's say your subject placed at a power point is a male cardinal illuminated by the sun at a feeder with a female cardinal and sparrows. While the other birds harmonize with him in general *shape*, *size*, and perhaps *value*, he dominates the motif because his bright-red hue contrasts with their drab *color*. He'd further command attention if he were larger in the foreground than the other (smaller) birds more distant in space, and the scene's background elements, such as tree shapes, contrast him in color or value (or both).

The female cardinal, more drab but the same shape, could be placed at a power point diagonally opposite him. In the same foreground space she'd therefore be the same size as he, yet he'd still be the focal interest. He might be in profile while she faces forward for variation. She's a visual link between him and the drab sparrows.

A colorful blue jay is a *distracting* element in this scene because its chroma is similar to the male cardinal if placed nearby and at the same scale as he, but a *supporting* element (similar shape) if placed in shadow (value difference) or smaller in the distance (size contrast).

If a large, round boulder is a dominant shape in your motif, *contrast* it with small round or angular rocks (size, shape differences) and *harmonize* all with a similar color, texture, or value. Similarities relate subject and background spaces. Train your eye to notice harmonizing and contrasting elements, or try to incorporate them intuitively.

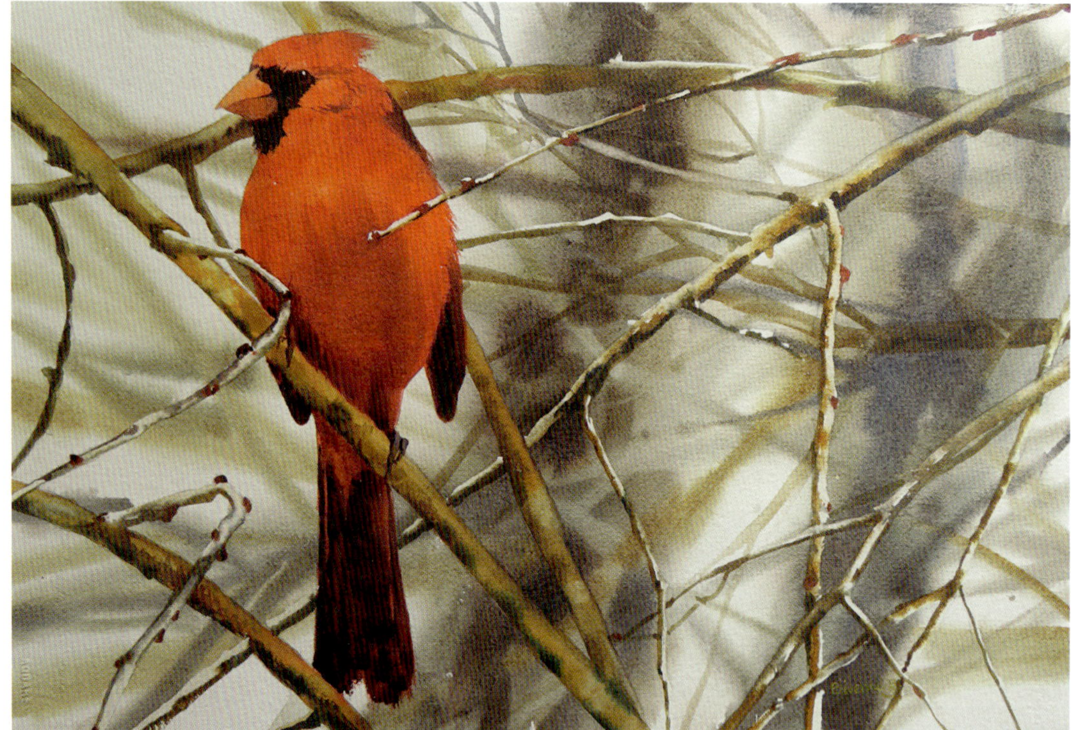

Red Finery, 15" × 22"

A very dark green background emphasizes both the bright flower and the gray bird; both are also supported by the bright green emerging leaves. Note shape repetition, and color and value variation.

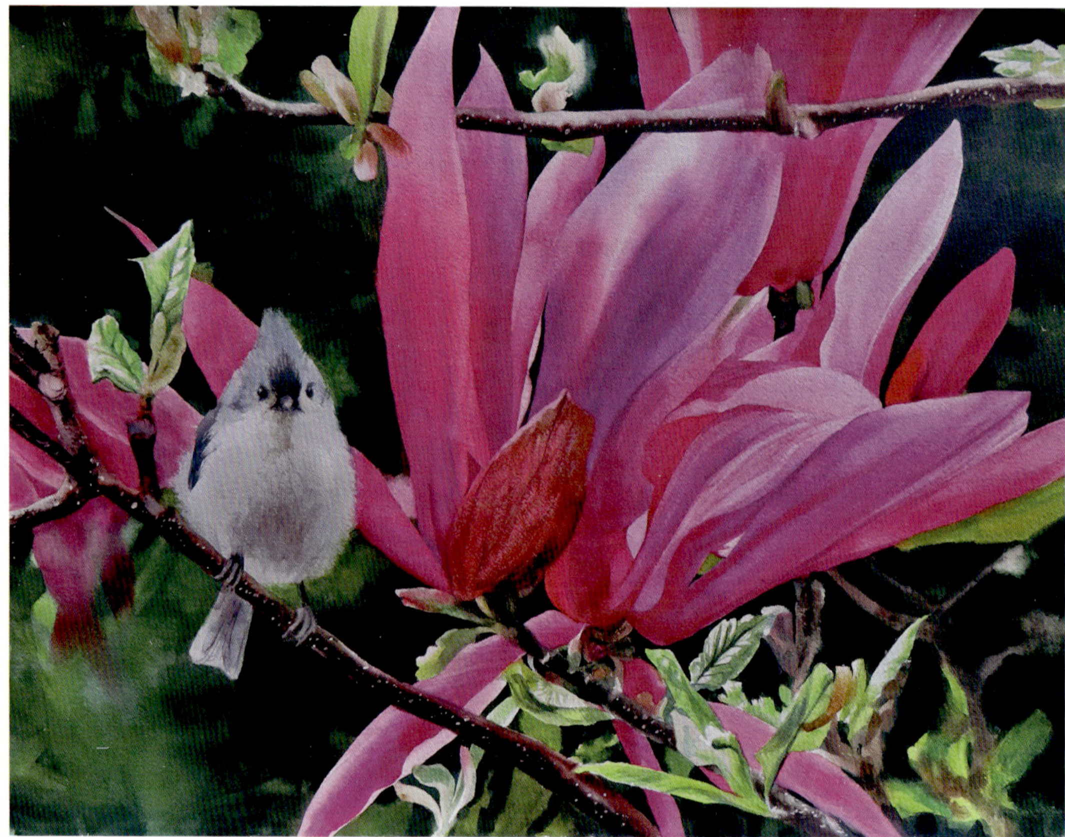

Titmouse in the Magnolia, 22" × 30"

ASK YOURSELF THE FOLLOWING

- Can the subject itself stand on its own as truly compelling in its elements, or are the background's elements more fascinating? Would the subject benefit from being larger?
- Does the subject's size affect its position in the composition space and the background's degree of complexity?
- Which background elements support or enhance the subject, and how, by harmonizing and leading the eye to it or by contrast? Which distract? (Eliminate or minimize distractions.)
- What color, value, shape, pattern, or other element(s) *dominate the subject*, and how and where can that particular element or combination be incorporated into the background to a lesser degree? Which of these should contrast with the background for greater impact or should otherwise be altered?
- What color, value, shape, pattern, or other element(s) *dominate the background*? Do any harmonize or contrast with the subject? Should any be altered to benefit the subject?
- Where can the eye rest? Is there empty *space* in the background or in the subject? Is that empty-space shape itself interesting? Can any of its elements vary?
- Do defined and suggested *lines* that compose background elements guide the eye to the subject and around the composition? Do they have a dominant direction and do they vary in length, width, color, value, direction, and texture? Which support the subject and which distract? Do some intersect edges of adjacent shapes in a compelling way?
- Which elements in both subject and background, if any, should be included, altered, or eliminated?

Objectively planning how you'll adjust elements in these spaces will ultimately bring interest in the whole design. This effort facilitates painting! Keep the principles in your head as you paint, so you won't lose track of that vision.

Bottom Line:

A plan encompassing the subject with supporting background elements establishes a solid compositional foundation on which you can rely without much further thought as you paint.

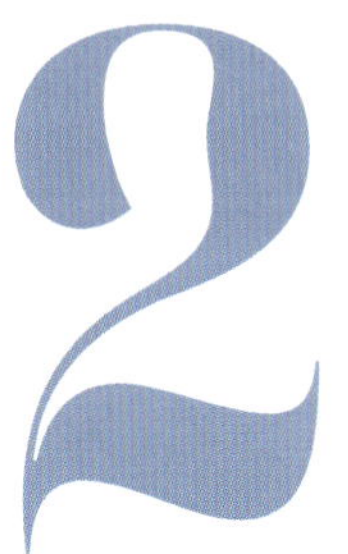

Sketching the Motif

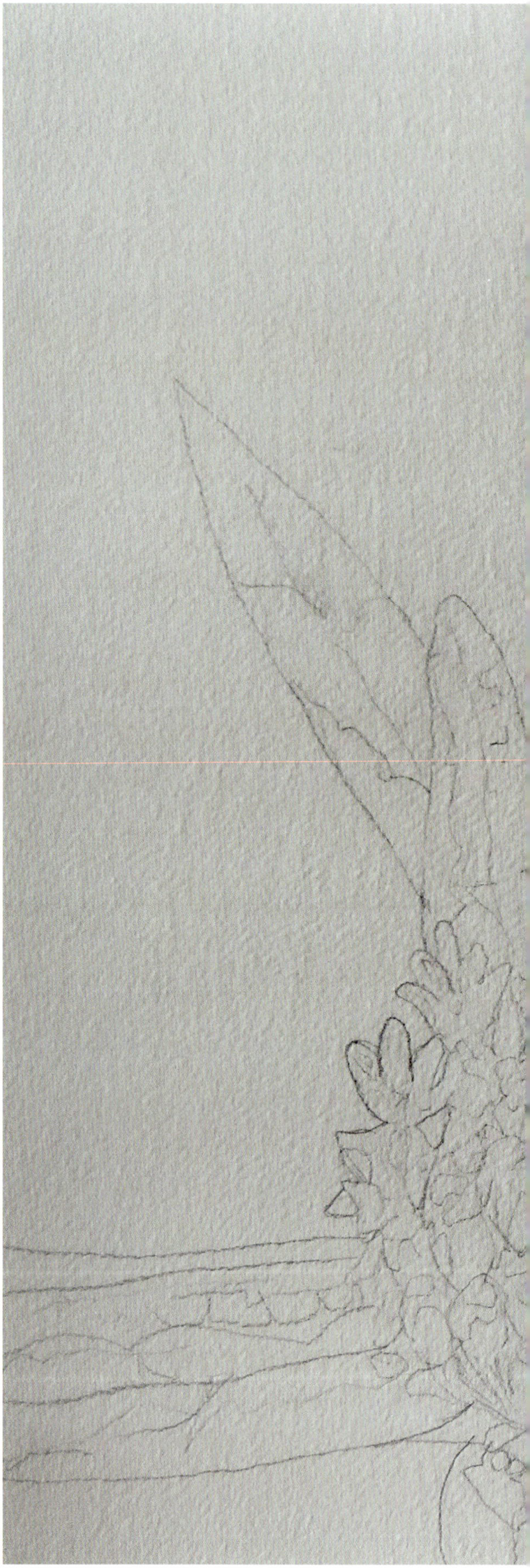

Drawing is the basis of painting. Developing the outlines of essential shapes is often most of the effort in creating a great watercolor painting. It makes your plan easier to express, and painting straightforward and quick.

Before rendering your contour drawing on watercolor paper, it may help to make some smaller preliminary line, color, shape, and especially *value* studies on sketch paper. Use a soft lead (2B, 4B, or greater), *conté*, or charcoal pencil and perhaps colored media to asymmetrically balance key elements through their apparent or implied edges in an imaginary triangle, spiral, or zigzag design. Isolating key elements separately helps prevent any single one from visually dividing the composition in half or from keeping the subject centered. These preparatory sketches accent potential design problems. Better to make mistakes here than on the watercolor paper.

Isolate value by depicting shadow only on, next to, between, and around objects. The overall dominant value shape and object forms will be apparent. Balance one extreme value asymmetrically with its opposite.

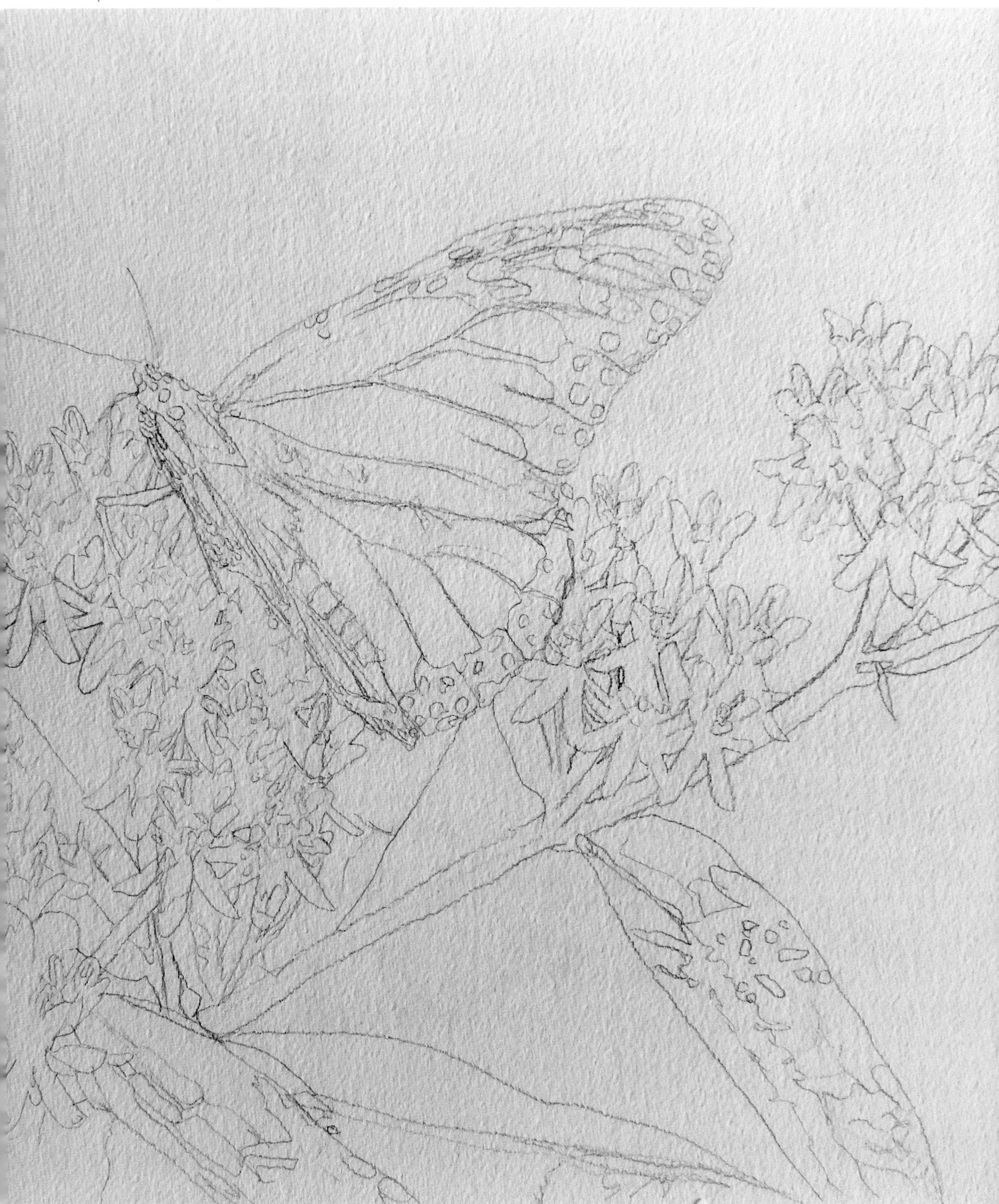

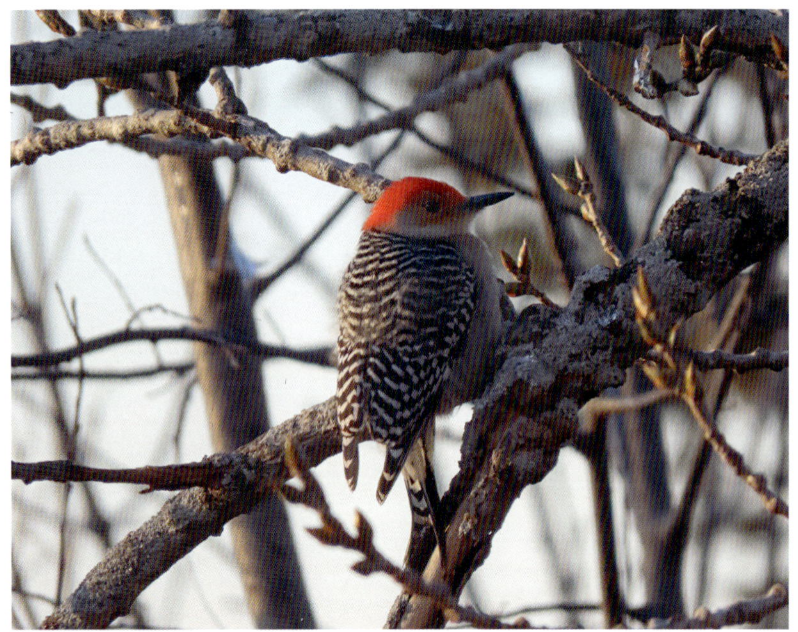

Next, single out color temperatures (see page 52). For instance, represent all warm colors with orange and all cools with blue and balance them asymmetrically, such as a large warm shape and a small cool. Plan to use no more than a handful of colors in any one painting if possible; black, white, and blending don't count. Many paintings are created with variations of the three primary colors of red, yellow, and blue.

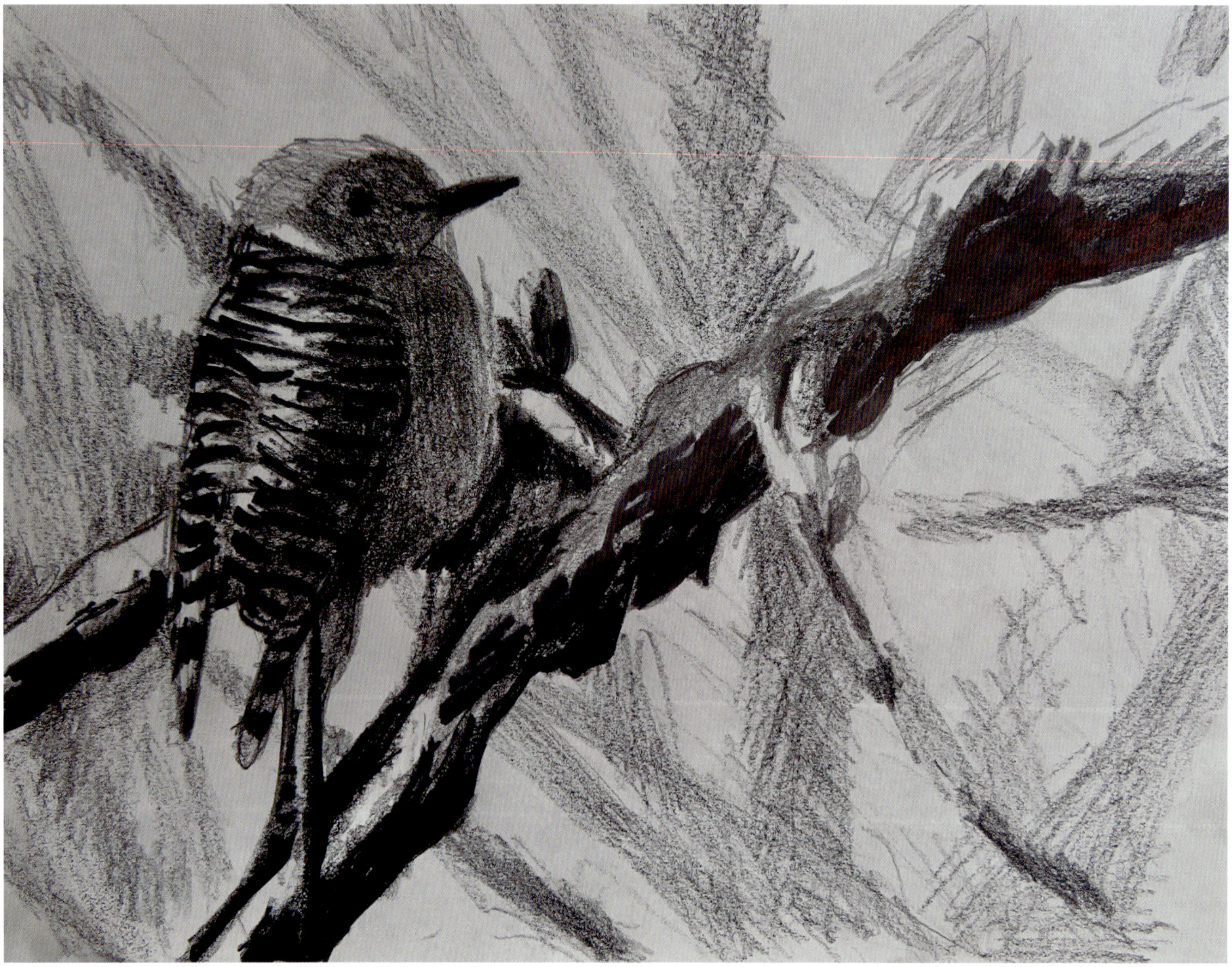

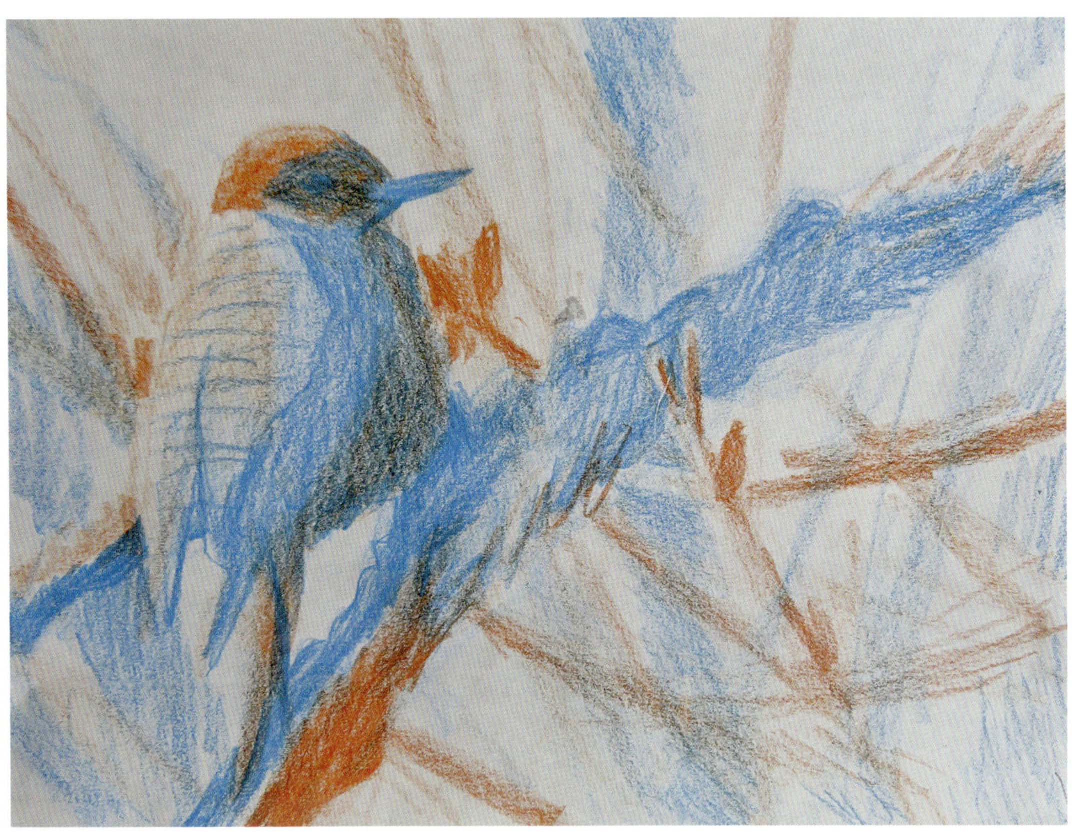

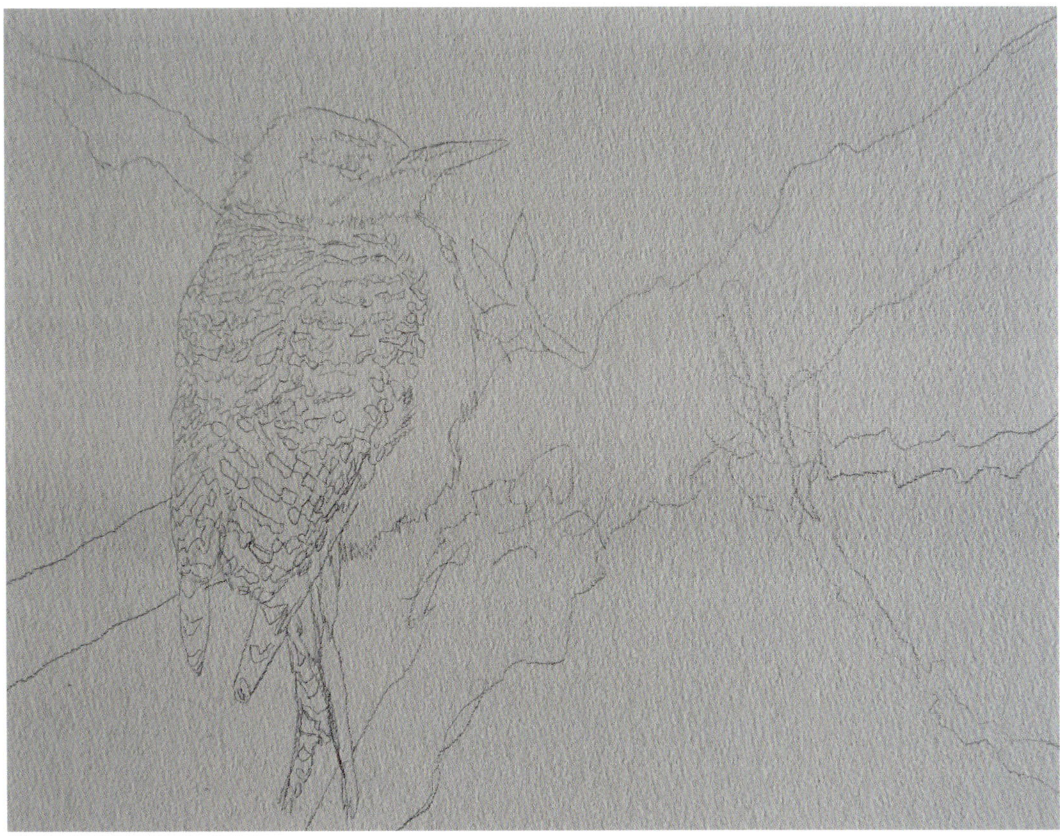

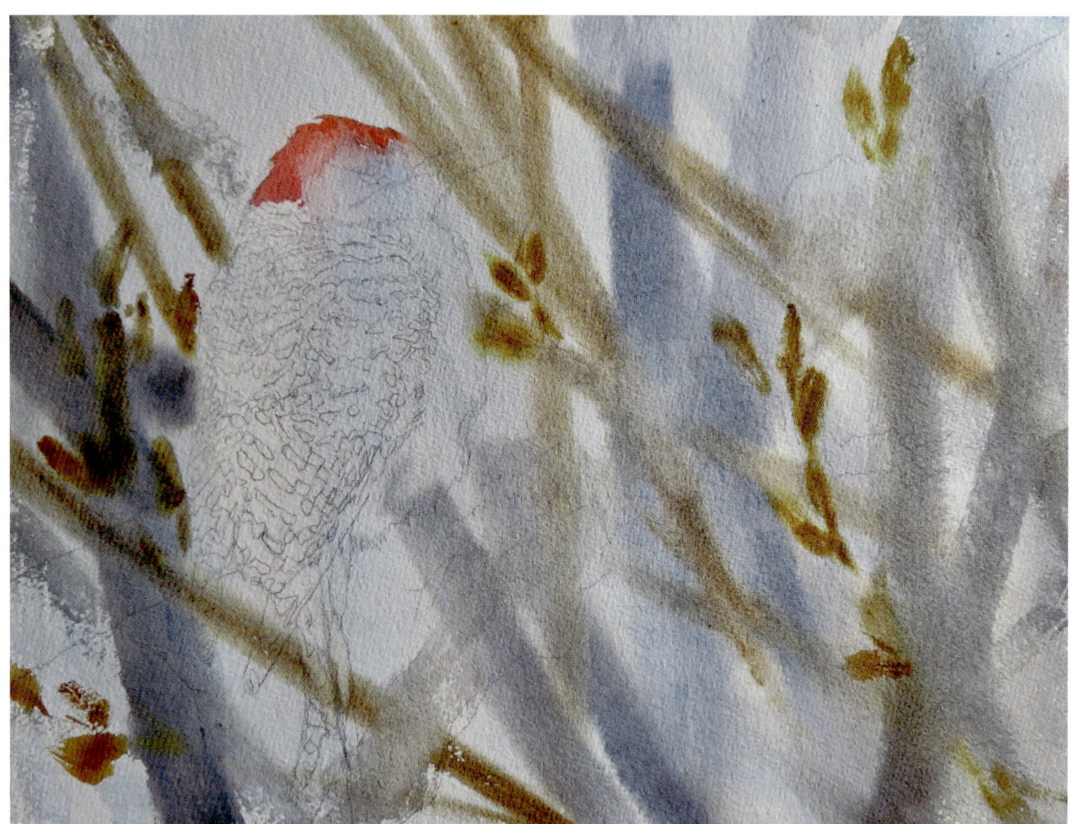

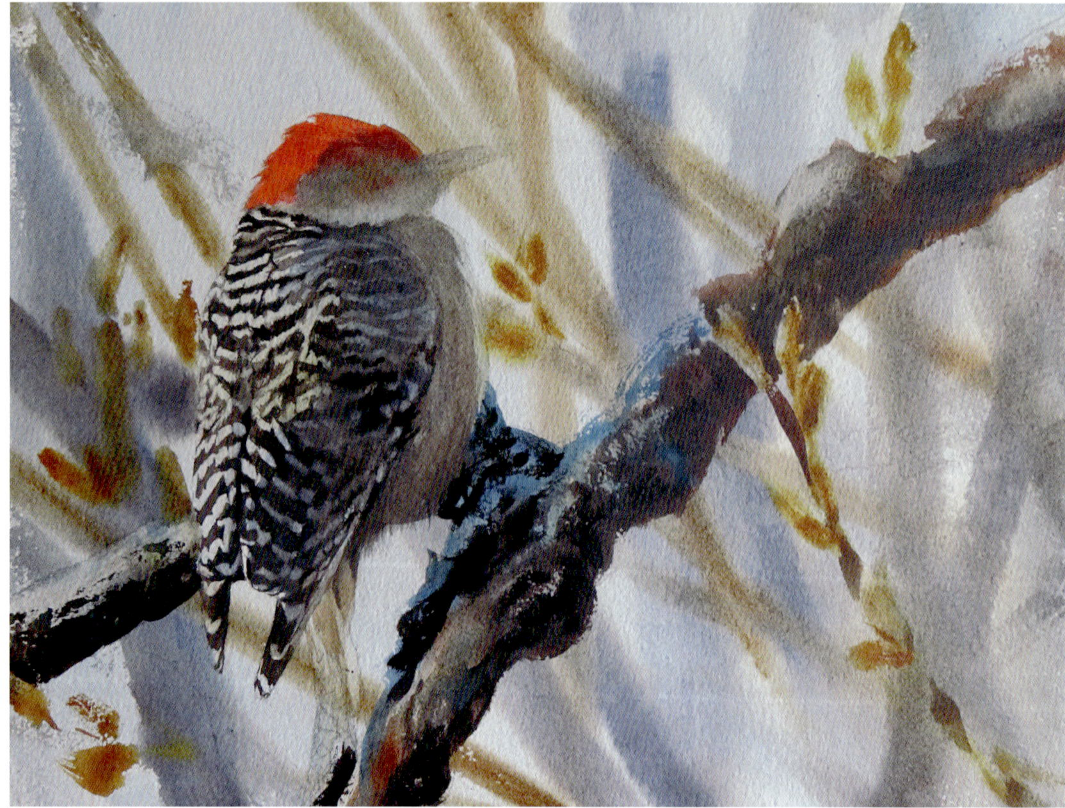

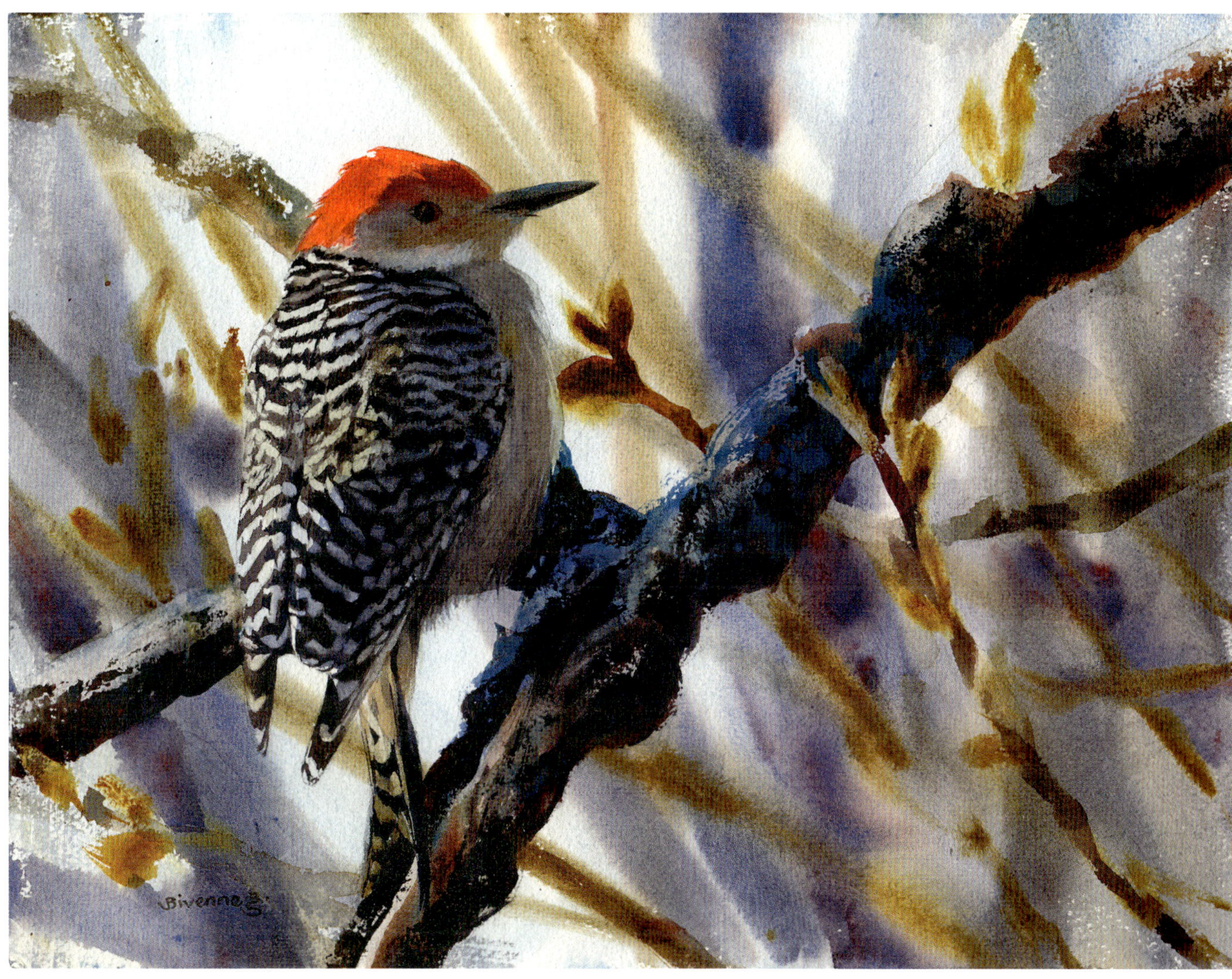

Yellow-Bellied Sapsucker, 12" × 16"

Value and color temperature differences may not always be immediately obvious, as shown here. Establish a value range first, then warm and cool colors. Sketch primary and secondary shapes in contour, but not areas of less consequence, such as distant branches. Painting stages 1, 2, and 3 are shown on these two pages.

Hold preliminary sketches up to a mirror; you might notice mistakes or an imbalance more easily. Pieces of cut or torn colored and black and white paper suggesting shapes, or sticks and brushes representing linear elements, placed across the composition sometimes help iron out design problems.

Simplify your motif down to its essence; namely, its dominant object, shadow, illumination, and background supporting shapes.

When you're satisfied with your design, use a regular 2B pencil to sketch the *outline shapes* of the subject, its pattern and details, supporting surrounding shapes, those of light *and* shadow, and even of color differences on the watercolor paper. Delineate a few key details that jump out. Plan to let them sizzle. This may seem like a lot, and sometimes it is, but taking the time to carefully indicate these saves potential painting headaches later.

Fortunately, not every mark, line, shape, or pattern (such as each blade of grass in a field) needs to be sketched! Instead, draw the major shape silhouette, such as (in this example) grasses at the field's periphery that contrast in a fascinating way with another (background) shape. Draw the fur silhouette of an animal and wherever light and shadow alter its textural appearance, *not* each hair. Contour lines of key shapes, especially where contrast occurs, help remind you where a change is necessary as you paint. We notice change.

Do not add shading or indicate soft-edged shapes. Don't press too hard or draw too lightly on the paper.

Minimize corrections, but if you must, use a white eraser, which is less likely to leave streaks. Remove any heavy pencil lines as much as possible before painting, especially those delineating yellow shapes.

The background elements of color and line support the small subject by harmonizing with it in color and directional lines of goldenrod stalks and leaves. These guide the eye toward the bird, placed at a power point.

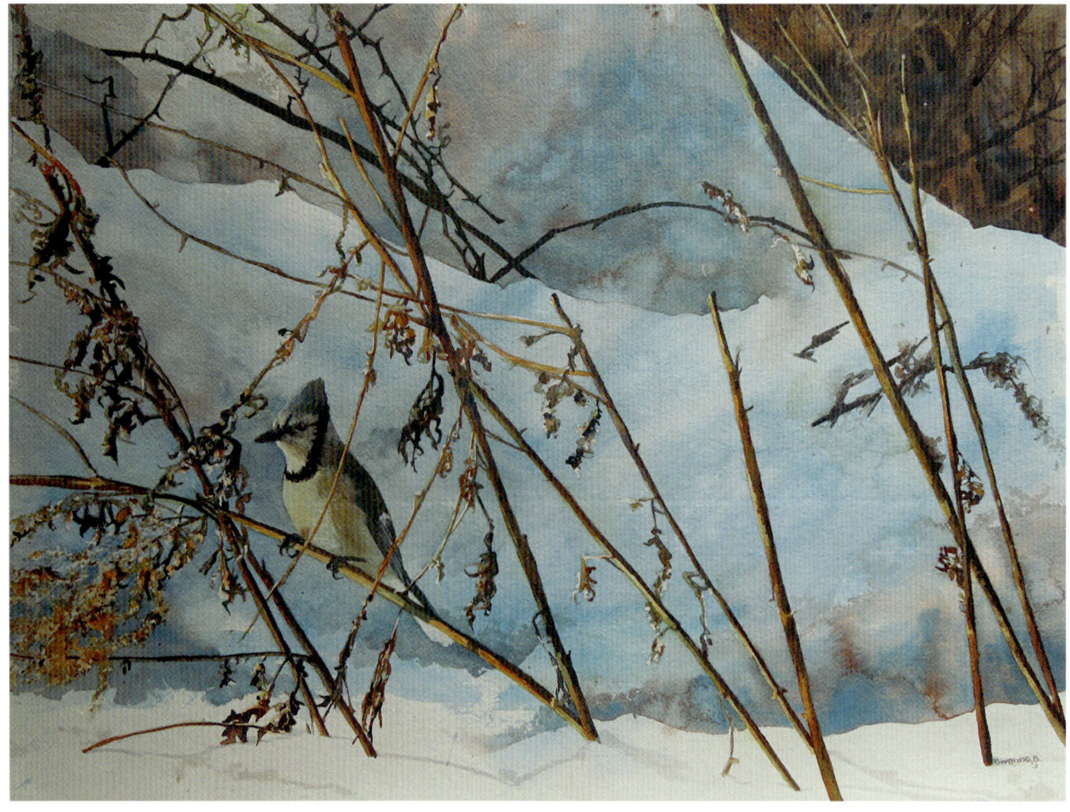

Blue Jay on the Goldenrod, 22" × 30"

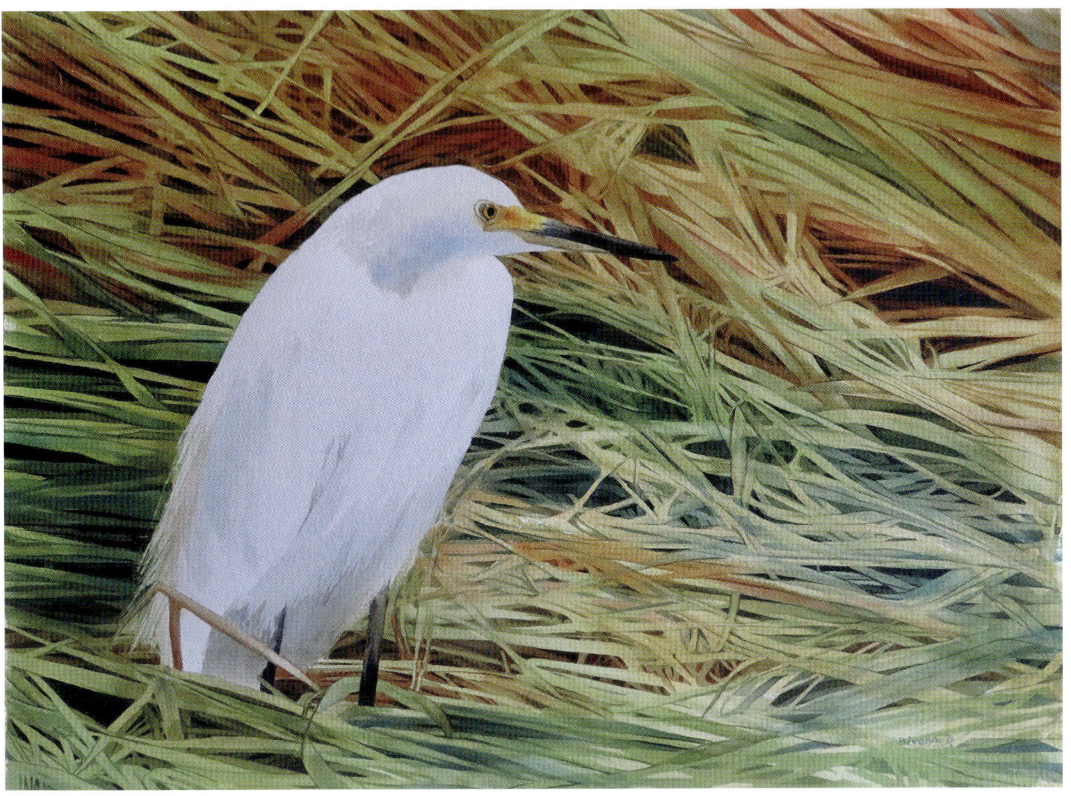

The egret subject's shape, color, value, and plain (or nonexistent) pattern and dominant line direction contrast sharply with the same elements in the background.

Snowy Egret in the Reeds, 22" × 30"

Outlines are not required for soft-edged shapes such as clouds; simply make a mental note. When a reminder is needed, though, draw a faint dotted line and erase it before painting that area.

Not all major elements may necessarily carry the eye around the design in every painting, but at least one element should. Always make that a composition goal and plan to vary elements as you paint. Since you may add, eliminate, or alter subject *and* background elements, here are tips to help you draw from observation a pleasing motif in contour:

Choose a viewpoint and stick with it. Observe, study, and, if necessary, research characteristics of your subject and its key surrounding objects. Train your eye and your mind to record *shapes* of color and value rather than of particular things such as leaves, petals, or eyes. Shape edges create lines.

Draw contour lines of largest shapes, including background space shapes, before any detail shapes. The big picture is more important than tiny particulars. Intersect and interrupt large shapes or long lines with others.

Start with an easy shape, and as you do so, pay particular attention to where another neighboring shape's line, value, or color begins or ends, and briefly divert back and forth between the two. For instance, where does a shadow shape begin and end on one and on adjacent, nearby, and distant shapes? Where on the stem does the leaf begin—at the bottom, middle, or top? Where do cast shadow shapes begin and end?

Make sure your subject comprises at least one dominant shape, color, value, size, pattern, or other element. If possible, let one or more contrast with the background. Record two contrasting values or colors (or both) and note how they compare in value and color to the next. Do they compete for attention? If so, eliminate or plan to tone down insignificant ones, possibly later with paint.

Note which harmonizing elements the subject

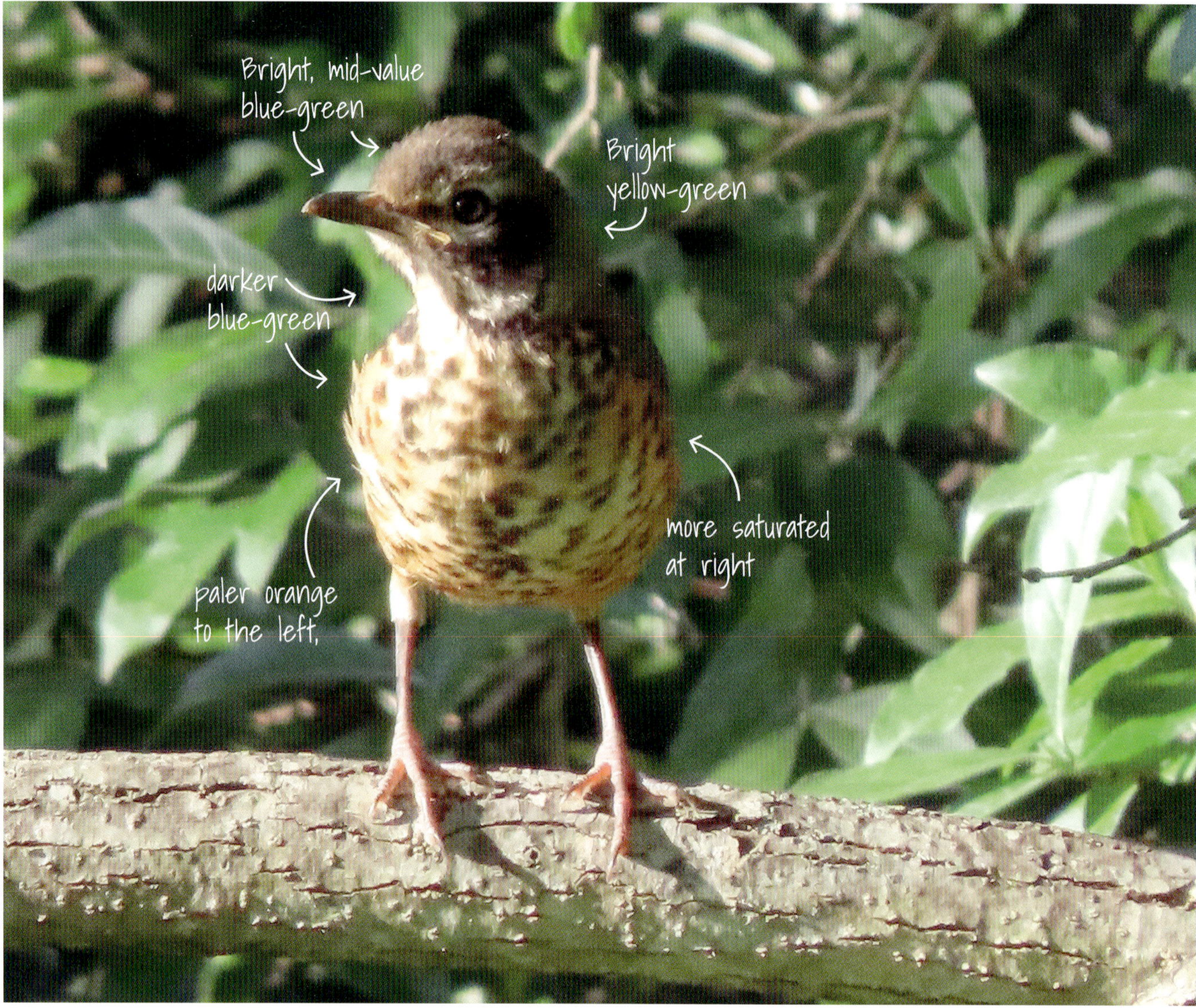

The busy leafy background would not be delineated because its *pattern* contrasts too much with the bird. Instead I'd alter background elements by adding more blue-green foliage (*especially at left*), softer branch and leaf edges, and darker (background) value to the left of its belly to contrast it.

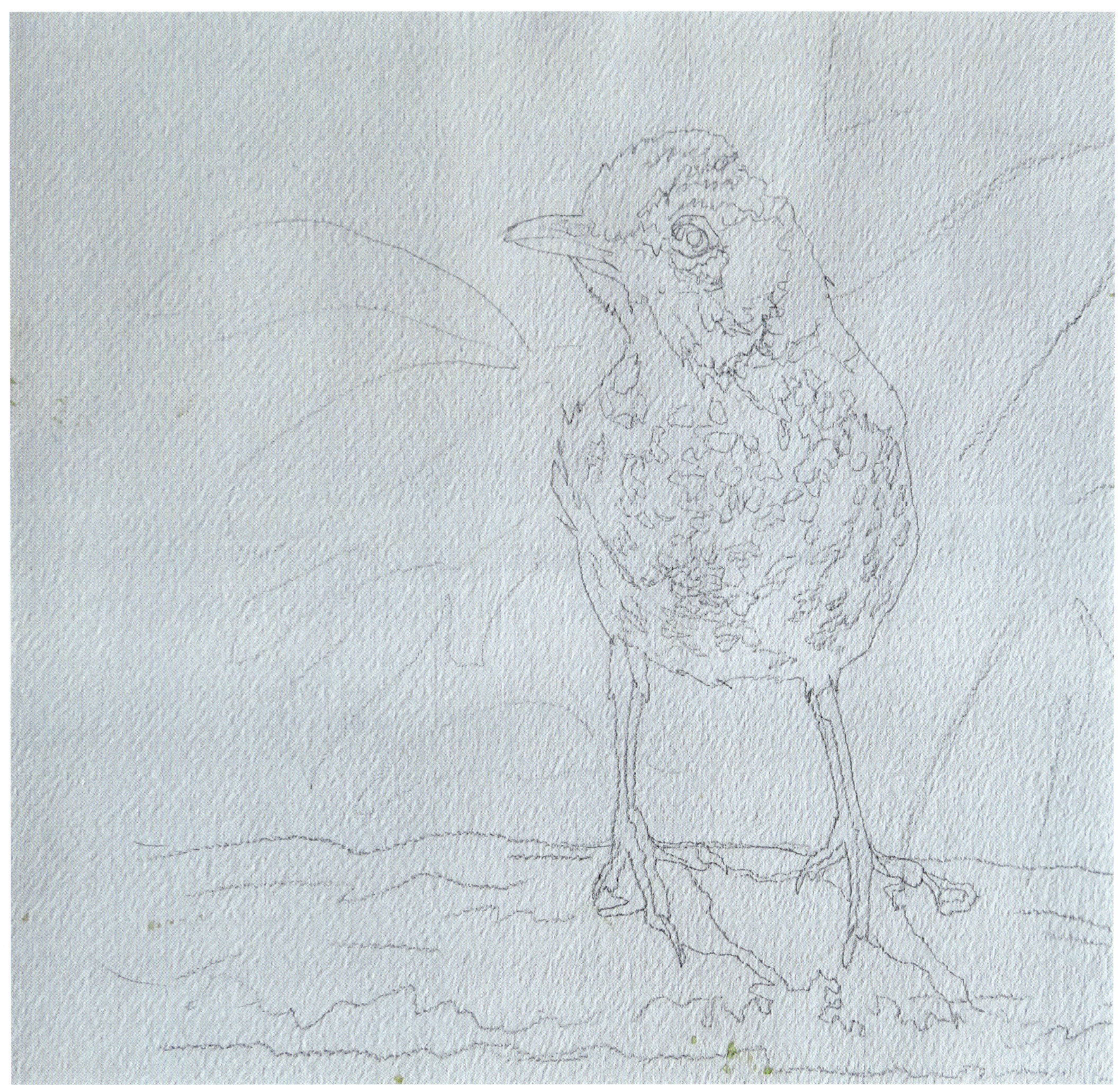

and background share, particularly common colors, values, and lines, but draw *contrasting* elements. Color and value similarities will give you a head start with painting. An orange subject shares *yellow* with its green background, but orange and green are different hues.

If the source of light's position is unapparent, introduce one. This means creating light and shadow *shapes* as they fall on, around, and perhaps through object contours. Such shapes establish form, a critical element in representational painting and already begin to connect your subject to its background!

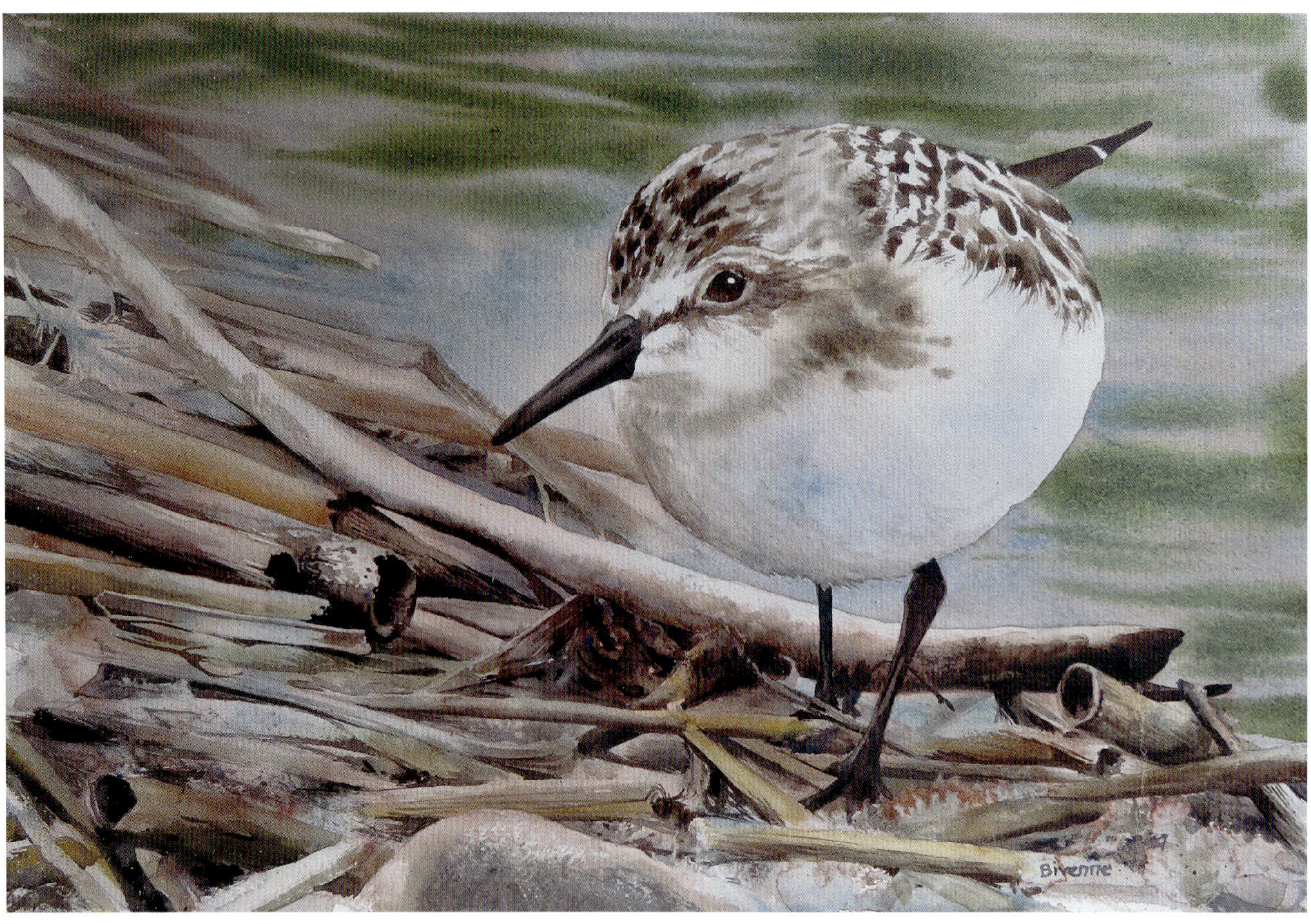

Semi-palmated Sandpiper, 12" x 18"

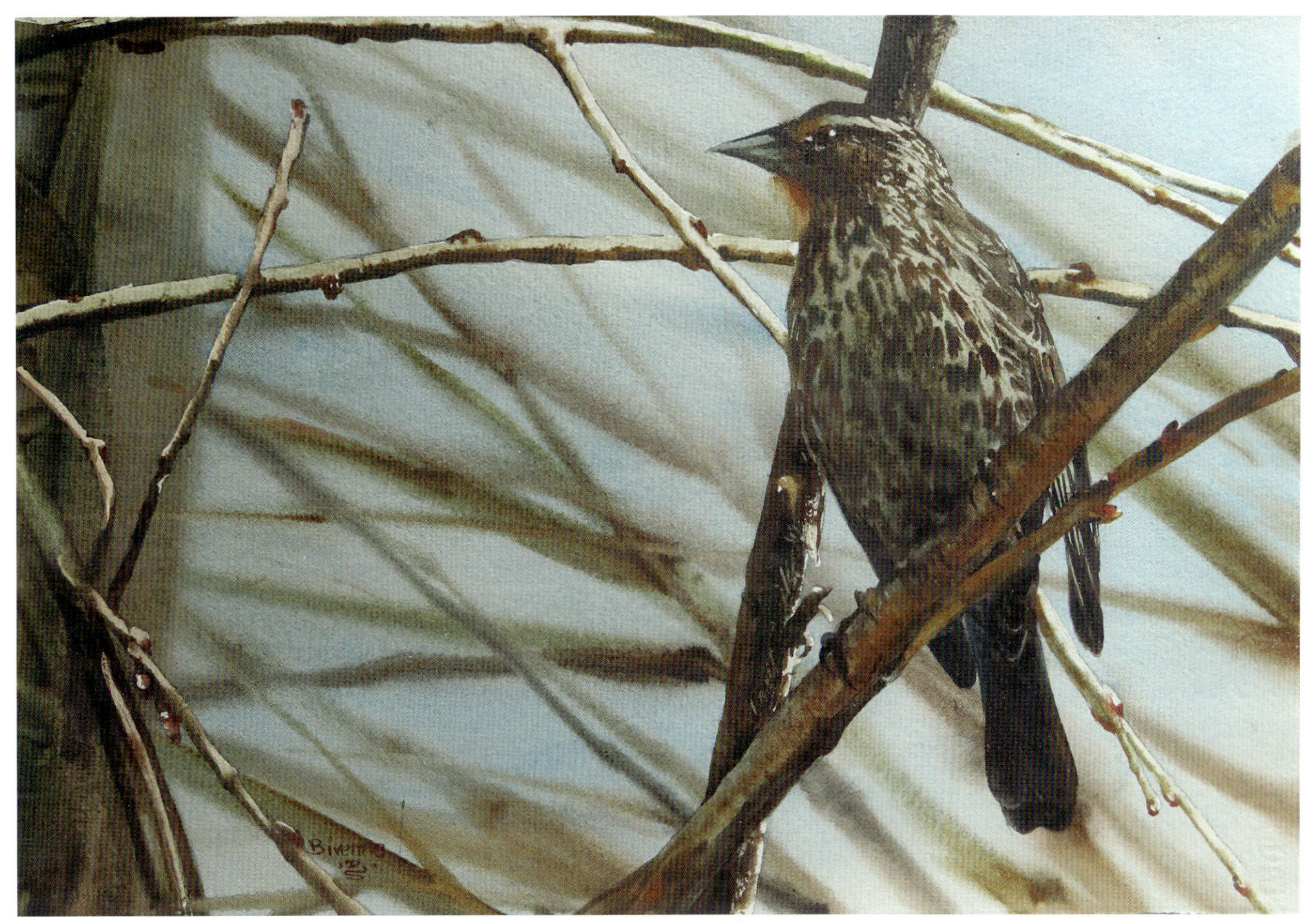

Female Red-winged Blackbird, 15" x 22"

Create line dominance, curved, linear, or diagonal. Draw directional background (or subject) shapes that most support or direct the eye to the subject. Eliminate or redirect obvious distracting shapes that cross a face or lines tangent with key subject contours. Use painting tricks to remove or reduce most (or all) of the rest.

The cattails support the bird subject because their oval shapes are similar. They also emphasize the subject because their texture, color, and value contrast it. Soft-edged shapes suggesting distant cattails create shape repetition and visually connect defined cattails with the bird subject.

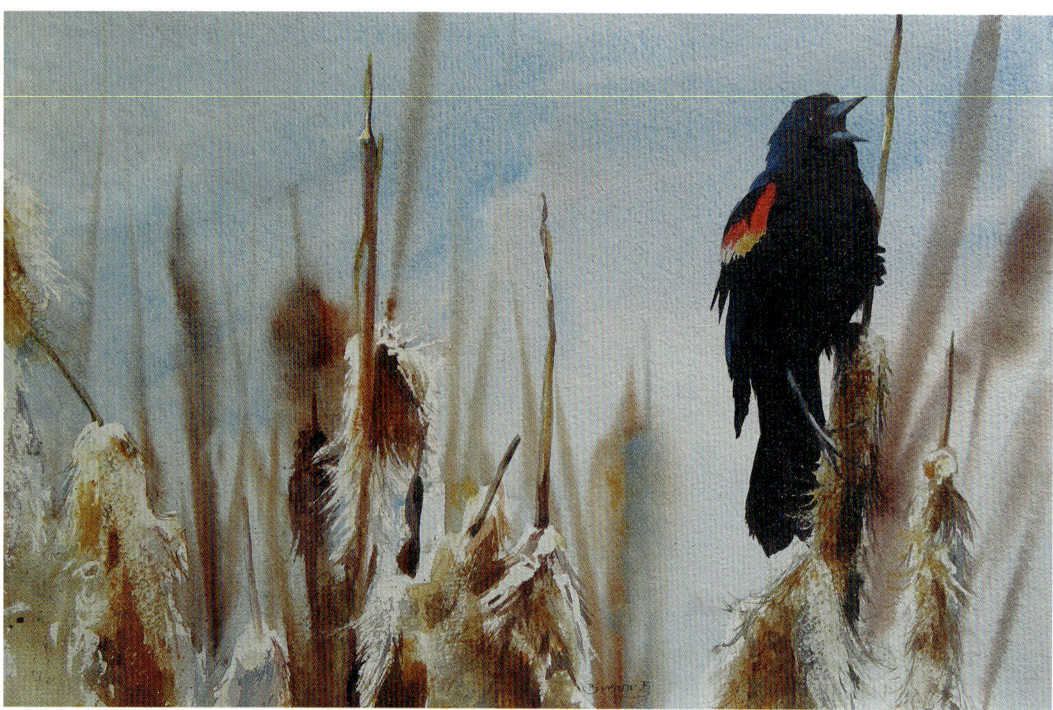

It's My Territory!, 15" × 22"

Surface textures of focal objects may need particular delineation, especially where light meets shadow, but not always, because, for instance, rounded objects generally have less obvious light-and-shadow shape contrast, and rough textures—such as that of certain rocks—need not be drawn. Timing and techniques to paint them vary. Subtle differences may be hard to notice, but if you need a reminder, indicate them with a faint or dotted line.

Draw delineated shadow shapes to visually connect disparate objects in space. Or, if you're planning to connect such shapes with soft-edged forms such as clouds, don't draw anything. Instead, plan to connect them later with paint in subtly varied background color, value, or shape edges, like the distant cattails in *It's My Territory!* (above) and branches in *Two Nuthatches* (page 45). It's better to visually connect many shapes into one large one than with many (unrelated) bits.

Determine where shape edges can be less discernible, perhaps from inky shadow or very bright light. Draw a slightly heavier line where shadow will mostly obscure them, and a paler or dotted line where light or similar color conceals edges. Similar textures, colors, value, or patterns might also obscure edges.

Take your time, understand your subject, and render not what you *know* but what you actually *see*. For instance, we all know that cats have whiskers and people eyelashes, but they're generally obscure to the greater mass of cat or person. Eliminate or minimize nonessential details you don't actually see!

As you draw, double- and triple-check proportions, an important composition principle.

Take the rough length measurement of one distinct shape, such as, in a bird subject, its beak, tail, or leg, and compare the length, width, and angle of every other part, and even key background elements, to that one unit. For instance, if a long beak is one unit, its head might be half that; its body, three or four; its tail, three; and its perch, five or six, depending on the species and angle of view. In a flower subject you might use a leaf, petal, or stem length as your standard unit. Don't use a different unit in the same painting!

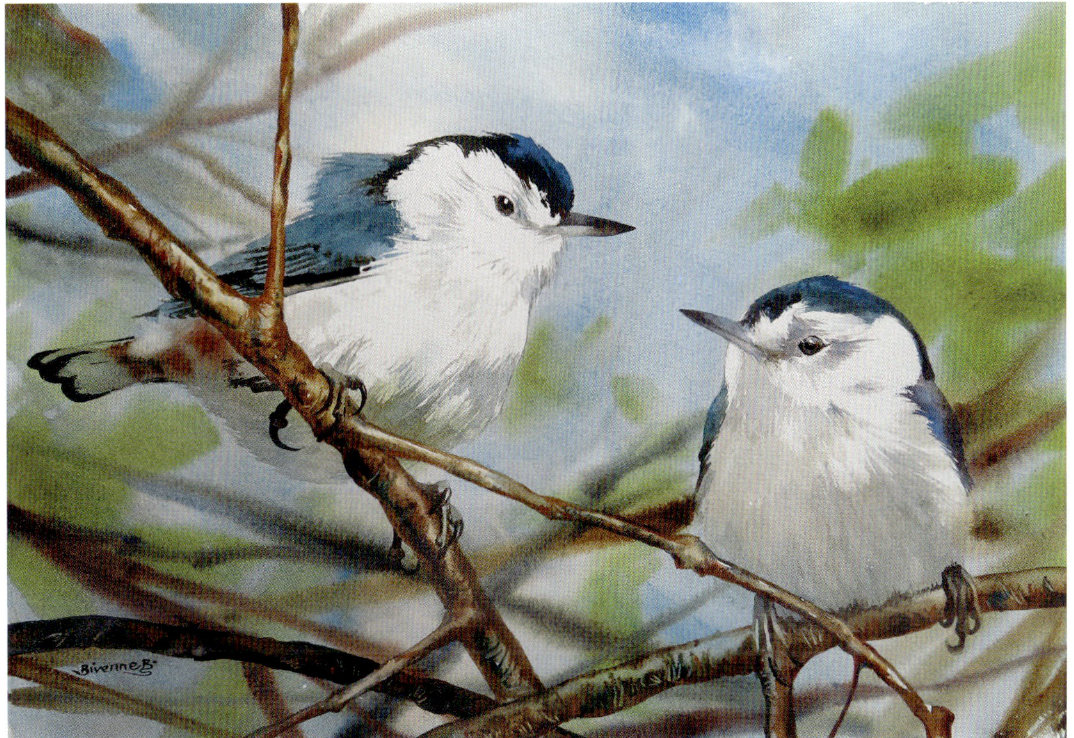

Two Nuthatches, 15" × 22"

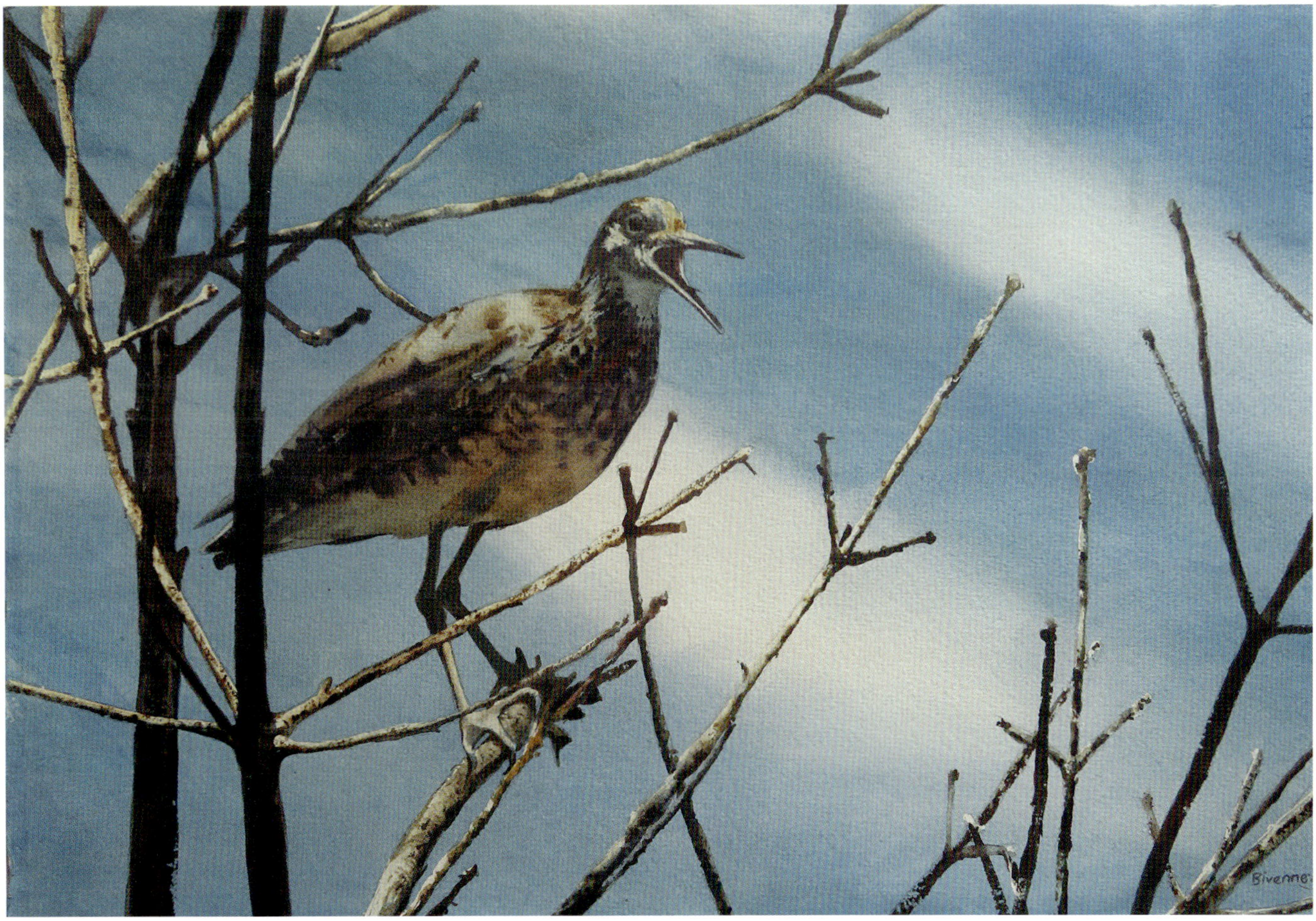

Willet, 15" × 22"

One unit of measurement was used to determine the spacing, size, and placement of the eye and particular markings. It can also be used to calculate the length, angles, and width of supporting background elements.

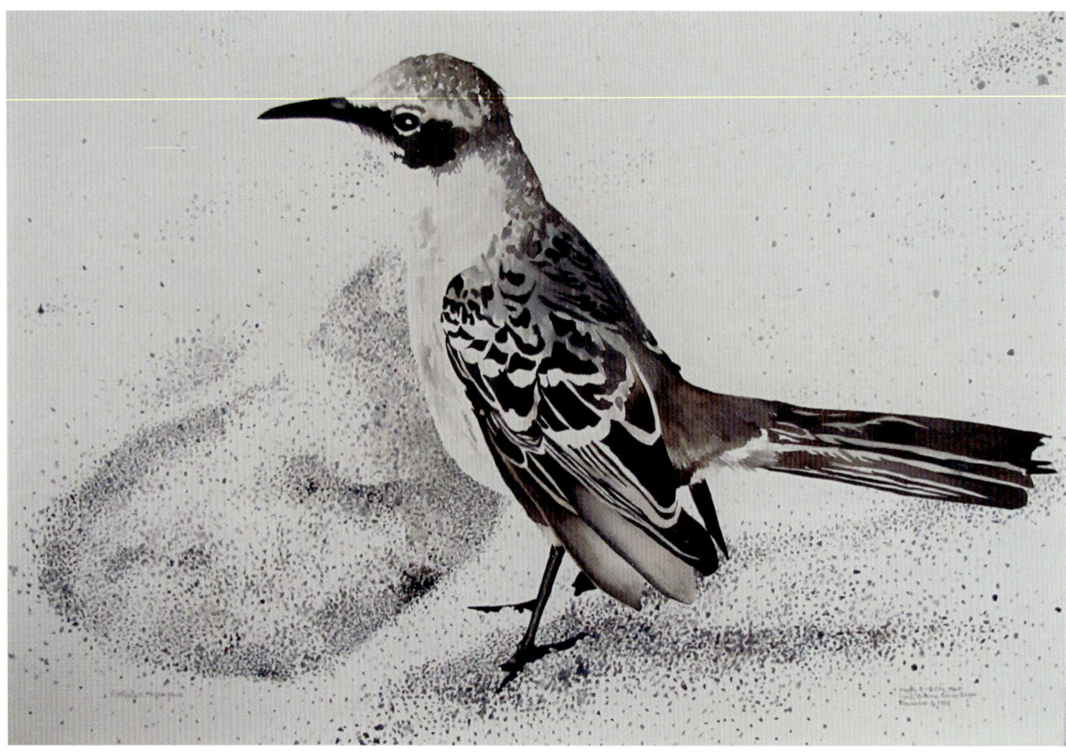

Galapagos Mockingbird, 15" × 22"

Head feathers are usually short, though sometimes they are long in odd places, such as a crown at the top. Back and chest feathers are often slightly longer, and in some, such as ptarmigan, feathers even cover feet. Wing and tail compared to body feathers of flying birds are long, as seen in *Galapagos Mockingbird*.

Note the length, thickness, and position of (nonrepresentational) color and value shapes, and always compare them to supporting and other background shape elements. Don't ignore shadow and illumination shapes. Careful comparisons are key for a solid drawing and eventually a great painting.

The line length and direction of hair, fur, and tail—or of branches, stems, and leaves—often help determine the position of the next (object) shape and guide the eye around the composition. Do you see how the long hairs encircling the chin in *Oo la Zsa-Zsa!* (page 47) and the whiskers and markings in *Feline Friendly* (page 47) direct the eye back up to the face and eyes, respectively? Look for such cues in your subject and background supporting shapes and indicate them in your contour drawing.

Sketch linear, man-made object shapes freehand, because the eye picks up even the subtlest error made with a straight edge.

If a particular shape is challenging to sketch, try drawing only negative-space shapes that surround it, such as the shapes between fingers, branches, tail and legs, flower petals, or leaves. Take your time to get characteristics and placement within the composition right. Always think of *shapes*, both positive and negative, as you go back and forth from subject to background, rather than of such specific things as a leaf or foot. Add details last.

Or with a photo reference, refer to and draw the motif upside down; this forces your eye to focus on shapes. You might make a grid on it,

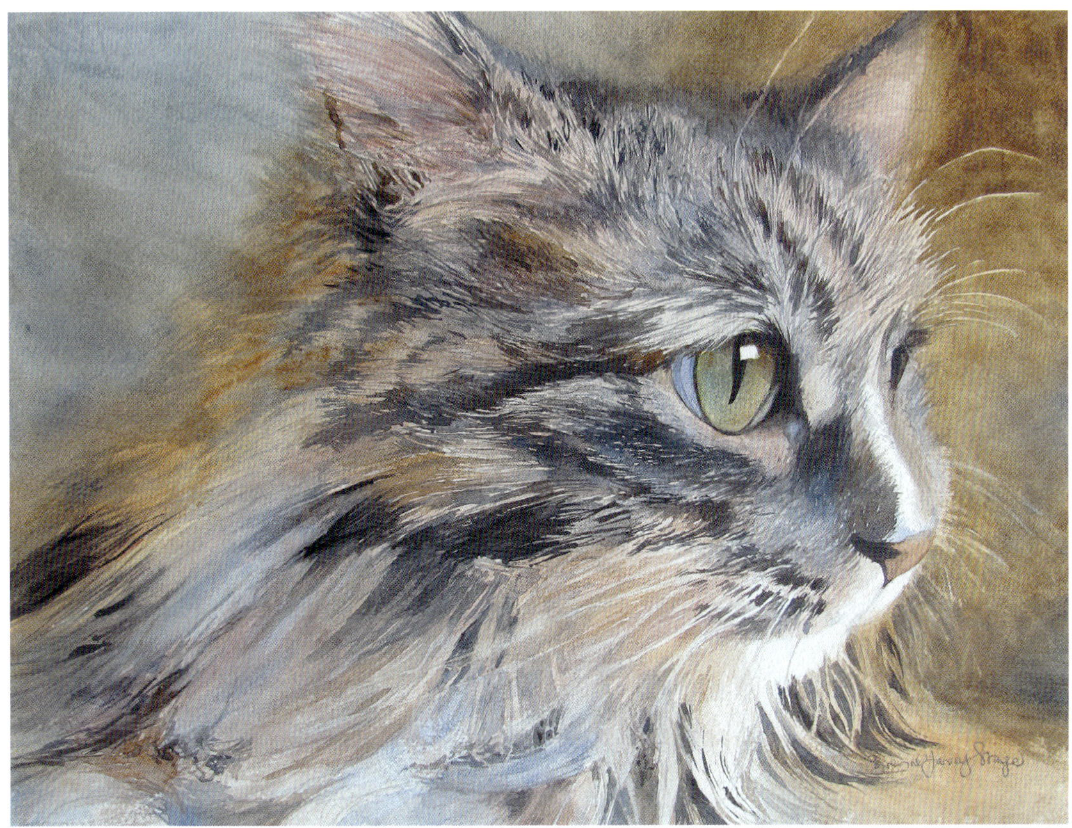

Feline Friendly, 11" × 15"

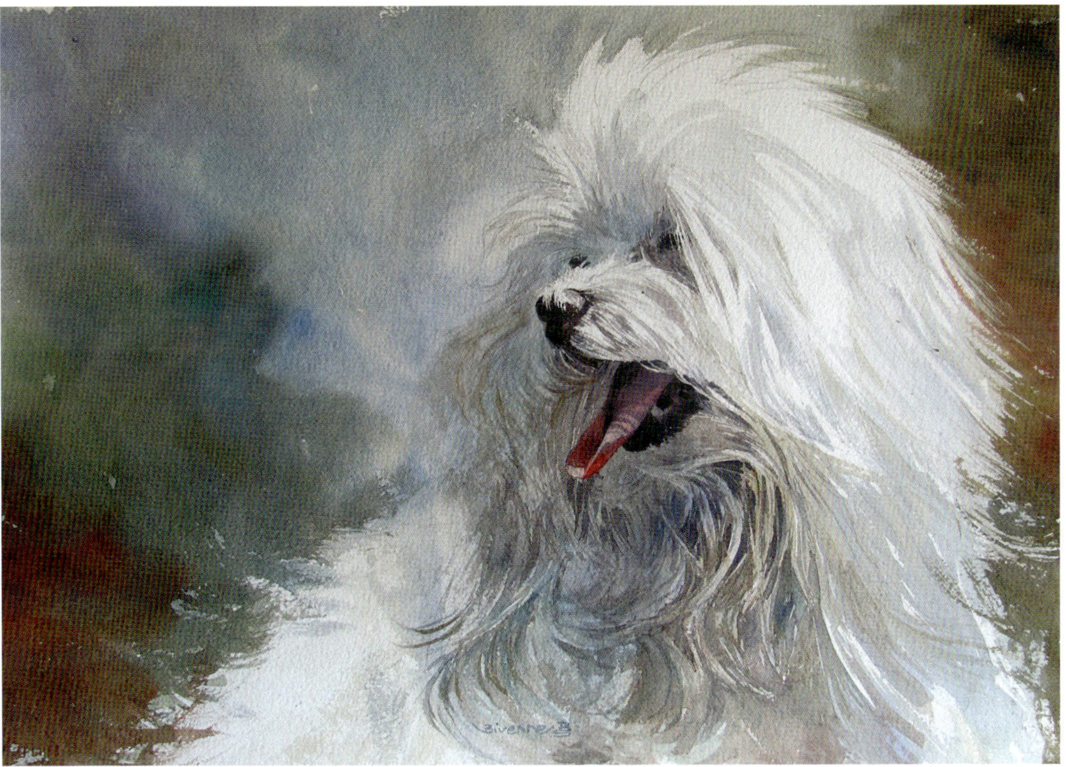

Oo la Zsa-Zsa!, 15" × 22"

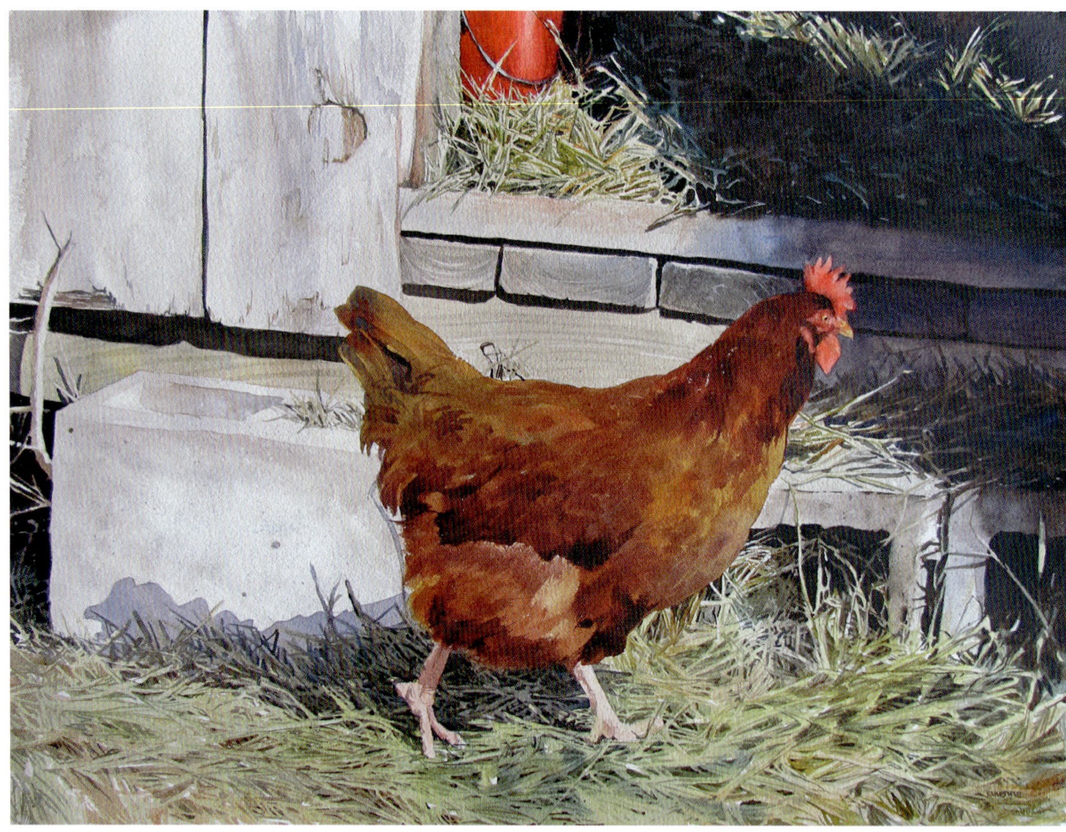

Poultry in Motion, 22" × 30"

The cinder blocks in this motif were drawn freehand. Note that cast shadow shapes, key feathers, and the wood grain in the panels but not all the hay stalks are outlined.

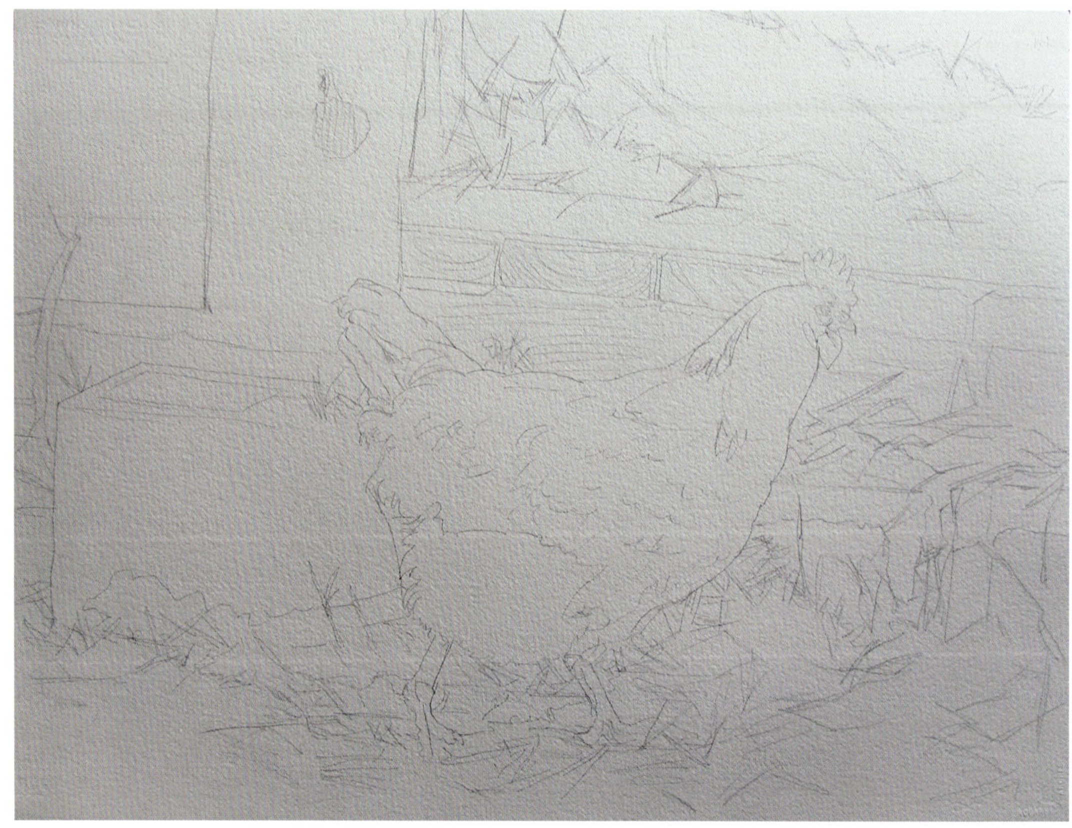

which you can use to scale your subject up or down on the watercolor paper. Then draw the shapes as they appear in each square. *Don't rely on grids* once you become familiar with drawing. Erase the grid before painting!

Now step back. Hold the contour drawing up to a mirror to double-check proportions and angles. Do edges of key shape, color, value, and other elements guide the eye to the subject and around the composition?

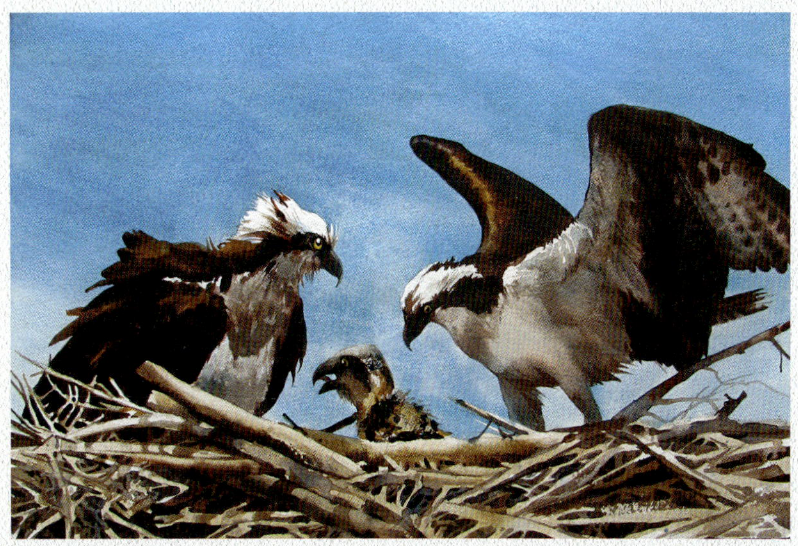

Proud Parents, 15" × 22"
Though empty, the blue sky is an interesting shape, and value varies from medium to light. The simple, open-space background balances the complex nest pattern, warm colors, and dynamic subject shapes.

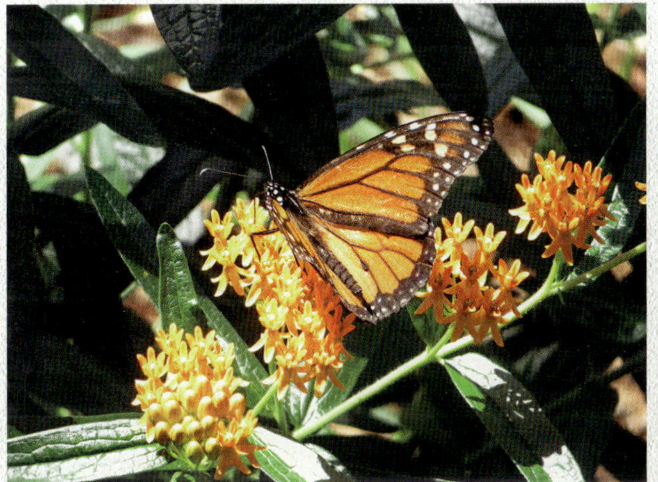

To sketch a motif like this, begin by cropping from left and top. Note similarities in leaf and butterfly wing shapes. Plan to initially harmonize orange butterfly/flowers and green background with yellow, because orange and green contain yellow.

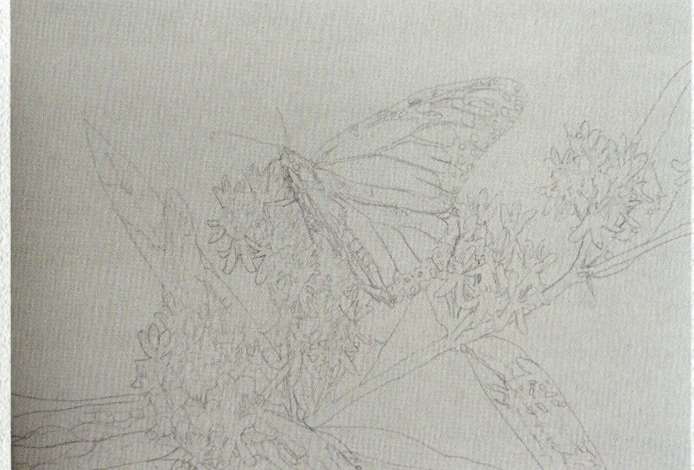

I ignored most of the busy, dark background leaf patterns, which compete with the butterfly wing markings, and sketched insect, flower, leaves, stems, and cast shadows on leaves. The butterfly visually connects the evenly spaced flower spheres, while the leaves and stem act as secondary supporting shapes.

Bottom Line:

A contour drawing represents your carefully planned design and acts as a structure for painting. Let the fun begin!

MATERIALS

Dragged across bone-dry paper, sandpaper helps suggest highlights on rough rock or sand surfaces, the sun's sparkle on water, or blizzard-driven snow.

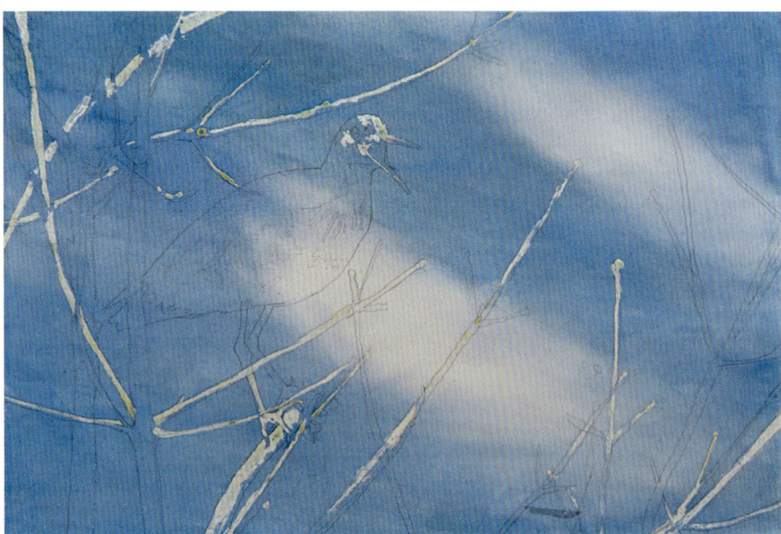

Use the best materials you can afford.

Paper: Bright-white, cold-pressed watercolor paper; I use D'Arches 300 lb. Its weight should not be less than 140 lbs., to reduce warping. Since I manipulate, twist, tilt, turn, and dry the paper as I paint, it's unattached to a board or table.

Brushes: A large assortment, rather than one or two, allows more options for additional colors and simultaneous applications.

- brights (or flat brushes) by Princeton Art & Brush Company and Regency Gold Series 500 from 1/8" to 2";
- Robert Simmons White Sable #7 script used for fine detail work;
- small, medium, and large rounds;
- Princeton Art & Brush Company size 4 fan brush;
- old toothbrush to spatter or remove paint.

Palette: Ideally, this should be white with large wells surrounding a large mixing surface; it shouldn't wobble on a table. Arrange pigments around the palette in color wheel order. Mine, by Creative Mark, has a cover and still serves me well after thirty-five years.

Other materials: water bucket, 2B pencils, white eraser, tissue, paper towel, Q-tips, medium-grit (#80–#100) sandpaper, frisket, sponge, spritzer, salt.

Frisket (or masking fluid) is a type of resist. Follow directions for use, then paint freely over it, as shown. While laborious to apply, it leaves defined edges (some of which may later require softening) but saves time and effort painting around or behind many tiny white or pale details, such as dots or stripes. Nevertheless, refrain from relying heavily on it, especially for *large* areas that are easier to paint around. When the paper is dry, remove with an eraser-like *frisket pickup.*

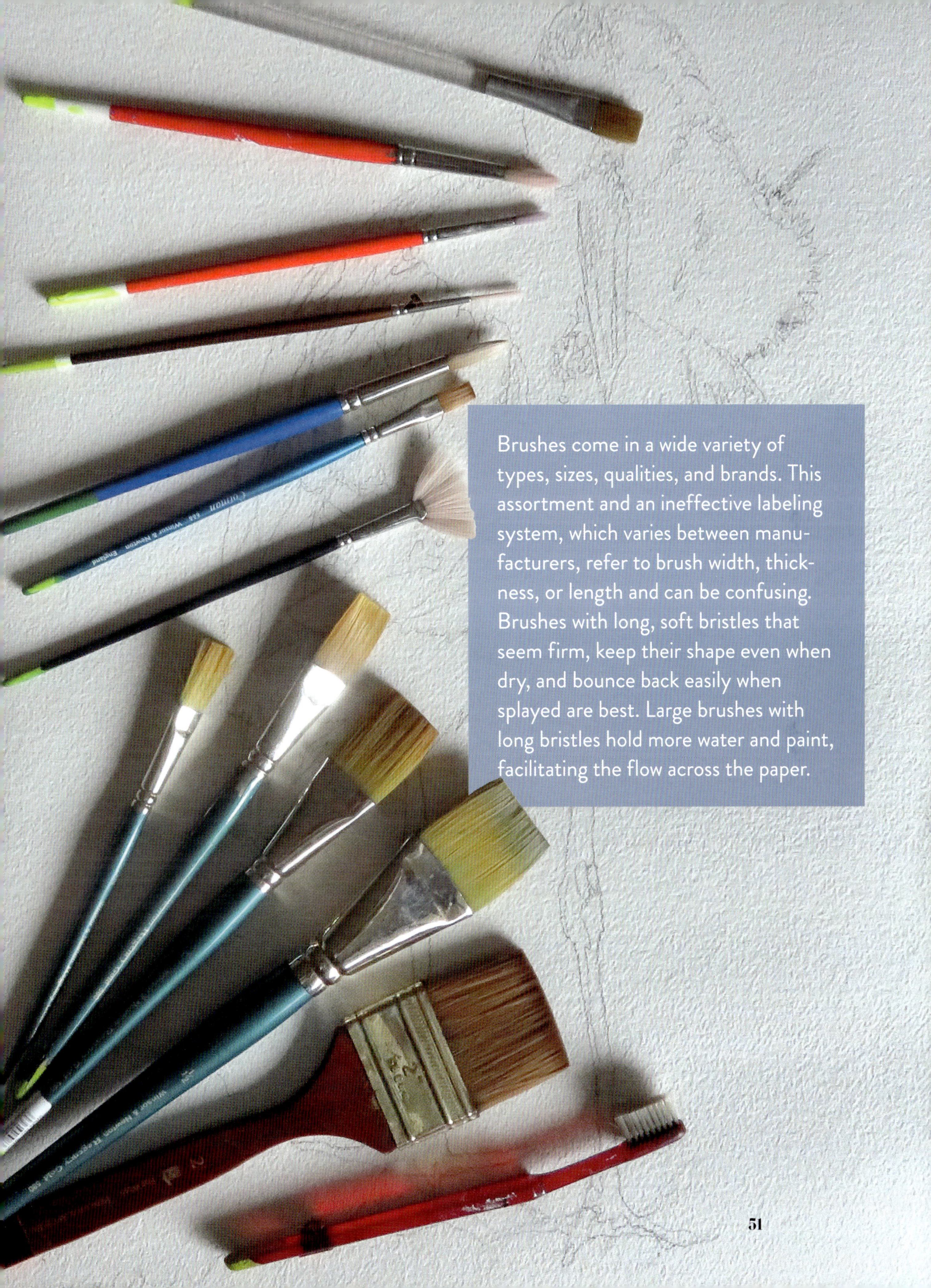

Brushes come in a wide variety of types, sizes, qualities, and brands. This assortment and an ineffective labeling system, which varies between manufacturers, refer to brush width, thickness, or length and can be confusing. Brushes with long, soft bristles that seem firm, keep their shape even when dry, and bounce back easily when splayed are best. Large brushes with long bristles hold more water and paint, facilitating the flow across the paper.

COLOR THEORY BASICS

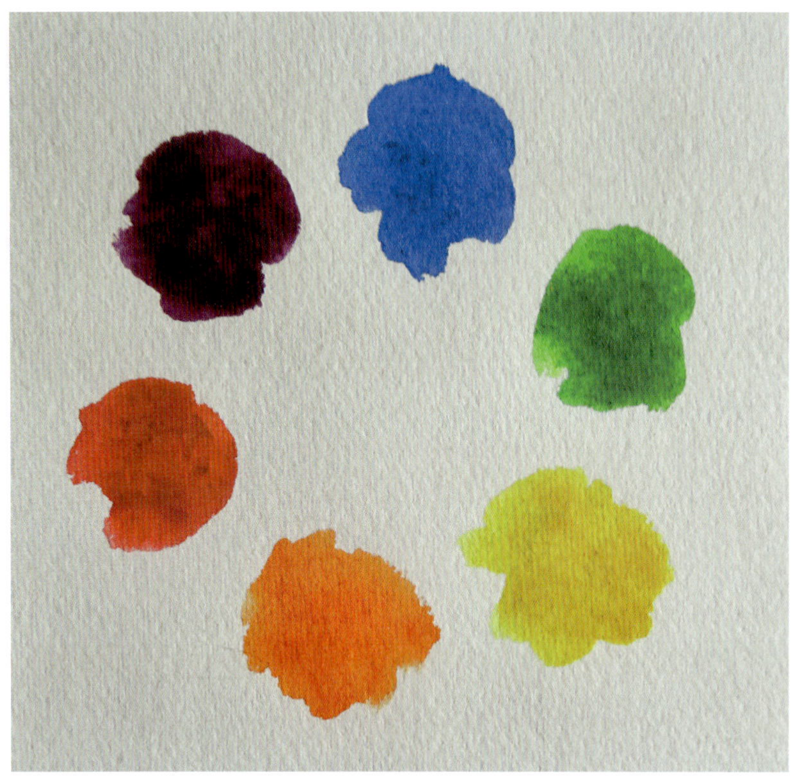

Colors (and pigments) are relative in temperature and value to each other. In any value, yellow appears warmer and paler than purple, which has (cool) blue and no yellow in its mix, but only slightly paler (and cooler) than orange and warmer than green, because both contain yellow.

Color, which is subjective, has four major properties: hue, chroma, value, and temperature, all of which are most apparent when compared to other colors. Light and shadow affect color.

Hue refers to individual colors such as red and blue. Organize paint around your palette in color wheel order of red, orange, yellow, green, blue, and purple. Place brown paint near red/orange or yellow/green.

Chroma is the quality of a hue's purity, intensity, brightness, or saturation. White (or, rather, *water* in watercolor), black, or the color's complementary (opposite) changes chroma. Fire engine red is high in chroma, while pink is low (red + white or *water*).

Value, which is subjective, is a color's lightness (tint) or darkness (tone, shade). The lighter a color is, the higher its value. Change value by increasing or decreasing the amount of paint *and* of water (white *paint* in oil) and often the quantity of a harmonious dark color. Squint to see value nuances.

Confused? By adding water (or, in oil, *white*), color becomes lighter in value *and* loses chroma (saturation). But by neutralizing it with gray/black or its complementary of the *same value*, the hue loses chroma, not value. It becomes less bright, less colorful, but *not* less dark. An object that is gray or neutral or of low chroma only appears to increase or decrease in value as shadow and light change.

Temperature, which is subjective, is a hue's warmth or coolness and affects chroma. Orange, red, and yellow are warm (think fire and sun) relative to cool blue, green, and purple (think water, grass, sky, shadows). An opposite temperature dulls chroma. Open your eyes wide to see temperature nuances.

Perhaps adding to further confusion are *temperature* differences between various hues around the color wheel *and* between hues within a family. While red is warm and blue cool, yellow and purple can be either. Yellow *warms* green, purple *cools* red. In the blue family, Ultramarine, because it has hints of red in it, is warm compared to Prussian blue, a greenish blue.

Similar colors, particularly those difficult to differentiate, are harmonious. Orange harmonizes with both yellow and red because both produce orange. Major temperature differences such as (warm) orange and (cool) blue painted next to one another contrast. Combined, they neutralize, creating a gray and reducing the chroma of both. Using one temperature maintains bright chroma, but introducing the other dulls it.

Don't mix a reddish blue with yellow if you want bright green.

Don't mix a greenish blue with yellow if you want dull green.

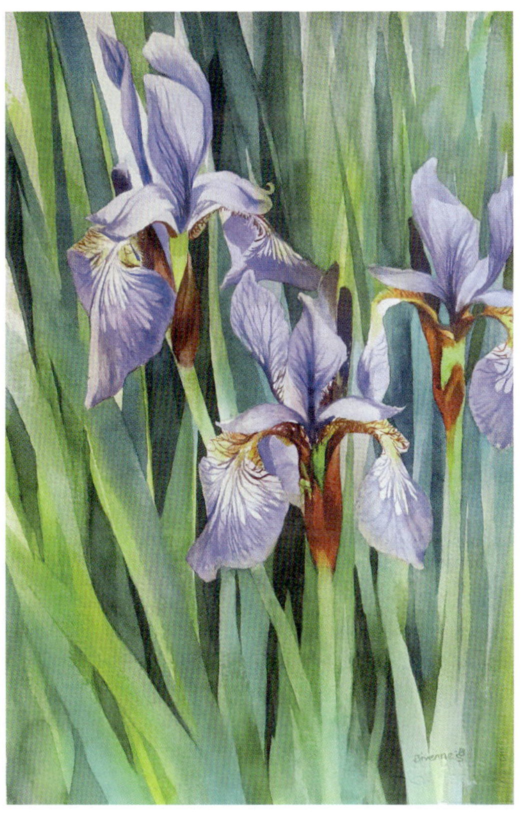

Siberian Iris, 15" × 22"

MIXING GREENS

Always create green with a yellow first and then a blue, since the former is paler. Green appears more natural when mixed, and you can control color properties.

- *Bright* greens are attained from lots of bright or cool yellow, such as Aureolin, and *hints* of bright blue or green, such as Cobalt Turquoise Light or Winsor Green.
- *Dull* greens contain some red.
- *Warm* or olive greens contain brown.
- *Cool* greens have more blue in them.
- *Pale* greens are attained with lots of water, less paint.
- *Saturated* greens result from lots of paint and little water.
- *Dark* greens derive from lots of dark, staining pigment and very little water.

Bottom Line:

Get to know your paint! Familiarize yourself with color theory and pigment characteristics, because both are essential to painting. Efficiency is key to watercolor! You'll make wonderful discoveries by experimenting.

PALETTE AND PAINT

Watercolor pigments vary in color, temperature, strength, chroma, and other qualities. They are transparent, opaque, staining, reflective, granulating and/or lift easily. Stick with a brand that performs the way you like and expect. I use Winsor & Newton professional grade watercolor paint with mostly transparent pigments and a range of characteristics.

Arrange paint in color wheel order (red-orange-yellow-green-blue-indigo-violet) and label your palette with each. Keep the palette in the same position when you paint.

Some pigments fill multiple wells, and formerly empty wells accommodate extras, such as Cerulean at the top of my palette. Those that appear black are actually Ultramarine, Winsor Violet, and Prussian. ***Note:*** Labels are not necessarily adjacent to their respective colors.

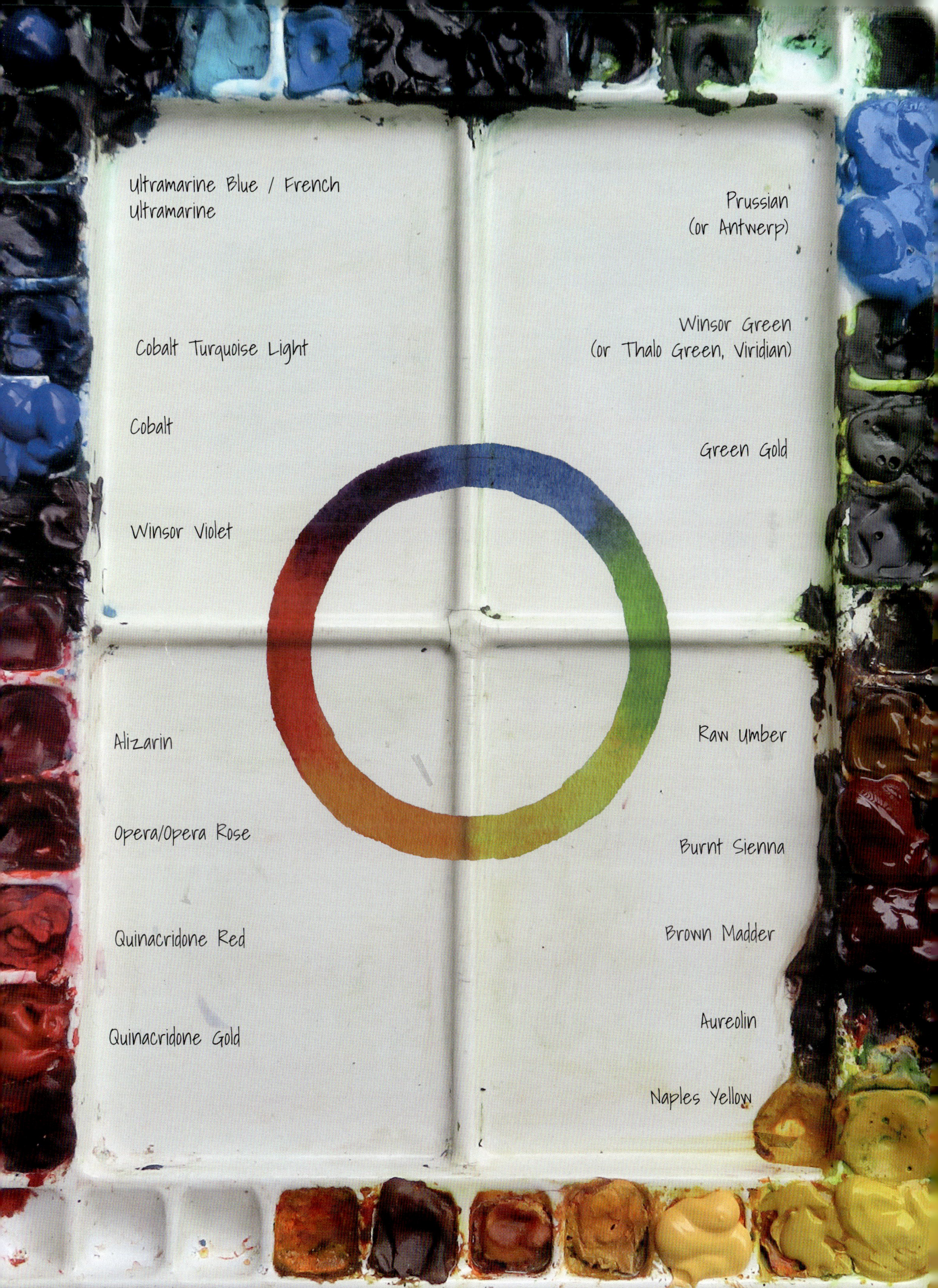
Ultramarine Blue / French Ultramarine
Prussian (or Antwerp)
Cobalt Turquoise Light
Winsor Green (or Thalo Green, Viridian)
Cobalt
Green Gold
Winsor Violet
Alizarin
Raw Umber
Opera/Opera Rose
Burnt Sienna
Quinacridone Red
Brown Madder
Aureolin
Quinacridone Gold
Naples Yellow

PART 2: Painting

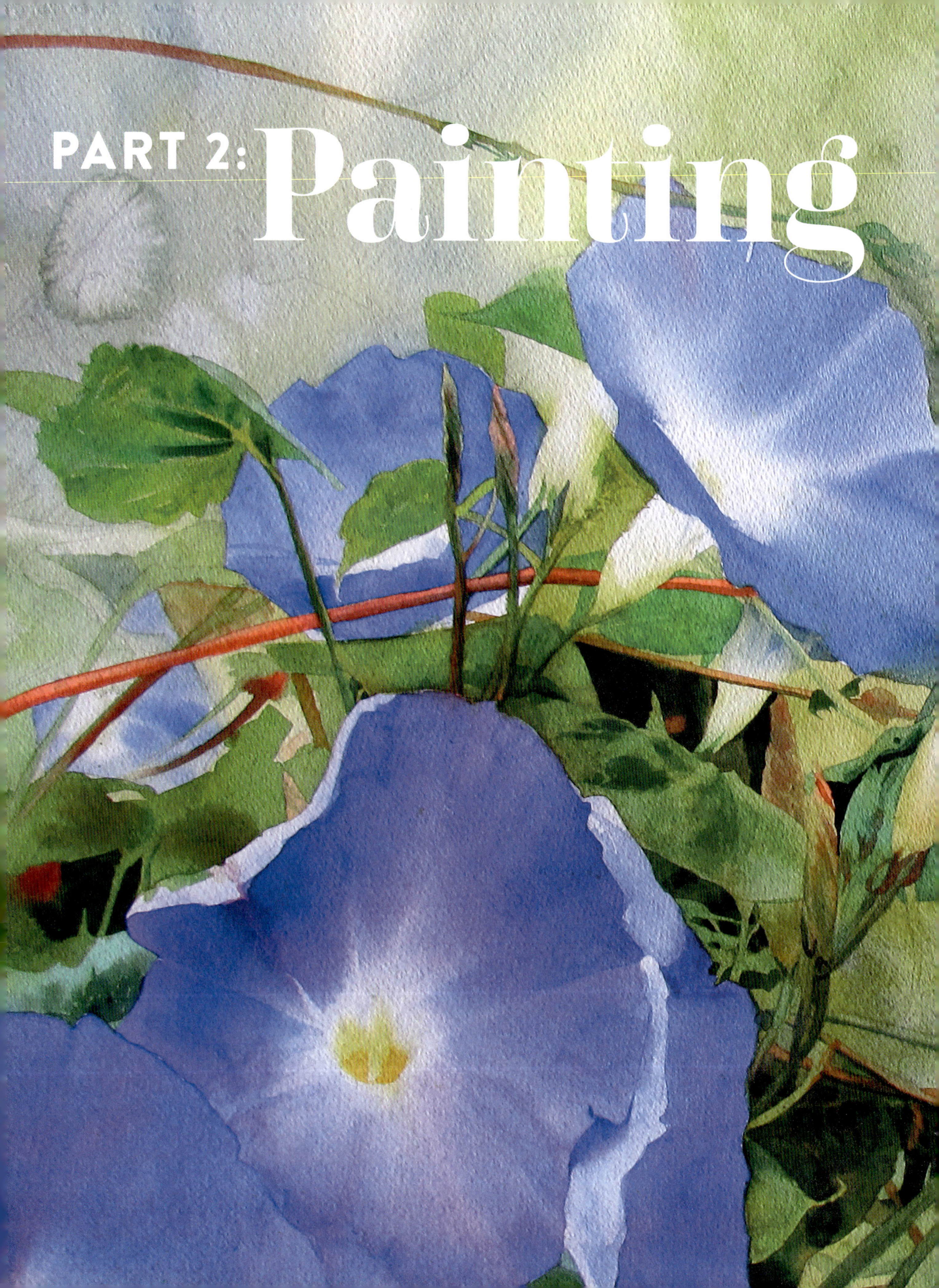

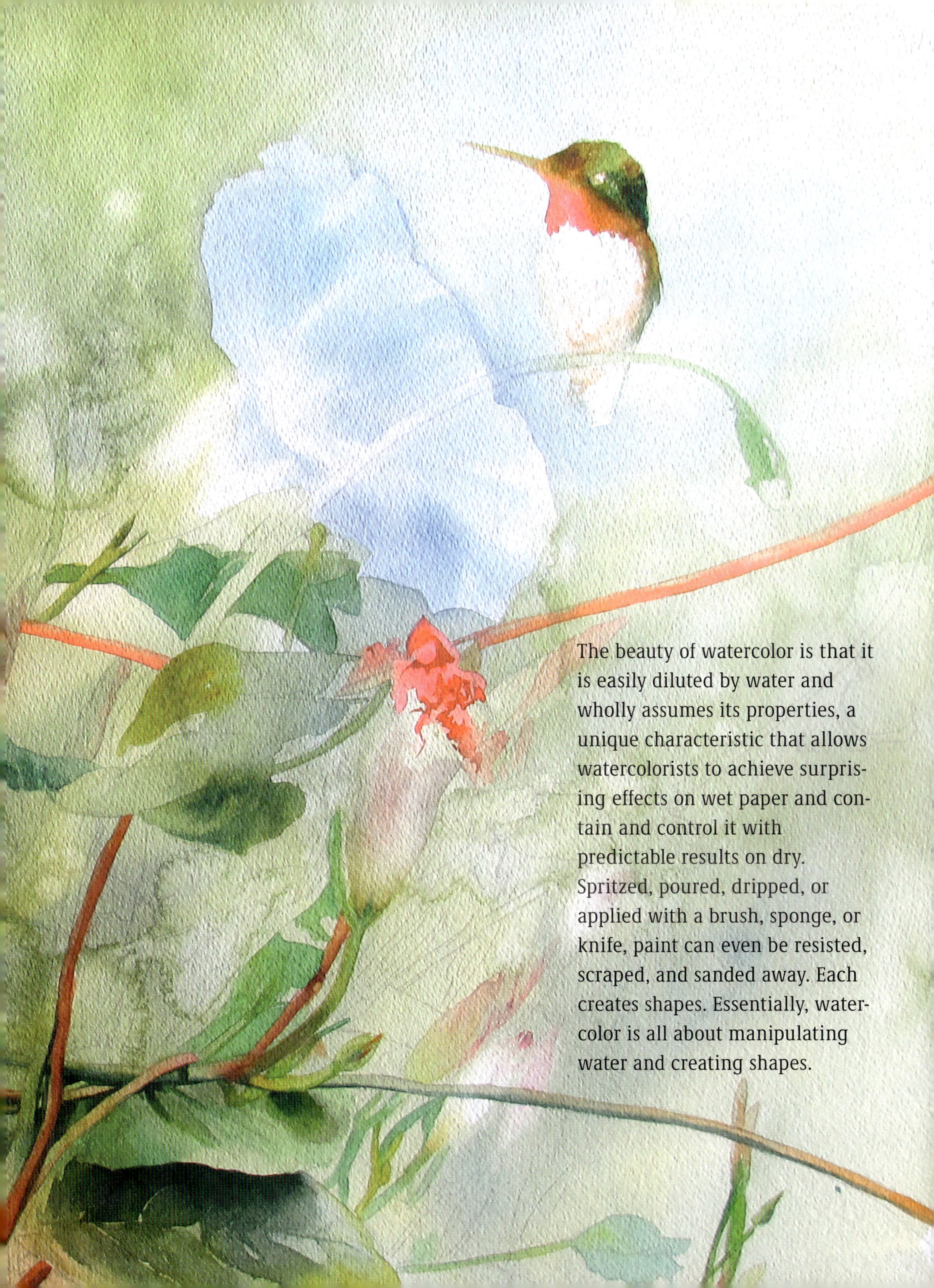

The beauty of watercolor is that it is easily diluted by water and wholly assumes its properties, a unique characteristic that allows watercolorists to achieve surprising effects on wet paper and contain and control it with predictable results on dry. Spritzed, poured, dripped, or applied with a brush, sponge, or knife, paint can even be resisted, scraped, and sanded away. Each creates shapes. Essentially, watercolor is all about manipulating water and creating shapes.

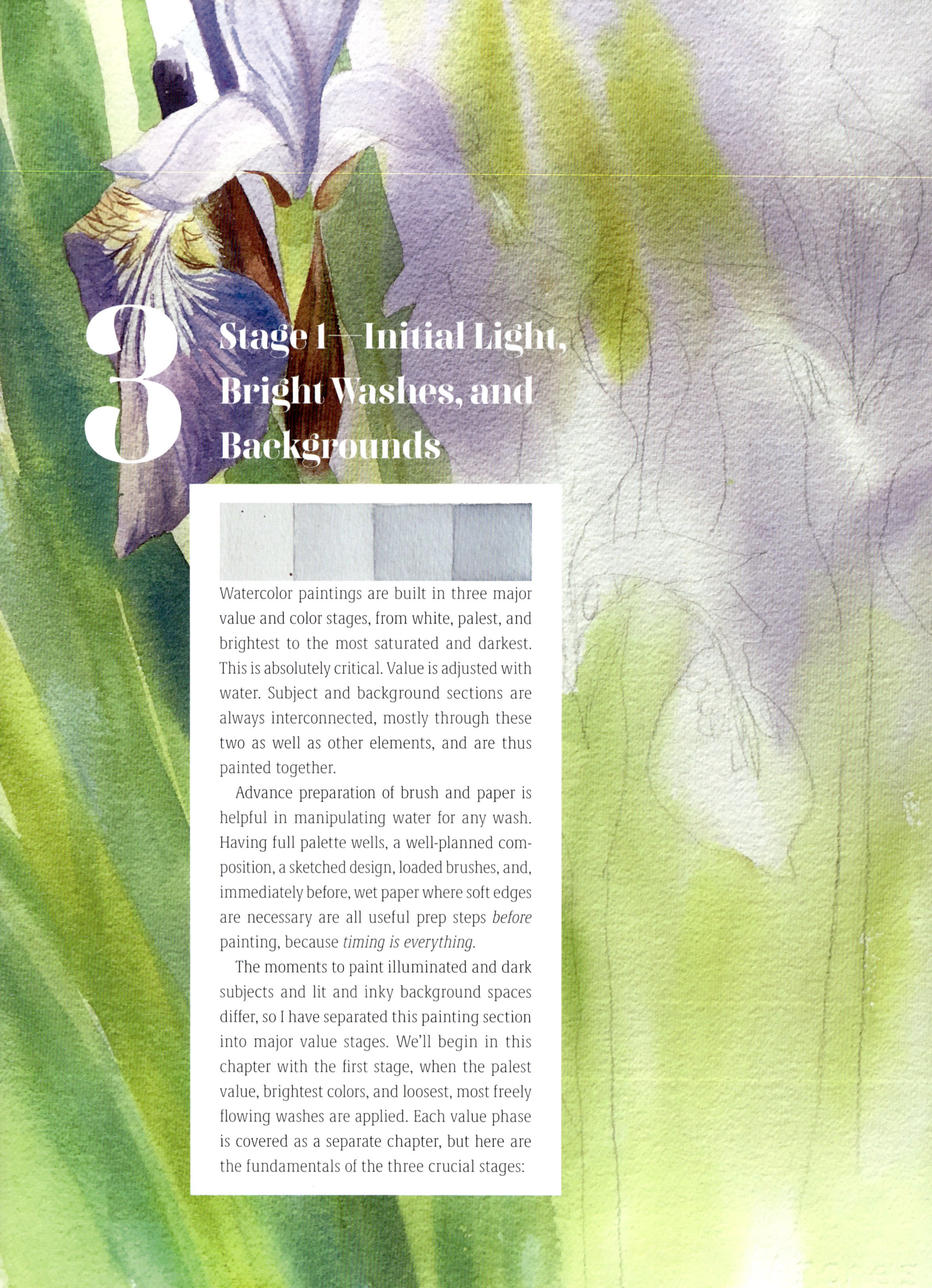

3 Stage 1—Initial Light, Bright Washes, and Backgrounds

Watercolor paintings are built in three major value and color stages, from white, palest, and brightest to the most saturated and darkest. This is absolutely critical. Value is adjusted with water. Subject and background sections are always interconnected, mostly through these two as well as other elements, and are thus painted together.

Advance preparation of brush and paper is helpful in manipulating water for any wash. Having full palette wells, a well-planned composition, a sketched design, loaded brushes, and, immediately before, wet paper where soft edges are necessary are all useful prep steps *before* painting, because *timing is everything*.

The moments to paint illuminated and dark subjects and lit and inky background spaces differ, so I have separated this painting section into major value stages. We'll begin in this chapter with the first stage, when the palest value, brightest colors, and loosest, most freely flowing washes are applied. Each value phase is covered as a separate chapter, but here are the fundamentals of the three crucial stages:

STAGE 1

With brightly colored, pale-value paint, overlap *most* sketched shape edges.

Covered in this chapter, bright paint establishes the strength and might begin to suggest the direction of lighting on objects highest in value and chroma. Paint as thin as tea to as thick as cream is quickly applied with large brushes to mostly wet paper and is least controllable. Sketched subject and background shapes are loosely covered with harmonious color *except* where defined, *illuminated white* shapes must remain unpainted. Otherwise, no other shapes, colors, shadows, or dark values are added in this quickly painted stage.

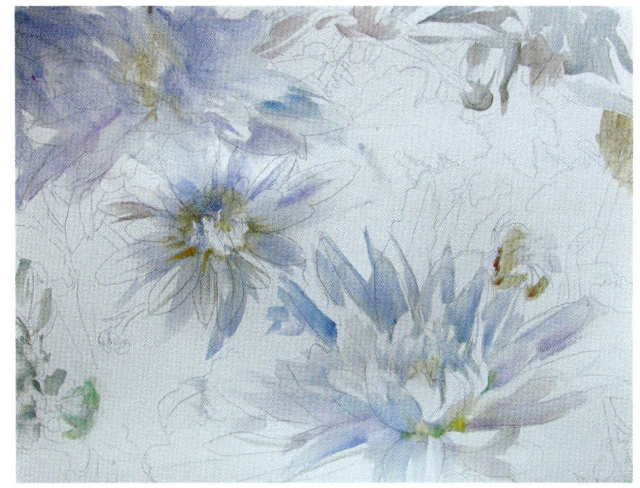

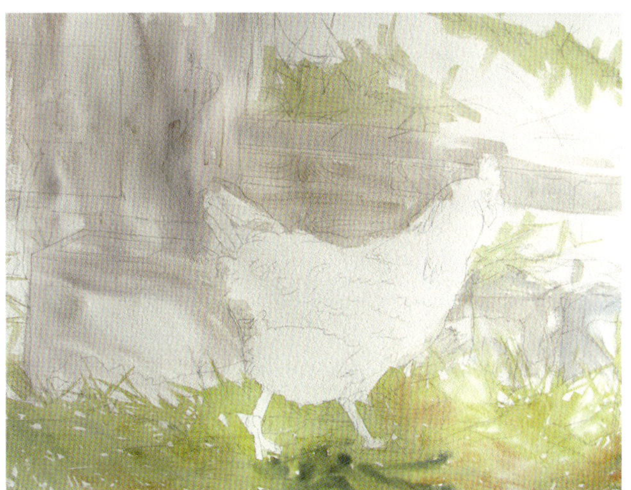

Muted, monochromatic, or low-chroma color evokes a quiet mood.

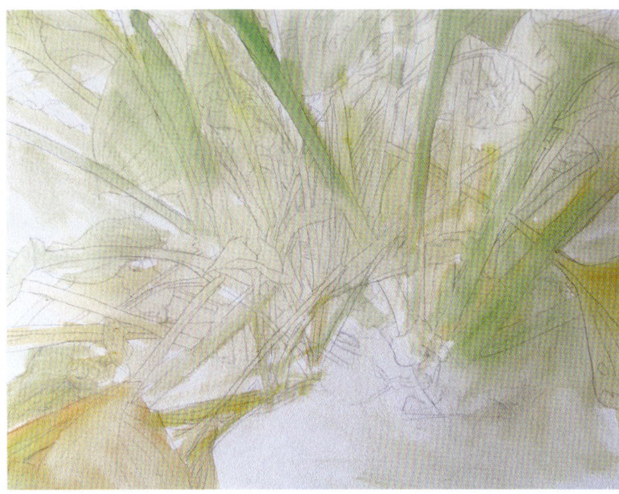

STAGE 2

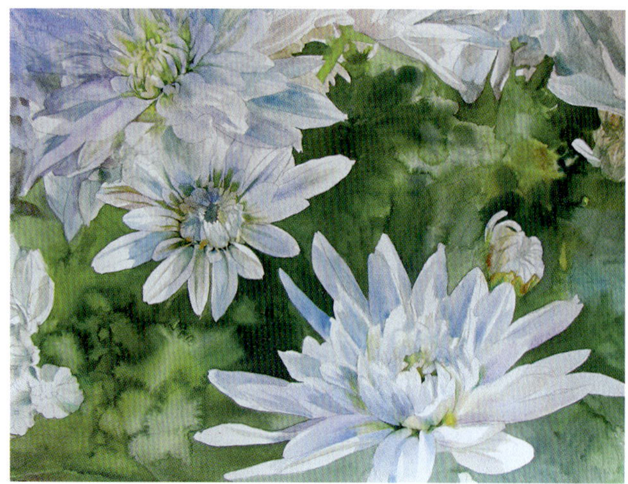

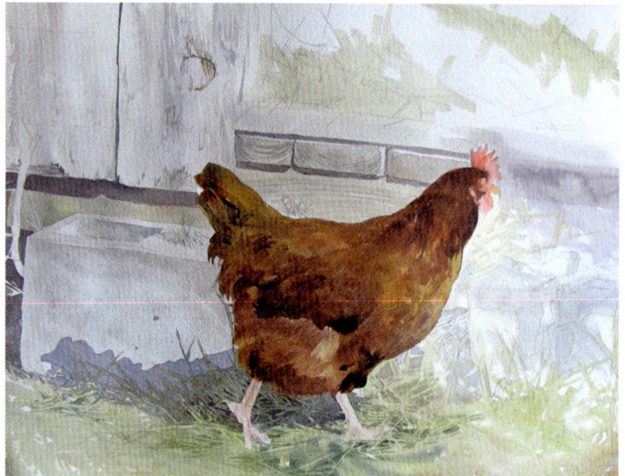

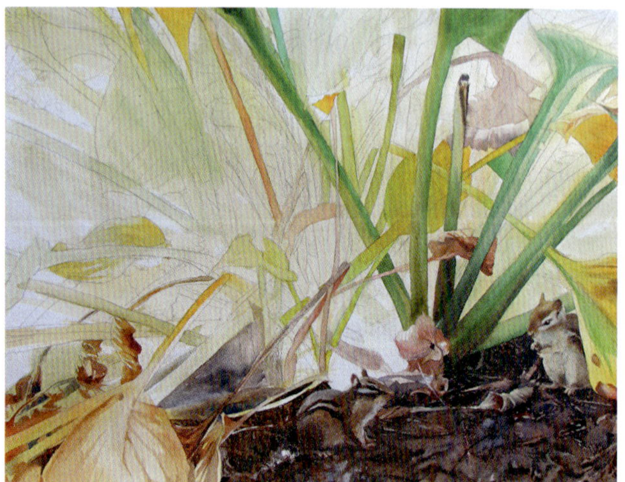

Paint midvalue or harmonizing color over *some* painted areas and some sketched shape edges.

Discussed in the next chapter, color is medium to high chroma and midrange in value. Basic subject shapes and simple details, dominant background color mass, form and cast shadows, negative space shapes, and some background supporting shapes are added. Paint in coffee or cream consistency is applied wet-on-dry and dry-on-wet with various brushes and other tools. Illuminated white and colored shapes are saved, but otherwise color saturation is enhanced. Depending on the composition's design, pattern complexity, and quantity of shapes and other elements, this stage can take time.

STAGE 3

Apply darkest, harmonizing, and sometimes contrasting color over *some* painted areas and shape edges.

Explained in chapter 5, darkest value is strategically placed within or around subject, supporting, and background elements to dramatically enhance lighting and color painted in earlier stages. Key texture, shape, and form details of subject and background, and shadowed depth and darkest negative space shapes are finalized. Pigment is more saturated, very dark, or even dull, and in generally a thick, creamy consistency. Most shapes are painted on dry paper except where dark, soft edges are required. A complex design, dominance of rich darks (which may require more than one layer), and many small, dark shapes can make this stage time-consuming. Always refrain from painting darkest-value shapes until completely satisfied with stages 1 and 2.

Painting in value stages from light to dark prevents dark defined shapes of color from bleeding into (wet) adjacent paler ones, because even dry paint seeps into a wet wash. Dark paint easily hides lighter-value paint, wet or dry. Beginning with bright color prevents future problems if you later need it where dark or dull already exists.

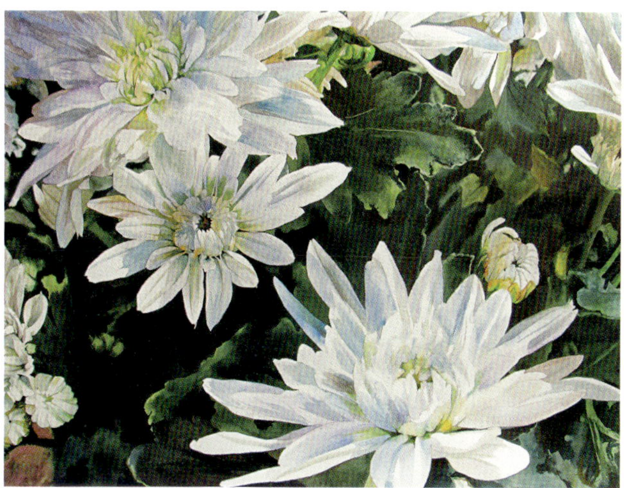

White Chrysanthemums, 22" × 30"

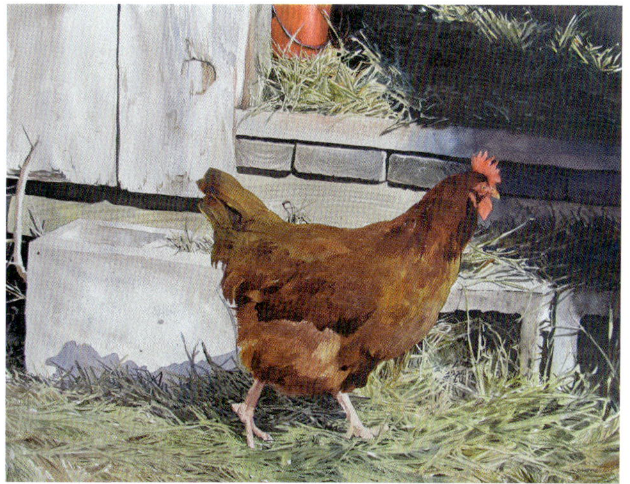

Poultry in Motion, 22" × 30"

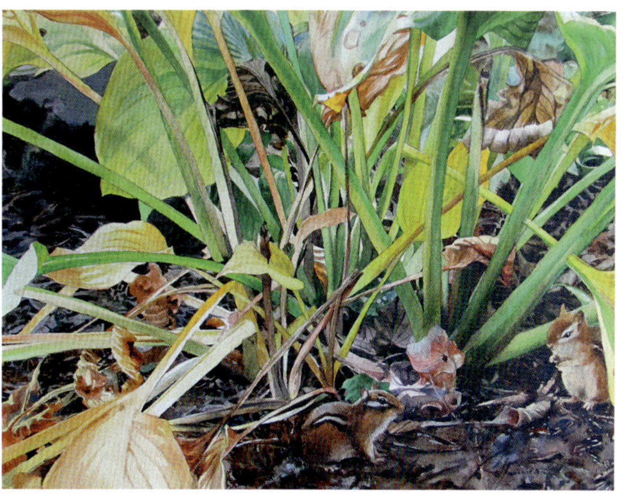

Hosta la Vista!, 22" × 30"

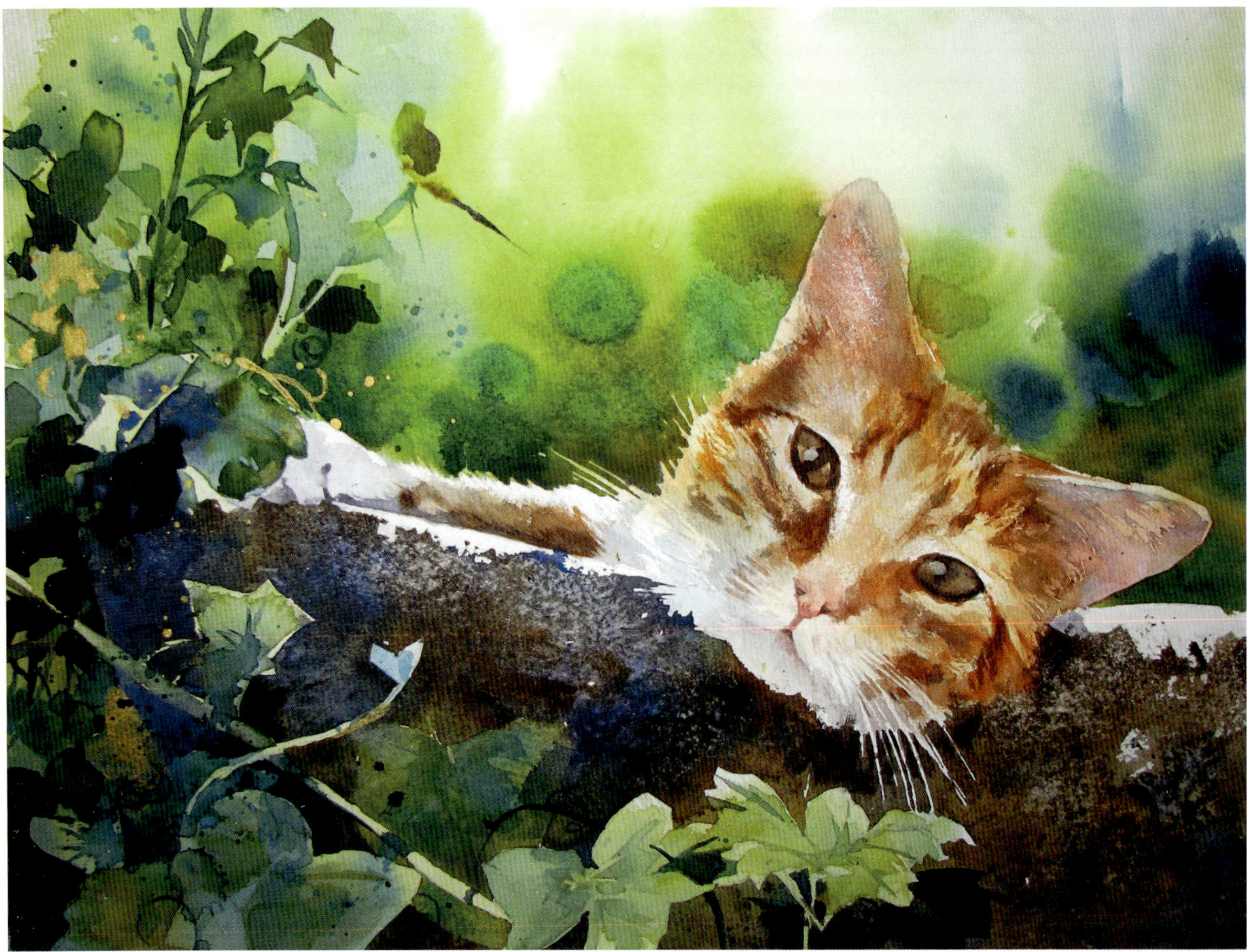

Topaz, 11" × 15"

Watercolorists thus paint around and behind illuminated white shapes (stage 1), then around, over, or behind illuminated white, pale, and bright colorful ones (stages 2 and 3), building value and shapes in this way until the darkest are finally added (stage 3).

Though lighting strength is first suggested through elements of color chroma and value in the first stage of a watercolor painting, it often becomes more apparent in stage 2 and is especially obvious in the last stage.

To preserve successful soft edges painted at any stage, paint them only once before continuing to the next stage and especially the last. This means often using more paint than you think necessary, especially on wet paper.

ADJUSTING VALUE IN WATERCOLOR

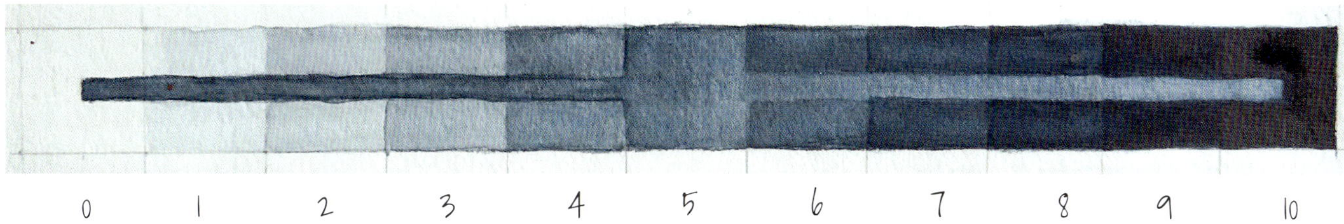

Varying color saturation and value depends on paint and water quantity. Both are gradually built in each successive painting stage with layers of paint.

Value is the relative degree of lightness or darkness of a particular color. White (being colorless) requires no paint at all (see "Saving White"), zero on a value scale of 0–10. Value, like color, is subjective.

Some pigments and colors, such as yellow, aren't darker in value than a medium range of 4 or 5. Each will seem its darkest when dry in the well, a clue to its usefulness in achieving very saturated dark value equal to black. On my palette, Aureolin is useless for this purpose, while Prussian blue is extremely effective.

Lots of water and little paint produce the palest washes at the light end of the value scale (1, 2, 3). Plenty of *bright* paint and little water yield saturated *color* (often midvalue of 4, 5, 6, or even 7), while *dark* paint and little water produce the darkest *value* at the other end of the value scale (8, 9, 10). An even mix both of water and paint produces the midvalue washes used in stage 2, with more water here for paler, and more paint there for darker midvalues. The ratio of water to paint on the brush affects value, produces various wash consistencies, and plays the most important role in attaining a value range.

> Water in the brush causes pigment to dry about 30% lighter on *dry* paper. Paint on wet paper dries *another* 30% lighter. Maximize dark value by using more paint on dry paper.

Water	+ Paint	= Value
None or clear	+ None	= White, 0
Some to lots	+ Very little	= Very light ("tea") 1, 2, 3
Some to lots	+ Some	= Light ("coffee") 3, 4
Some	+ Some to lots	= Medium ("coffee" to "cream") 4, 5, 6
Very little	+ Lots	= Medium dark ("heavy cream" to "thin mud") 6, 7
Almost none	+ Lots	= Very dark / saturated ("toothpaste") 8, 9, 10

This chart is likely challenging to practically interpret, so I suggest experimenting as much as possible using different-sized brushes and different ratios of water to paint, since no two brushes are alike. You'll notice that brushes with the longest and most bristles hold the greatest volume and therefore carry a wash farther. Observe the wash difference between a loaded brush and one with little paint.

Build value and color saturation, even with thickly applied transparent paint, by also layering washes, drying the paper between each. This method creates a wonderful, brilliant glow the way light shines through stained glass. But applying many thin, tea-like washes is a slow process because of the drying time in between, so it is far more efficient to use more creamy paint in two or three layers.

WHITE passages + midrange value + SATURATED COLOR + rich DARKS = ENERGY.

Colors, neutrals, and midrange values are enhanced by extremes of shadow and light.

Bottom Line:

Add more water to lighten a value, and more paint to darken it.

APPLICATIONS

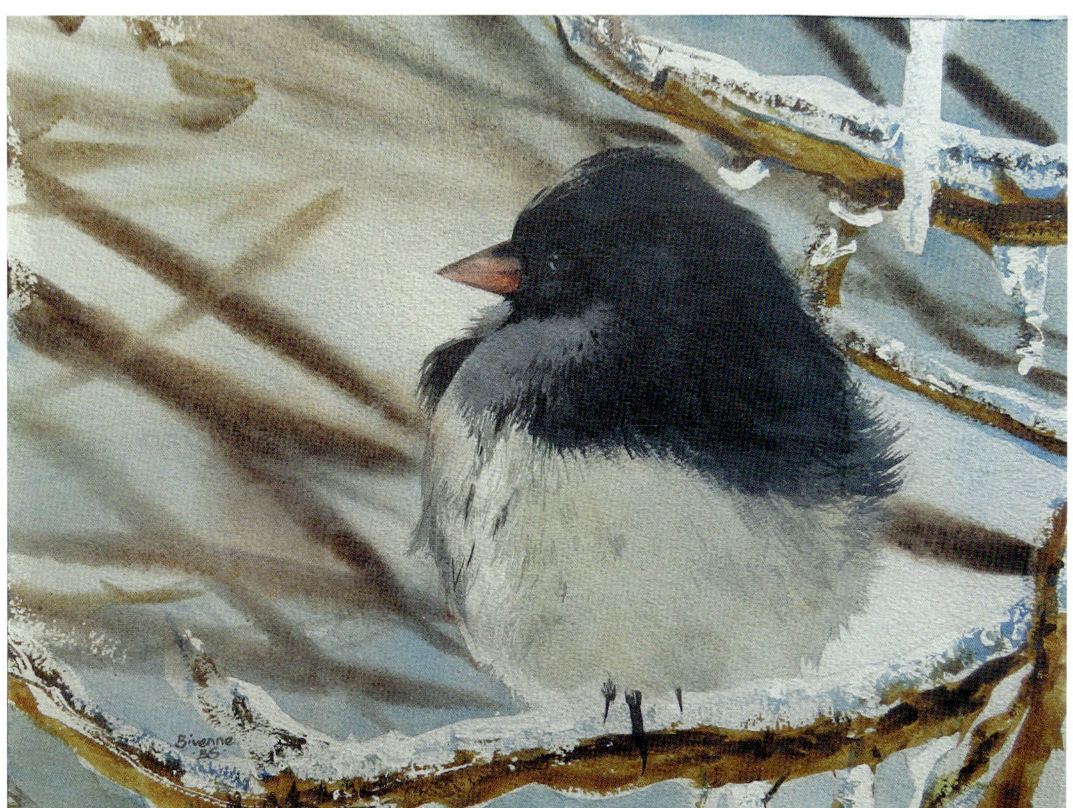

Slate-Colored Junco on Ice, 12" × 16"

Watercolor paint is applied to paper in four major ways; I begin most of my paintings with the first two and generally complete them with the last two. I also often use a fifth way in stage 1.

Each creates different shape, color, value, or textural *edges*, creating a feeling of spontaneity with some or defining details with others. Don't use one exclusively; in fact, try to use all to establish line variation and interest in your paintings.

The first word (for example, "dry") in the following refers to the *brush* (loaded with paint), and the last word (for example, "wet") refers to the *paper*:

1) ***Wet-on-wet:*** Applied mostly in stage 1, this leaves a fuzzy, diffused, undefined, or completely lost edge and is best for graded washes. Paint blends easily and freely on wet paper. Once applied, tilt the paper back and forth; don't adjust or otherwise touch the wash as it dries.

Always load your brush with copious paint *before* wetting the paper with a separate brush or spritzer. Then paint as fast as possible, spreading the paint before the paper dries—easiest with large brushes, almost impossible with small.

Water blanches a value like white lightens oil paint, so wet-on-wet washes dry much paler than they appear when wet. For more impact, increase the quantity of paint or apply to wet *painted* paper (or both). Adding extra paint now often precludes another value layer once the paper is dry. The lower sky and clouds in *Willet* (page 45) were painted wet-on-wet.

2) ***Dry-on-wet:*** Applied mostly in stage 1, this leaves a *controlled* lost edge suggesting fuzzy specific shapes such as dark clouds, mist and sea spray, fine fur, distant branches, light and shadow on round objects, and more. The brush, loaded with paint, is *damp*, with most of its water squeezed out. (Remove excess water by pressing the base of the bristles into a tissue; leave paint untouched at the tip.)

Dab thick paint (cream/toothpaste consistency) slowly to maximize control of and success with the dry-on-wet application. Dark paint applied to pale value or bright color is also effective. Don't adjust it as it dries.

Soft edges convey spontaneity and mystery in any medium. They ease the transition between two colors, shapes, or values, obscuring edges in shadow or bright light, or when melding background color with subject shapes. Wet-on-wet and dry-on-wet effects are unique watercolor characteristics, so *include them wherever possible in your paintings*. The green water shapes in *Semi-palmated Sandpiper* (page 42) and the branches in *Female Red-wing* (page 43), *Standing Out* (pages 82 and 83), and other similar bird portraits were painted dry-on-wet.

3) ***Wet-on-dry:*** Applied mainly in stages 2 and 3, this leaves a defined, hard, or found edge. Easily controllable with various amounts of pressure, angles, and twists of any implement, it suggests a variety of textures and shapes, revealing your unique painting style, because

Each application except the fifth was used in this painting.

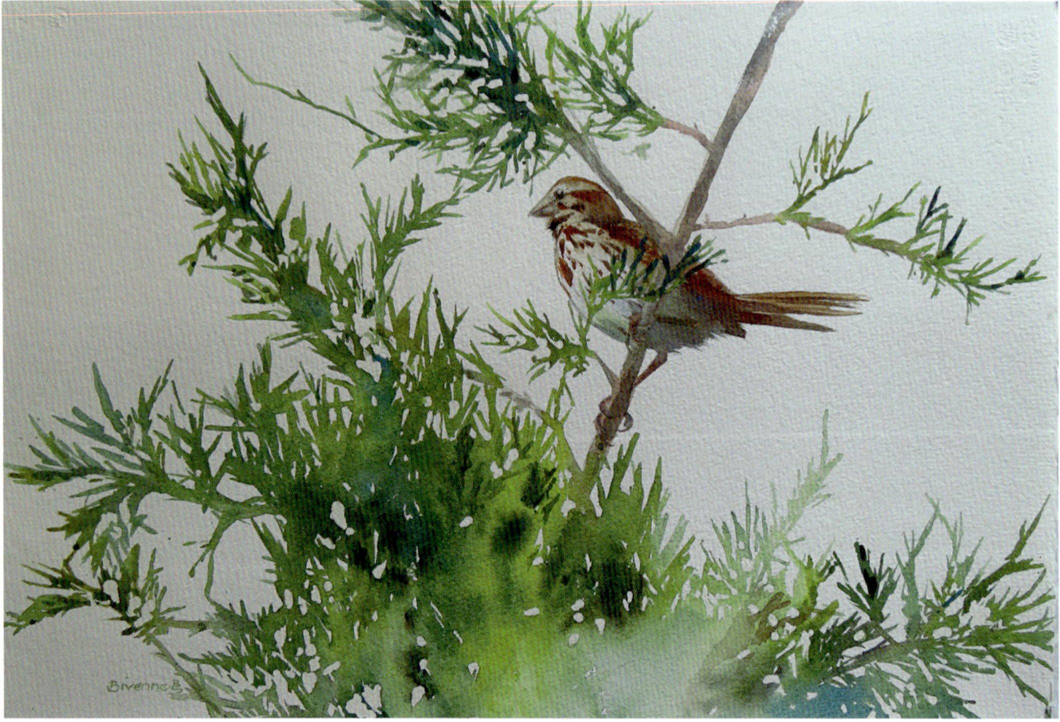

Song Sparrow, 15" × 22"

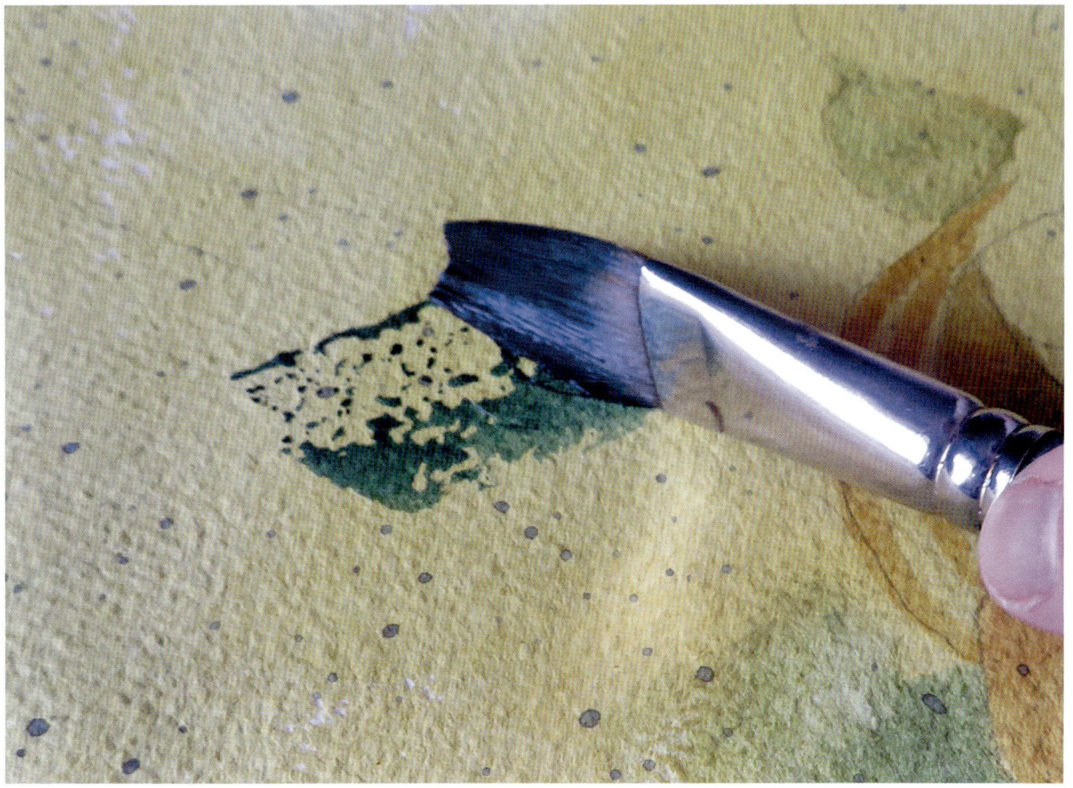

A dry brush effect is easiest to accomplish in small areas and generally with cream-consistency paint. Hold the brush at an angle and push or drag it lightly and quickly across the paper on its heel, parallel to the paper surface.

hard edges delineate shapes and create noticeable contrast. *Use this application in focal and other areas but not exclusively.*

4) ***Dry-on-dry:*** Applied when the painting is complete in stage 3, or wherever it can be left undisturbed by other washes, a damp paintbrush barely grazes the peaks (not valleys) of uneven, dry paper. Sometimes known as scumbling, it might suggest rough texture on bark or rocks, or sparkle on the sea.

5) ***Wet-on-damp:*** Less clearly defined and controllable than possible on dry paper or as evenly spread on wet, a drop of water applied early on *damp*, painted paper slowly spreads into a strange shape called a bloom. It's unapparent until it becomes lighter in value than the surrounding paint and develops a dark outline.

Though some watercolorists avoid blooms, they might suggest soft, mottled, and bumpy textures on shadowed snow, sand, and foliage; composite blossoms; curly fur; piles of sticks, bark, rocks, etc. When blooms occur by mistake, they can be challenging to remove.

Each application used in a single painting adds variation and especially interest to lines, shapes, colors, textures, and value throughout.

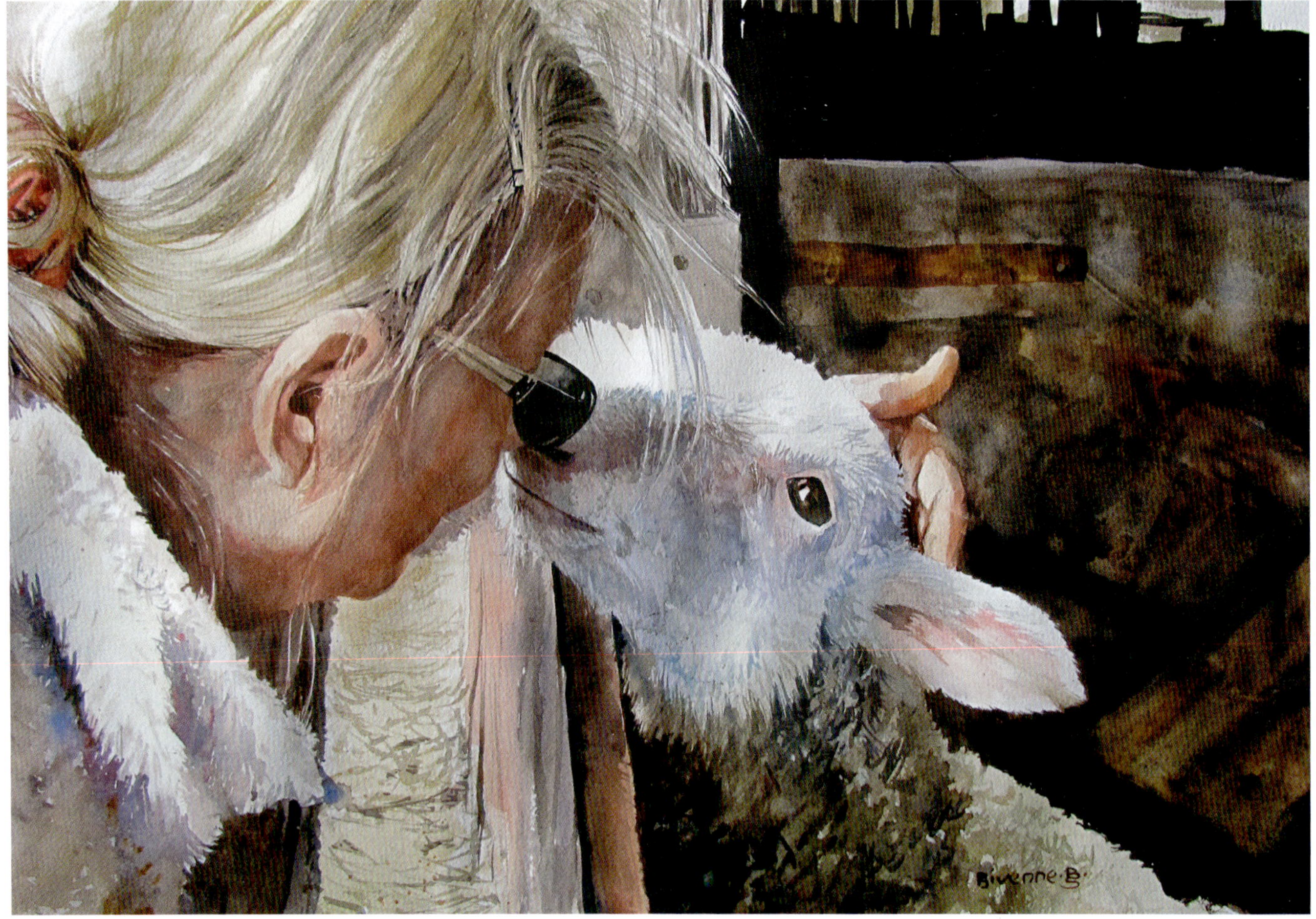

Mary Had a Little Lamb, 15" × 22"

SAVING WHITE

Conveying whiteness is easy. White paper acts both as a color and a value in watercolor. Unpainted, white is *saved* and suggests illumination. Both points are key for a strong painting because white is a value extreme that adds appeal to midvalues and contrast to darks.

Color from nearby objects reflects onto white objects, which of course cast shadows and have shadows cast onto them.

Identify where light is coming from, and save only the *lit* part of the white object's shape with masking fluid for multiple tiny white shapes, as was done in *Monarch* (page 119) or by painting form and cast shadows around or behind large, white (illuminated) shapes with clean, bright paint, as in *Peaceful Preening* (page 86).

White objects look best if both *reflected and shadow colors are bright*.

Note the hue, value, and chroma of color reflected onto a white object, such as the pale-aqua tint reflected from the green leaves above the flower in *Water Gems*. The rich interior reds of the flowers in *Peonies II* (page 114) reflect pink onto neighboring white petals. Its shadows are also clean and bright and highlights "saved."

Observe the shape, value, and color of its form shadow. Though it may appear gray, a white object appears whiter if its *shadow color is bright*. I suggest a clean, bright blue in a tea to coffee consistency, painted (in stage 2) once any reflected color is dry. Leave highlights unpainted. Typically, midvalues and darks added later (in stages 2 and 3) behind a white object shape make the latter appear especially bright, clean, three-dimensional—and white.

Cover a *completely shadowed* white object entirely with paint in stage 1, with generally a blue wash like the lower-left flower in *Pansy Pops* (*below*). Develop its form shadows in later stages. This may seem counterproductive, but when the shadowed white shape is juxtaposed with brightly lit or other darker cast and form shadowed nearby and background shapes, it will still appear white, yet in *shadow*.

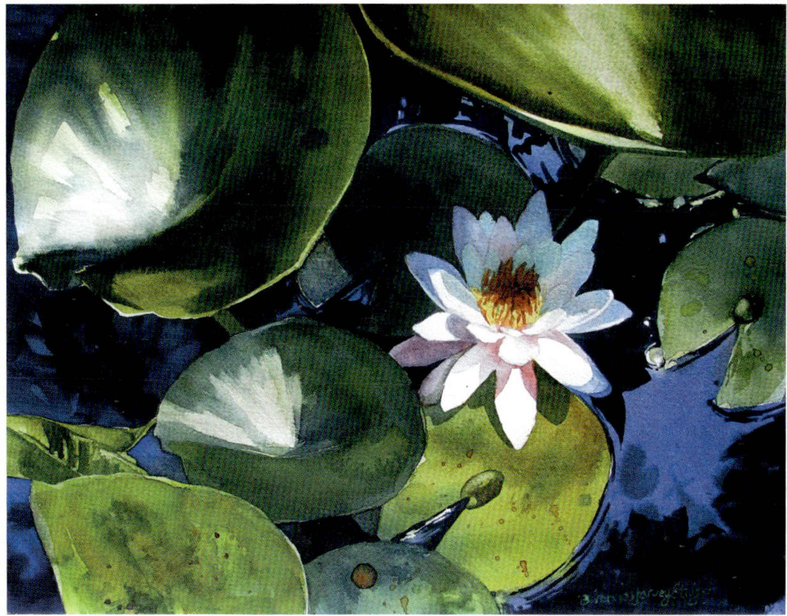

Water Gems, 11" × 15"

Avoid white paint, especially to fix mistakes or add highlights, unless you're suggesting snowflakes, or if most of the piece is liberally painted in an opaque medium such as gouache or acrylic.

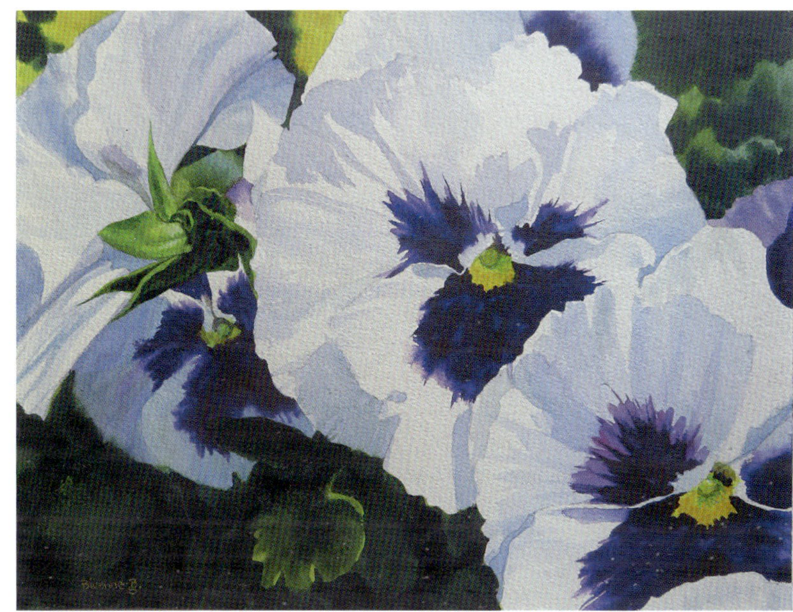

Pansy Pops, 12" × 16"

Bottom Line:

Identify light direction, save only shapes of illumination, and paint both reflected color and shadows with high-chroma paint. Try to save some illuminated white shapes in every painting.

PAINTING A "CLOSE-UP" SUBJECT WITH ITS BACKGROUND IN STAGE 1

The first step in painting a subject with its background is harmonizing them through color or at least a pale wash. This is a critical requirement in stage 1 and usually necessary as the painting develops throughout stages 2 and 3, because it not only forces loose, soft shapes but also immediately solves two undesirable *edge* problems:

(1) a white line where two adjacent defined shapes meet, or

(2) a dark line between the two.

The first happens when two proximate defined shapes don't quite meet neatly enough, while the other results from two layers of equal value overlapping sloppily. Both distract. This is not to imply that it's impossible to achieve an accurate, clean line separating two defined shapes. Rather, it's that painting them neatly side by side is challenging, especially when colors contrast. And besides, a painting with only defined edges has no line variation.

The solution is to initially paint them with a shared pale (bright) hue quickly and loosely across sketched edges, wet-on-wet and dry-on-wet, as shown in the examples throughout this chapter. Hide overlaps later (in stages 2 or 3) with darker value or another color, or lift while damp.

In the first stage of *Welcome, Zinnia*, a light wash of shadow color covers the white spots in the butterfly's wings (page 72). When dry, they and the few illuminated spots were protected with frisket, as seen here. Next, yellow was painted wet-on-wet and dry-on-wet across almost all edges, with bright light green confined mostly to the background. Orange and darker green, with more paint on a dry brush, were quickly applied dry-on-wet to suggest distant flowers, stems, and leaves—and for background shape and line variation, as seen on page 73. Do you see how the background is immediately integrated through a common color with the subject?

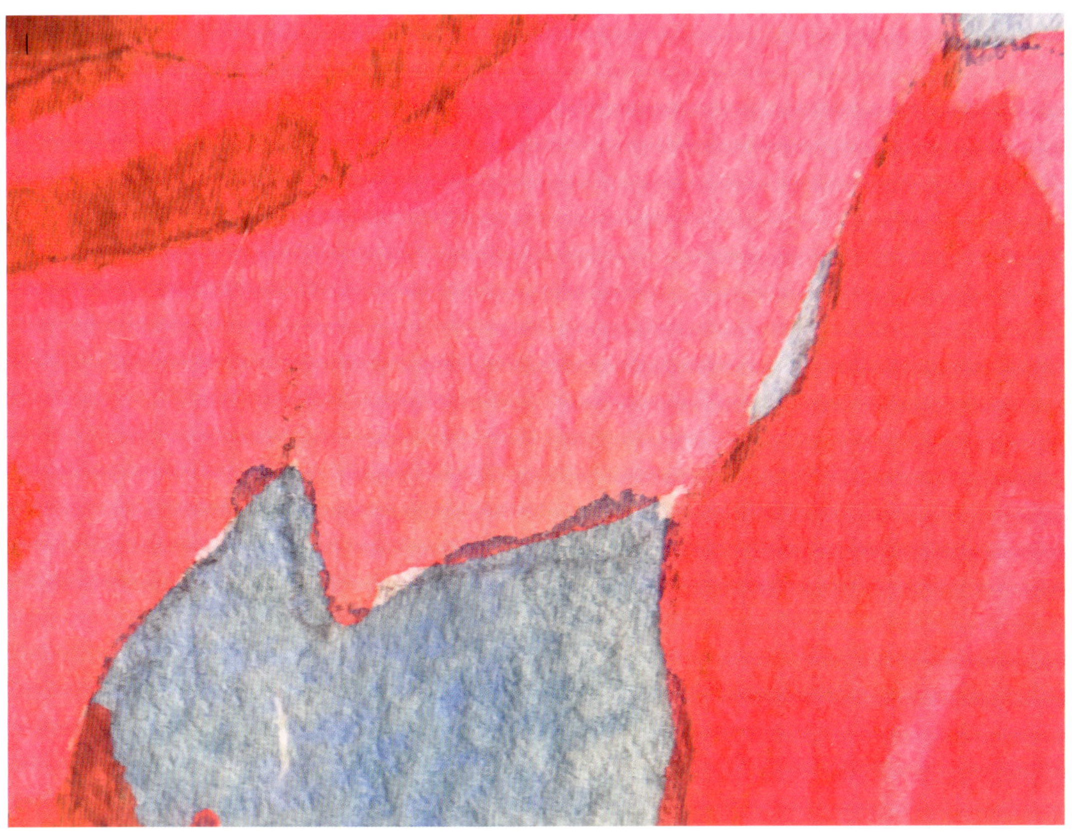
1

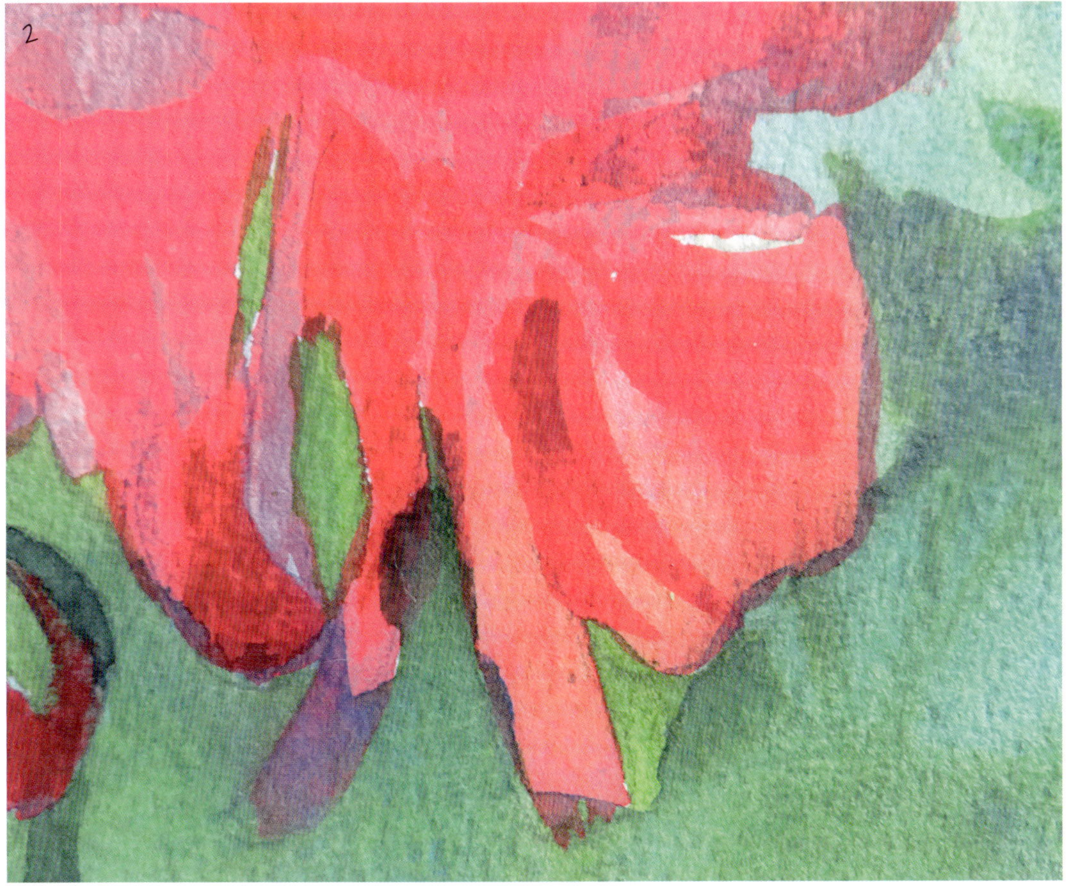
2

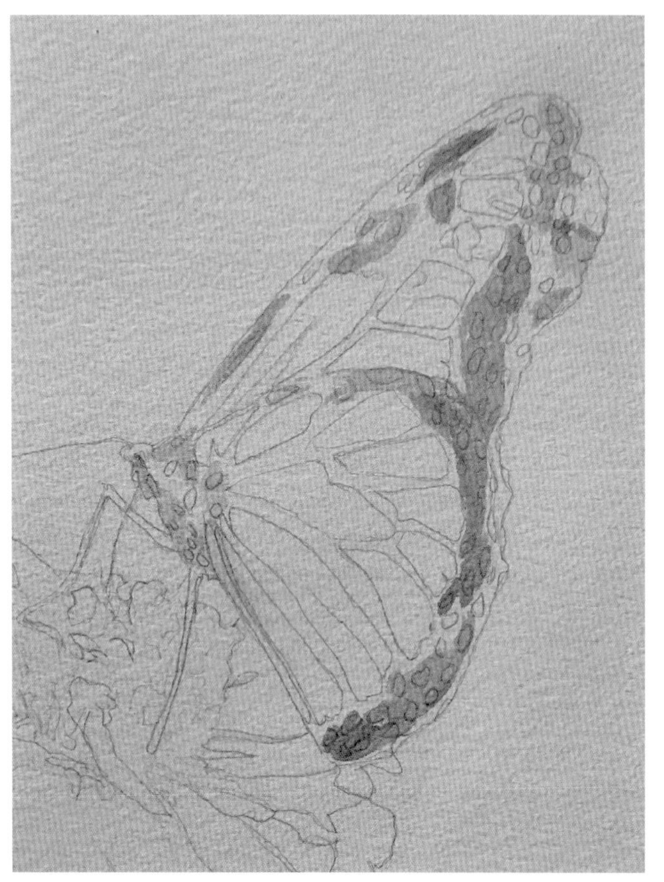

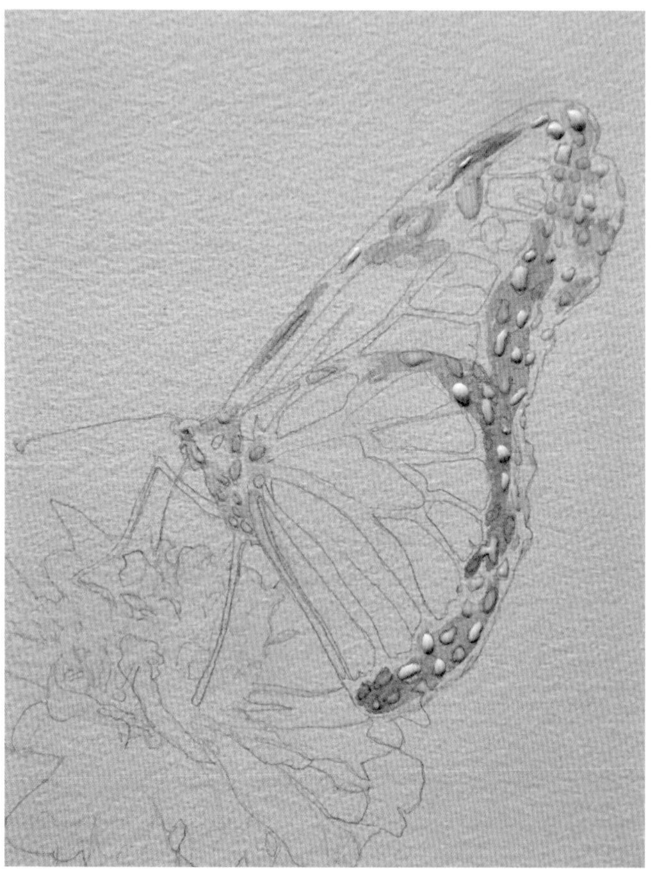

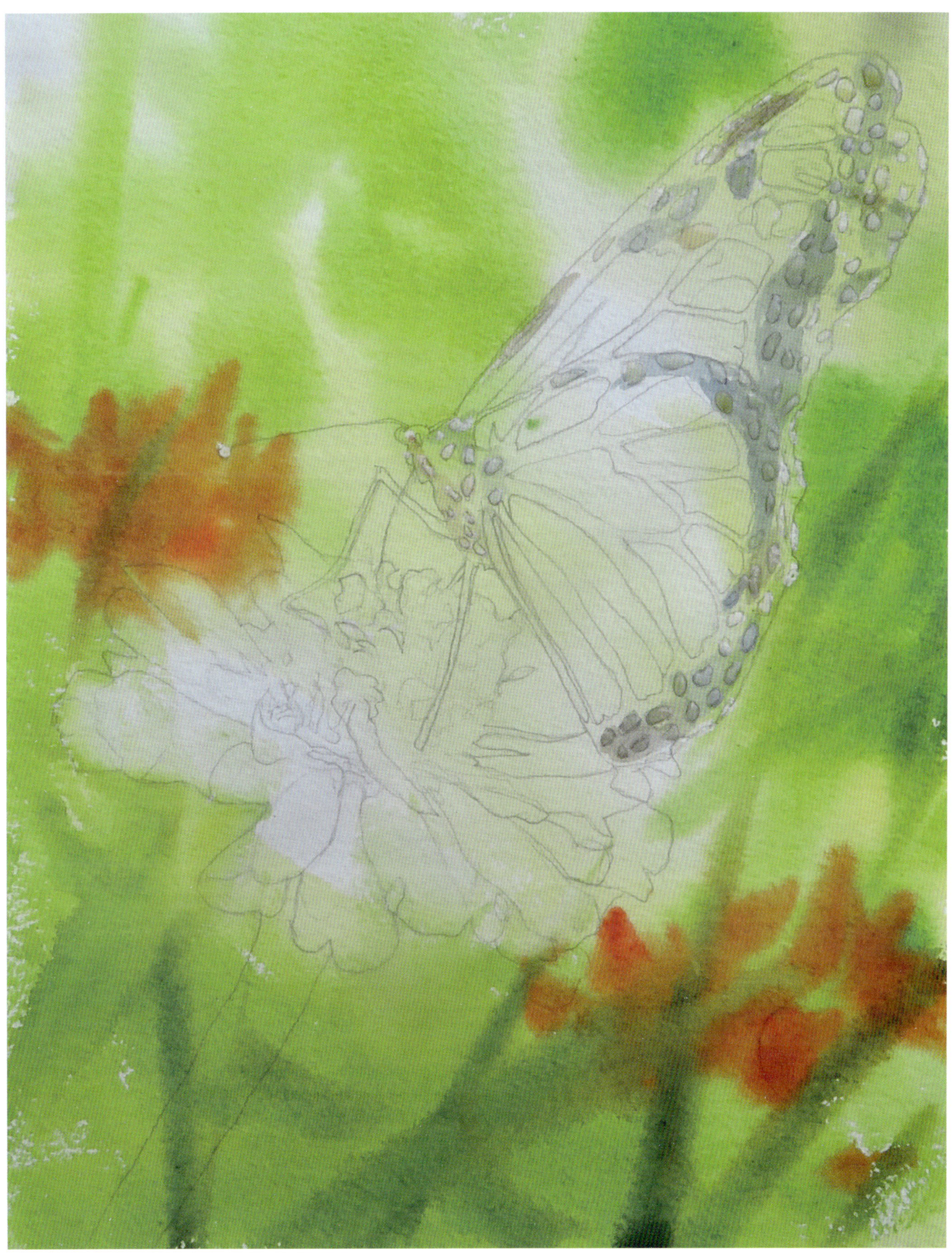

Here are some stage 1 recommendations to paint different color and value differences in subjects and backgrounds. The first word (for example, "white") in the following refers to the *subject* (up close) and the last word (for example, "midvalue") refers to the *background*.

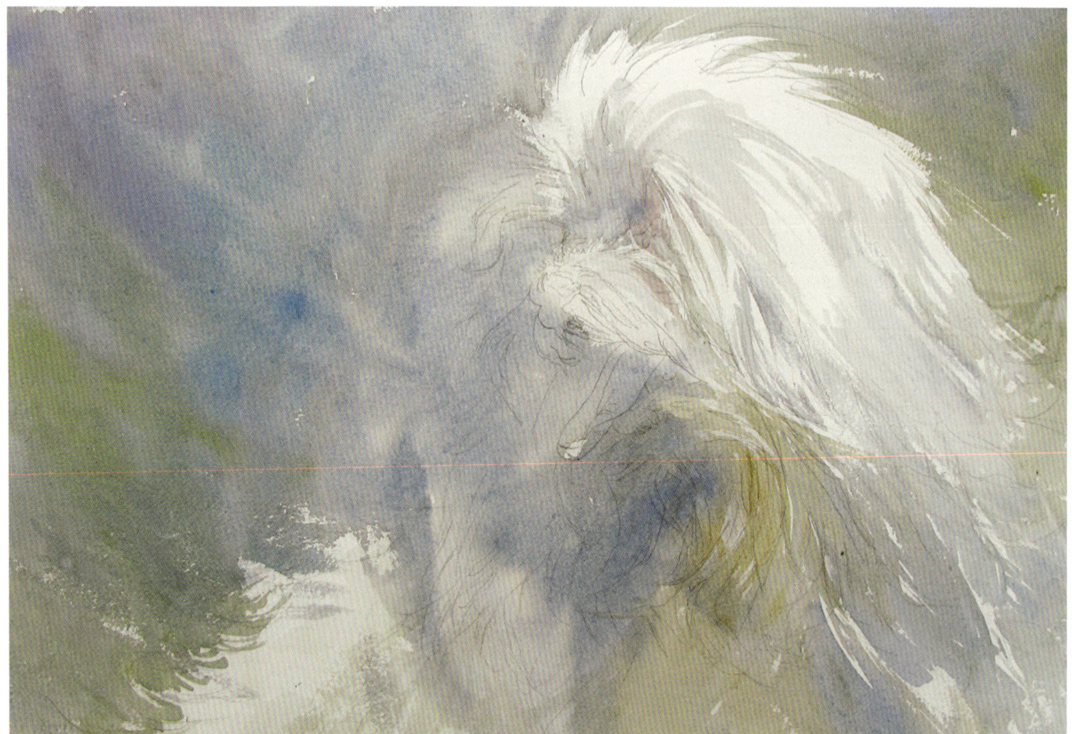

Clear water was added on the left side of the dog's head just before painting, and the ear was covered with a pale, soft-edged wash. I painted behind the dog's head on dry paper to control fur texture at right. Note color variation and white illuminated fur throughout.

WHITE / MIDVALUE

Save the illuminated shape. Paint any color reflected onto the subject with a clean, pale wash and let it dry. Load a brush with clean shadow color in a coffee/cream consistency. Wet the paper wherever shadows are soft edged; don't let paint wander to dry paper unless a defined edge is required there. Paint form shadows beyond the silhouette shape's edges. Don't paint midvalue tones or darks until you are ready for stages 2 and 3.

MID-DARK, DARK / PALE, BRIGHTLY COLORED

Load the brush with a bright or pale background color that harmonizes with the subject, if possible. Wet the paper across the subject *and* randomly across background space. Leave arbitrary background areas dry, because paint applied there will appear (when dry) more saturated than paint on wet. *Quickly* apply color, letting paint bleed into the subject, especially where colors relate. Lift or soften any hard edges within the subject as the paper dries. Don't paint details or darks until you are ready for stages 2 and 3. As you can see in the first stage of *Poultry in Motion* (page 59; final page 48), pale grays and greens were painted from the background into the hen's sketched shape, since I knew she would later be darker.

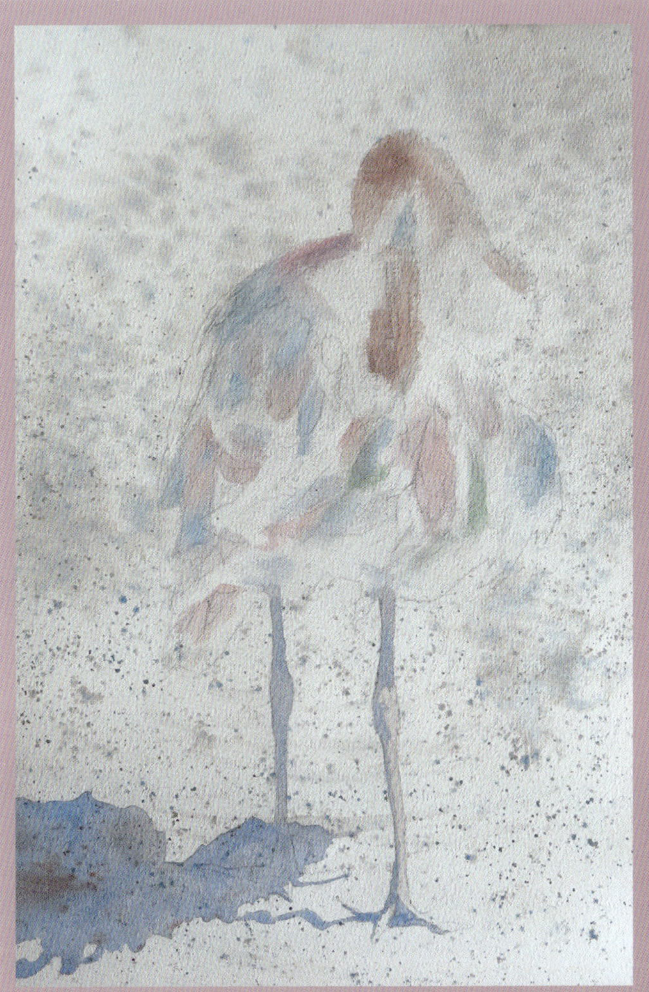

I spattered paint in pale primary colors into a partially wet background first, over the bird's edges, adding them also, dry-on-wet, to highlights in its feathers.

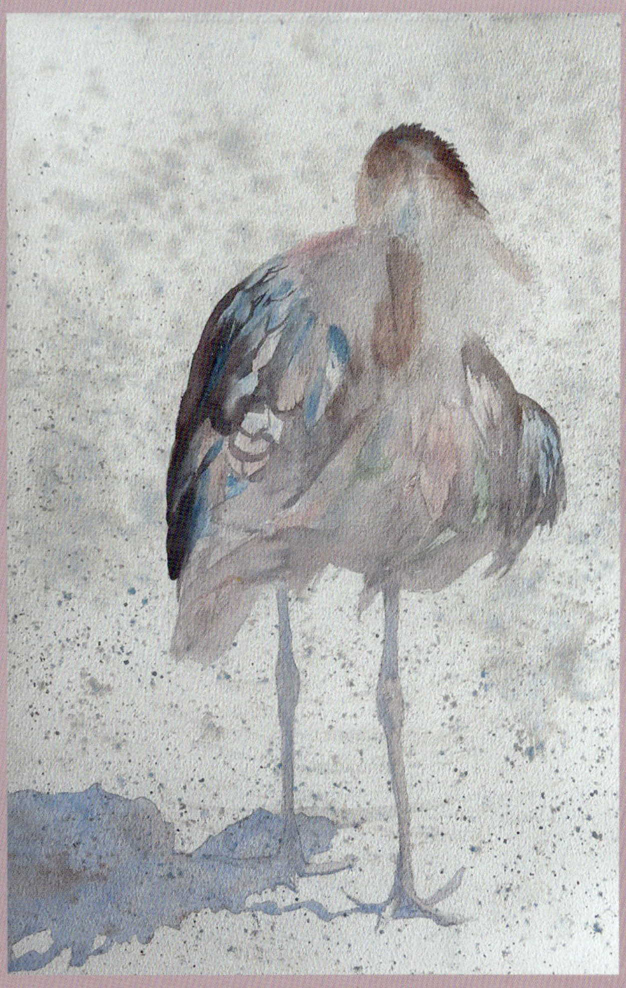

Here is an early pale wash of the bird's darkest value, painted around colorful highlights and the initial wash for its legs and cast shadow. Complete painting, *Glossy Ibis*, is on page 104.

For emphasis, contrast, and interest, the paler the subject's midvalue, the darker the background behind it should be, and the darker its midvalue, the paler or brighter (or both) its background should be.

Although this is in the midst of stage 2 here, bright green paint initially bled across the bird's shape, soft branch and leaf shapes were added while still wet, then any hard green edges were lifted within the bird in stage 1. Frisket still covers highlights on branches and leaves.

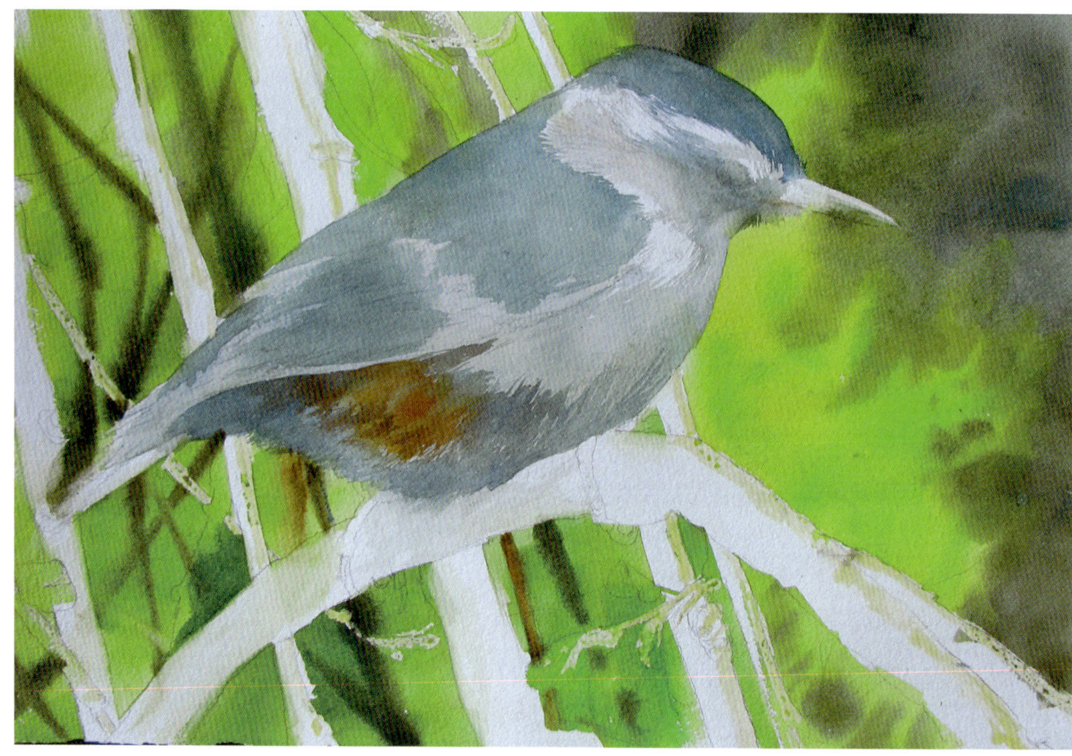

MIDVALUE, GRAY / BRIGHTLY COLORED

This painting sequence depends on which—subject or background—is lighter in value *or* grayer. It's a judgment call. Load the brush with the paler or brighter color. Wet the darker/grayer shape with clean water, then paint the paler/brighter wash. Let paint bleed from the pale/bright space into the wet space. Though the bird is paler than its surrounding cherry blossoms in *Song Sparrow in the Cherry Tree* (page 23) I let pink bleed into it because the bird is grayer *and* pink is reflected onto it. Don't paint any darks or build color saturation until you are ready for stages 2 and 3.

To suggest light on *focal* perching branches, flowers, or leaves (or a combination of these), apply masking fluid to lit parts only, and when they're dry, paint surrounding background elements such as sky and distant organic shapes right over them. Later, follow stage 2 techniques to define their local colors, shadows, and details.

SATURATED COLOR, MIDVALUE, DARK / WHITE

Paint the interior of the subject out to its silhouette accurately, wet-on-dry in its lightest value and brightest local color(s). Don't paint any details, midvalue tones, or darks until you are ready for stages 2 and 3, or *unless* some are soft edged within the pale, bright wash. The first washes of *Song Sparrow in the Cherry Tree* (page 23) and *Song Sparrow* (page 66) were painted this way, though dry-on-wet and wet-on-damp techniques were also used.

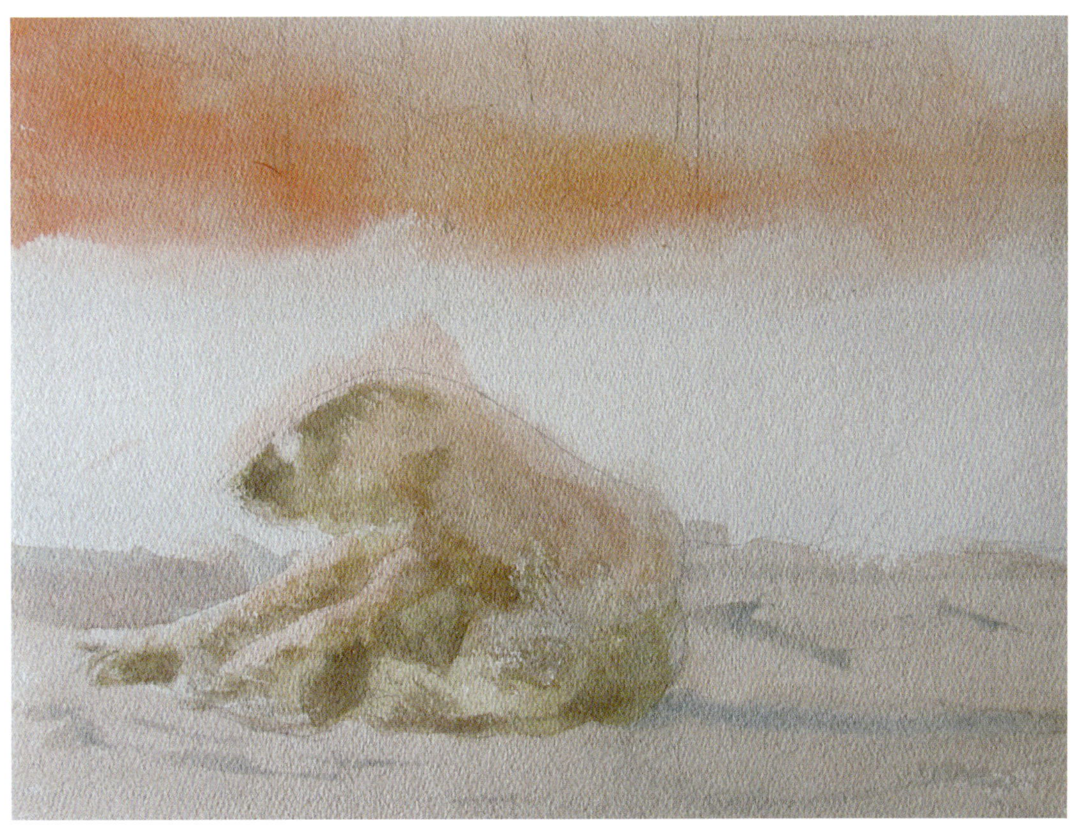

I painted warm neutral shadows on the bear's fur first, beyond most of its edges and into the snow it's resting on, then added orange and red to the fur and to the sky. Complete painting, *Taking It Easy* (page 115).

PALE-MIDVALUE, GRAY / VERY DARK

Paint the subject's pale values beyond its edges into partially wet background; let it dry. Do not paint midvalues or darks until stages 2 and 3, respectively. Gray or neutral-toned subjects appear bright if strongly illuminated against a richly saturated, dark background.

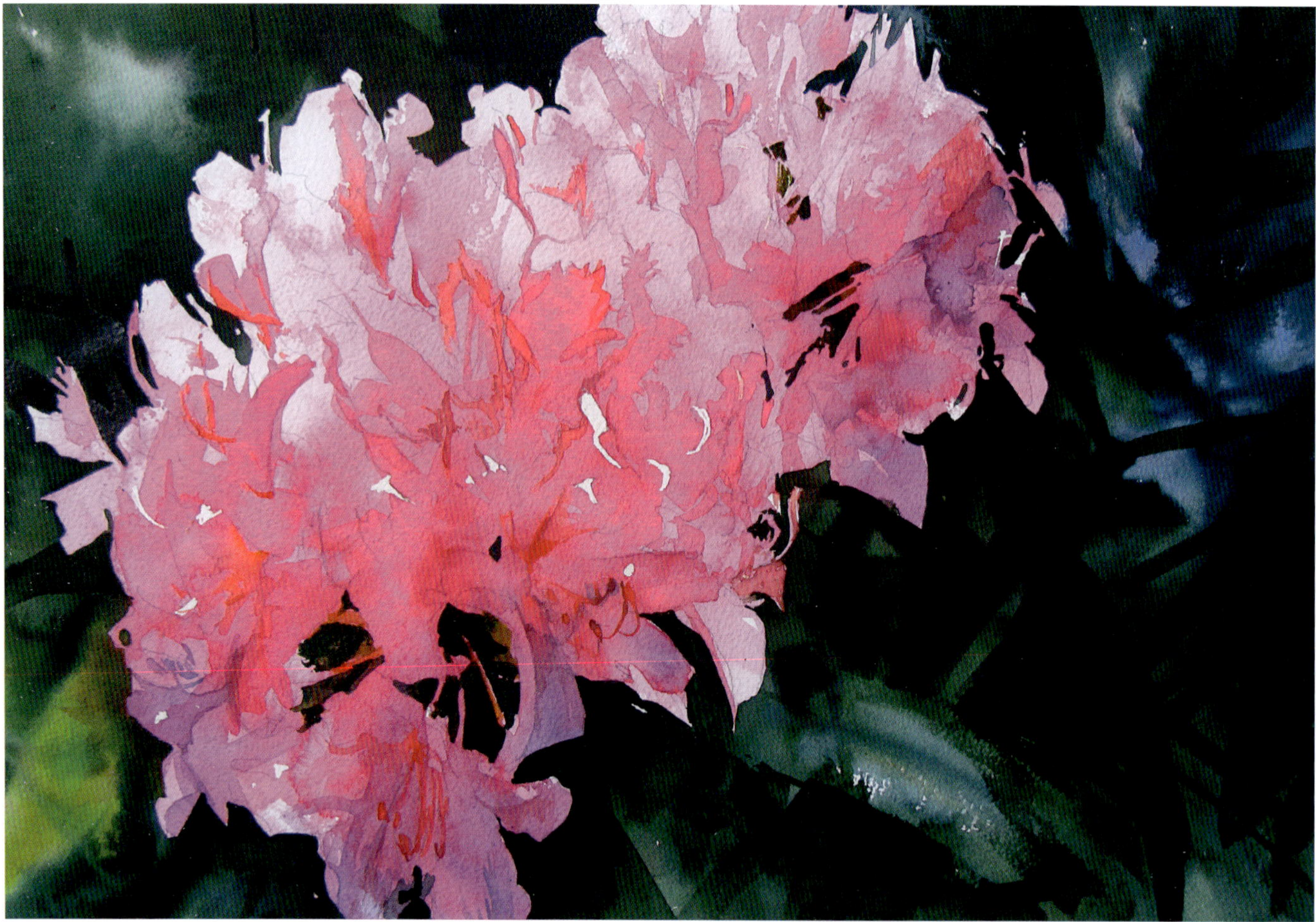

Pink Rhodies, 15" × 22"

BRIGHT / DARK

Use a harmonizing color if possible (though this is not necessary if the background will be very saturated and dark). Let bright subject color in its palest value bleed beyond its edges, out into the background. Though pink (in the red color family) neutralizes or dulls green, I let it bleed beyond the flower edges in stage 1 in *Pink Rhodies* (*above*) because I planned (and later painted) a very dark green, almost black, background, with varied color and value, to cover its excess.

BRIGHT, CONTRASTING COLORS / NEUTRAL, DARK (OR BOTH DARK AND LIGHT)

This is more complicated because there can be many contrasting elements that emphasize, diminish, or do both to subject shapes, as seen in *Peony Scenery* (page 107) and *Peonies II* (page 114).

Remember this book's title and always save (illuminated) whites, and paint the lightest, brightest washes first, wet-on-wet and dry-on-wet. Let (subject) color bleed into areas where the background will be dark. When dry, skip to stage 2 to build more saturated color value and define shapes. Don't paint a dark or neutral background until you are ready for stage 3.

Where parts of the subject motif, such as, for

example, some key flowers, are darkened by shadow, you might contrast them with a light-value background to help them stand out. Paint that pale background area now, in stage 1, as well, wet-on-wet, across sketched (dark) subject shapes. Or, if their dark shapes are insignificant and would appear better if they disappeared into an inky background, wait until stage 3 to paint them dry-on-wet or wet-on-dry in very dark values, as done with certain background leaves in *Monarch* (page 119). Value *always* affects painting timing.

Adding neutral and dark shadows while colorful, bright paint is still wet creates muddiness and an overworked appearance. Add shadows now in stage 1, dry-on-wet, *only* if they are soft edged. Otherwise, paint them in stages 2 and 3.

DISSIMILAR, CONTRASTING COLOR IN *BOTH* SUBJECT AND BACKGROUND

When subject and background colors contrast, one option to unite them is to use as your first wash nonstaining paint that's easy to lift. Another is to alter the value of one or both. Or choose a third color that might relate to both contrasting hues; for instance, yellow unites contrasting red and green, as seen in *Splash of Red* (page 80).

Often I combine the first two options; namely, I apply a pigment easiest to lift as a *pale* wash and paint it first, as was done in *Oranges and Mr. Blue*. Here the challenge was to make orange leaves appear bright against an equally saturated blue sky. Clean water applied over much of the lower part of the painting, where orange dominates, and roughly across other leafy parts kept the value light on the leaf shapes. Then Cerulean, a blue pigment easily lifted, was painted loosely across the paper. While it was still wet or damp, I removed any excess blue from the leaves.

Thick, creamy paint in bright yellow and orange next covered the entire leaf mass out to its silhouette and around the bird, as similarly described above in "Saturated Color, Midvalue, Dark/White." I intuitively added more red here and yellow there, and even brown, purple, and blue to this mass. Though done all in stage 1, the orange leaf mass is equivalent to painting the midvalue background mass described in the next chapter, stage 2.

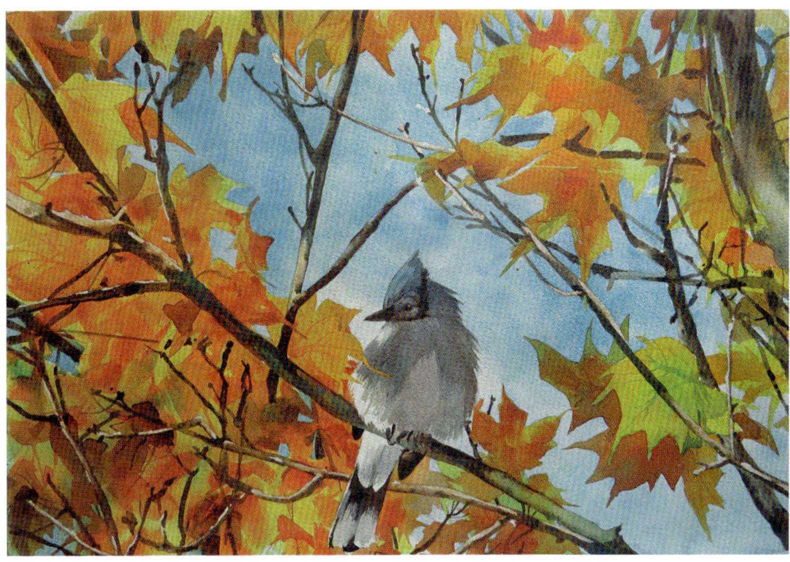

Oranges and Mr. Blue, 15" × 22"

The last option uses a third color such as yellow to unite opposites red and green. The latter two hide yellow because red is—like yellow, usually—a warm color, and with blue, yellow creates green. Paint the wash across the sketched edges. Remember, change the *value* of one or unify both with a related color.

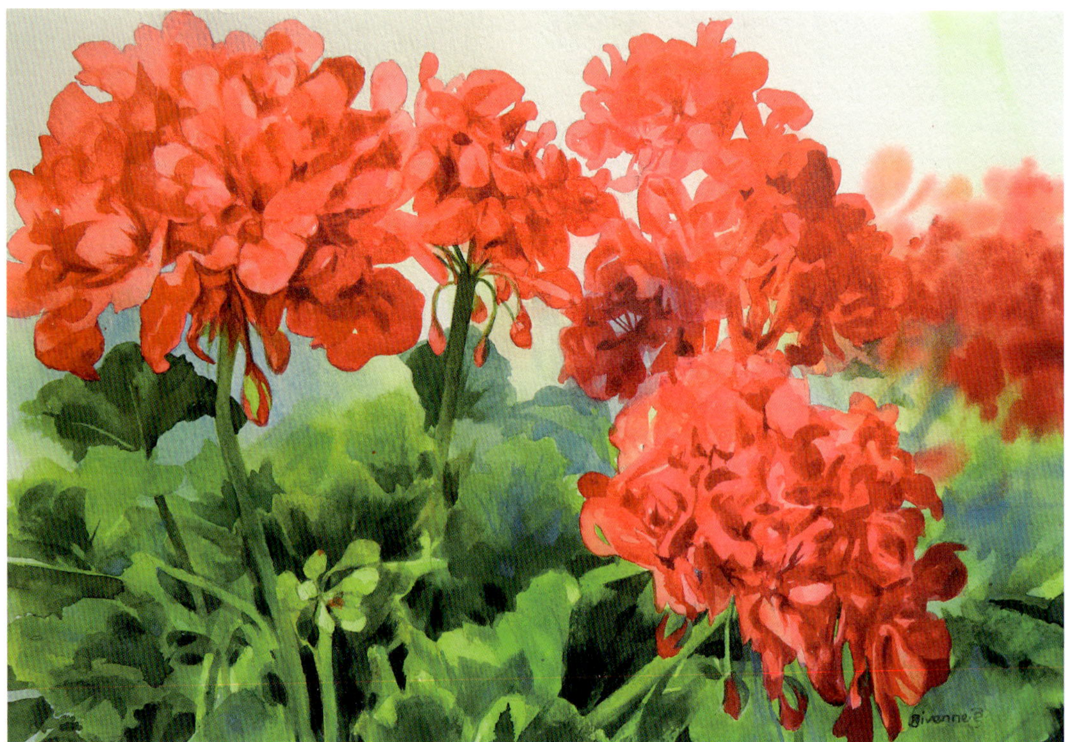

Splash of Red, 15" × 22"

Even with utmost care to avoid them, some overlapping edges occurred where a few red flowers and bright green background meet.

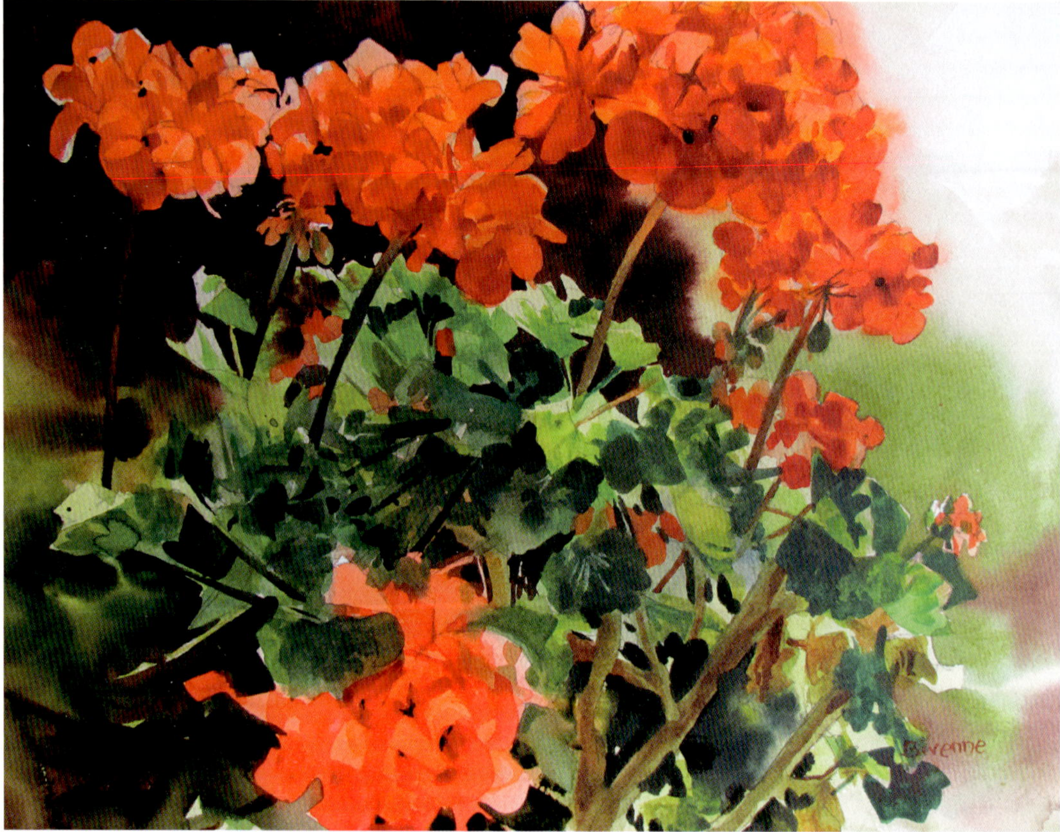

Scarlet Geraniums, 11" × 15"

BLACK AND WHITE (CONTRASTING VALUE) / MIDVALUE

Paint any shadows or reflected bright color on the lightest value (white) and let that bleed a bit into the background space. Lift or soften any defined peripheral edges that crossed into the background. Let it dry. Skip to the steps in stage 2 to paint a midvalue background wash up to the white or pale value subject shapes, and *across* the subject's (still unpainted) dark-value shapes. Don't paint any darks until you are ready for stage 3.

After all the meticulous planning and sketching, it might seem as if all control over the painting is lost by loosely bleeding color over carefully drawn shape edges in either direction, but in fact the opposite is true. These initial washes are not meant to make sense. You will not lose your penciled sketch unless color value is too dark this early. From the moment you put brush to paper in stage 1, color brightness and value immediately begin both to suggest lighting and to create a relationship between subject and background.

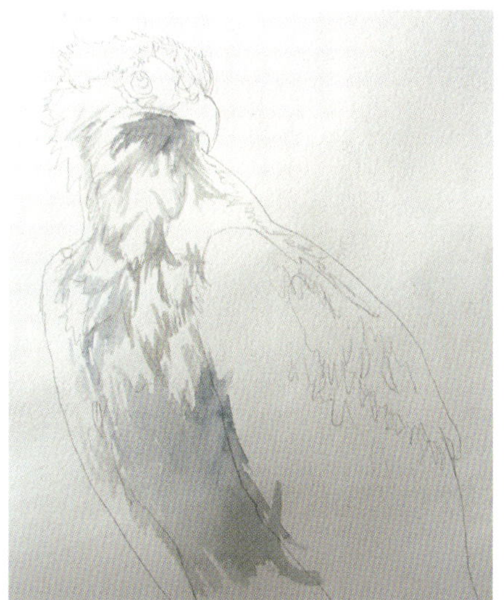

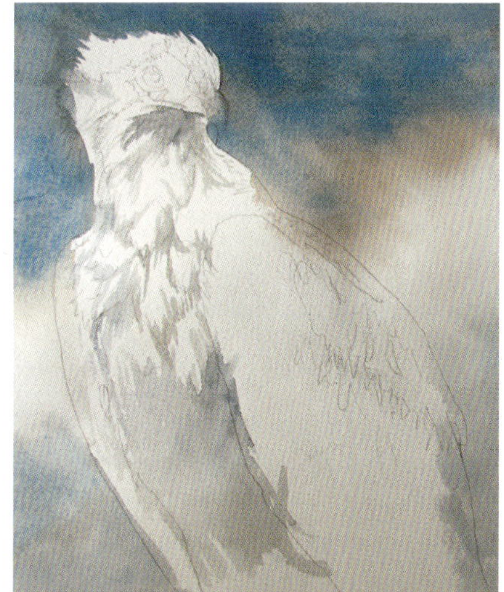

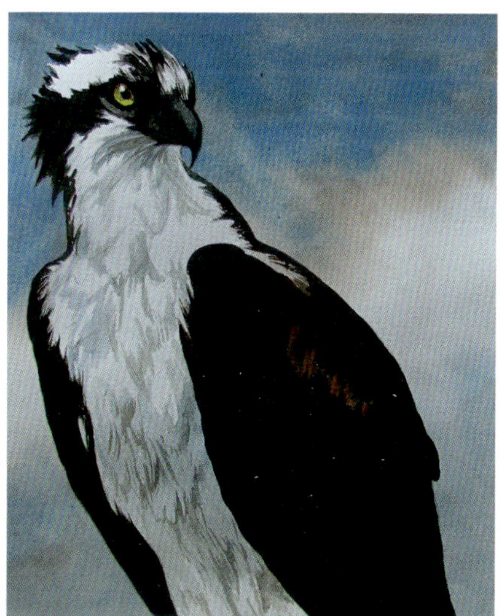

The Sentinel, 12" × 16"
A blue or gray sky is a great midvalue background for a subject with contrasting values, such as an osprey, because both value extremes pop against it.

Bottom Line:

Save illuminated white shapes. Paint the lightest, brightest value of illuminated colorful shapes or illuminated background spaces (or both) wet-on-wet and dry-on-wet across sketched shapes.

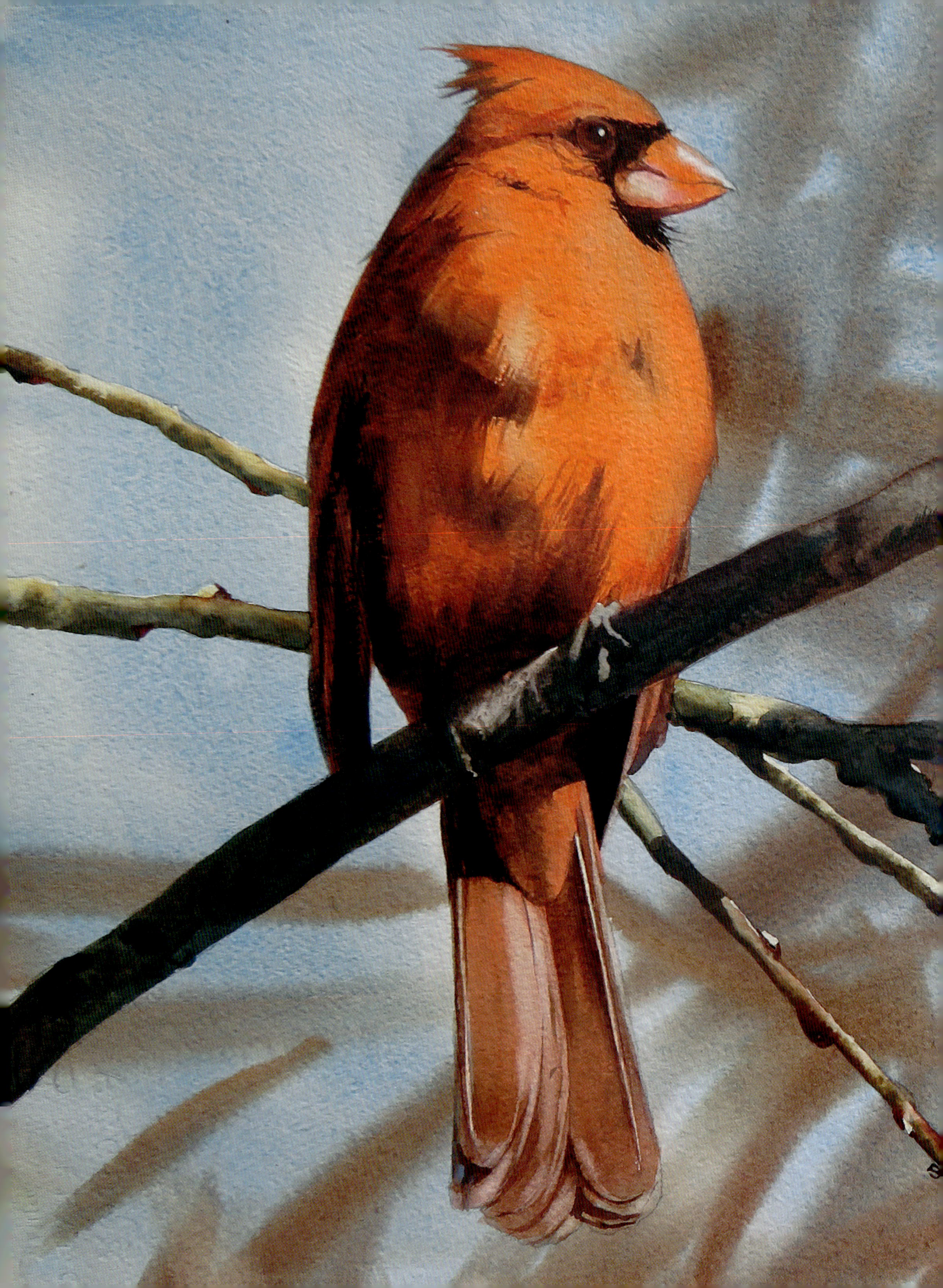

4 Stage 2—Midvalue Shapes, Colors, Shadows, and Backgrounds

Stage 1 set the stage for *lighting*.

Stage 2 now reveals the *direction* of that lighting. Certain illuminated white and colorful areas established earlier as a loosely painted wash now become specific saved shapes as the many parts of the painting develop via midvalue and saturated color washes. Though this stage has many variables, depending on the complexity of the design, the painting begins to take shape, quite literally, and your own personal style becomes more apparent.

Stage 2 is almost all about gradually building color saturation, midvalues, and more defined object and shadow shapes. The first wash of a dark background is usually established now too. This stage is complex because it's a push and pull between subject and background spaces, shapes, and value, lightest always before darker. Illumination shapes on white, brightly colored, or pale objects, as seen on page 84,

Standing Out, 15" × 22"

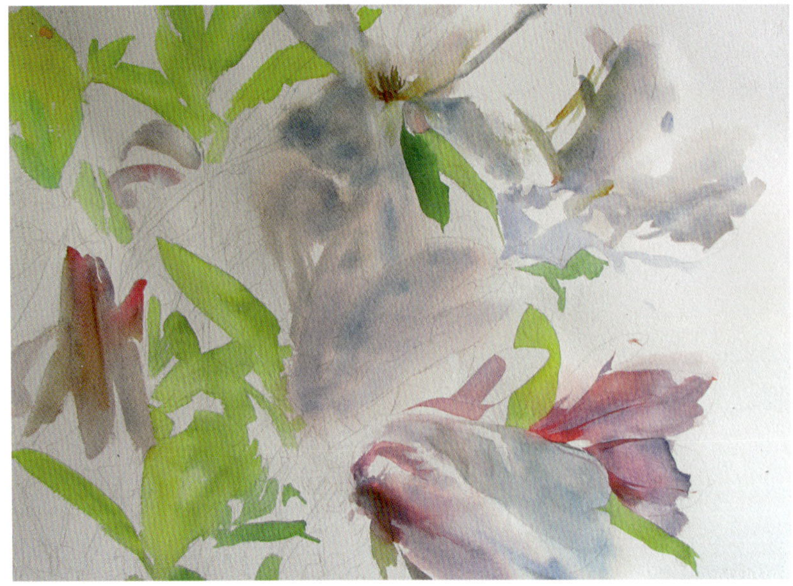

should not be completely covered with these midvalue shapes.

Those representing nearby or overlapping shadowed or more saturated colorful objects such as the hen on pages 60 and 61 crossing in front of her brightly lit shed (the painting's pale, dominant, background value) may cover parts of these illuminated shapes as long as they do not completely obscure them. This is key. Pale, bright shapes represent lighting on, around, behind, or through darker objects, and darker or shadowed shapes surrounding pale convey depth and three-dimensionality.

The sequence for painting all the various subject, background, and supporting object and other shape elements at this stage and the next depends on their value.

Paint the palest and brightest *mid*value shapes first.

Paint *around* or behind illuminated and pale shapes, such as a midvalue background color mass (covered in this chapter) around white or pale subjects. This may seem counterintuitive, especially after loosely crossing most sketched shape edges with paint in stage 1.

But this is crucial to watercolor and known as negative space painting (page 92). It's how form shadows are built around lit shapes, and how (darker) background shape elements define paler object shapes.

Painting the midvalue range in stage 2 is critical to the development of six major spatial elements; the timing generally depends on which is palest because it's painted first. Not every painting may have all of the following spatial elements.

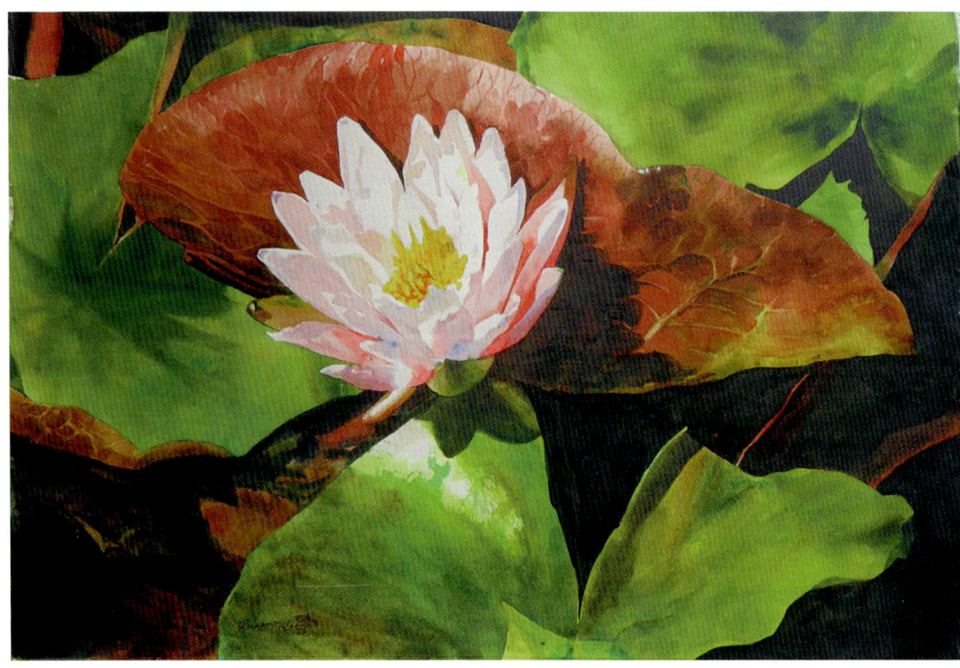

Peeking Out, 15" × 22"

1. SOFT-EDGED MIDVALUE BACKGROUND SHAPES

Depth may be conveyed in close-up work by suggesting background shapes with soft edges, such as distant branches, leaves, flowers, or other organic forms against sky. This is ideally painted in stage 1 *before* any midvalue or darker subject color; I include them in this chapter because their value is often dark or their color at least is very saturated, contrasting them against a pale background. So apply them, dry-on-wet, to a paler-value background shape. The wet paper makes the dark paint about 30% paler and the edges soft.

Before painting this, however, protect with masking fluid any *small*, white, illuminated, or yellow parts of your subject, and let it dry. I did this to the lit parts of branches in *Standing Out*, *Female Red-wing*, *Chipping Sparrow in Spring* (*below*), and other similar portraits. (Paint around *large* illuminated shapes.)

Thick paint consistency ensures a more successful, controlled effect. So load and set aside a separate dry brush in each color for the soft-edged background elements. Paint the pale background quickly with a large brush. Vary color for interest; don't let the paper dry. Quickly paint the soft-edged shapes across the space while the background is shiny wet.

As the paper dries, carefully lift any paint covering subject shapes with a damp brush, though this is not particularly necessary if it's very dark. Let the paper dry completely.

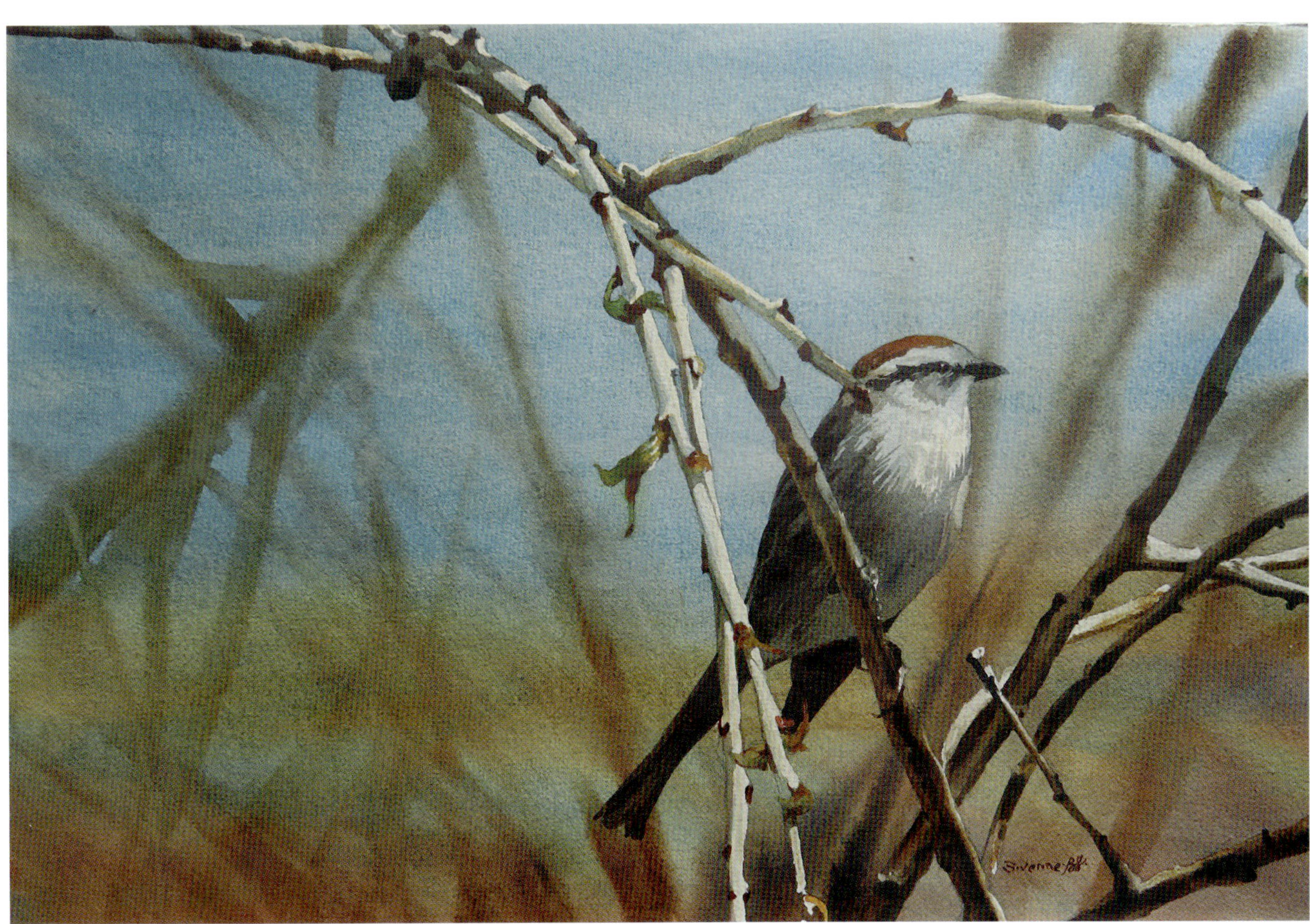

Chipping Sparrow in Spring, 15" × 22"

2. LOCAL COLOR AND SILHOUETTES OF BASIC MOTIF SHAPES

Once the bright green, orange, and yellow background was dry, I painted the local (orange) color of the butterfly and the zinnia, wet-on-dry. Orange extends across black butterfly markings, but only to the flower's outside edge. Pale blue covers shadowed white spots.

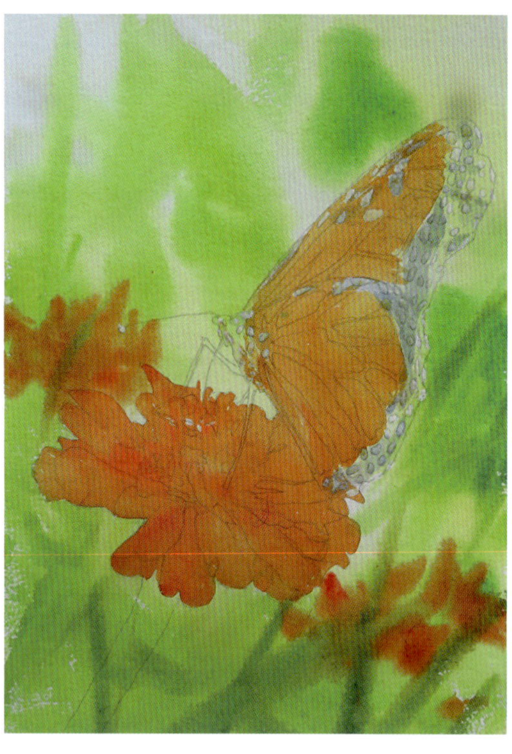

Local color is the dominant color of an object or shape in natural light and is added as its underpainting. A male cardinal is red, a sunflower is generally yellow, and foliage is usually green. It is also the dominant color of major background elements, such as all the foliage greens behind flowers, which I call a *background mass* (item #4, page 91).

With each shape's palest midvalue, apply more saturated local color to and within the object's silhouette, but around or *behind* previously painted illumination shapes (saving them). Color can be extended beyond edges wherever that adjacent space will be surrounded or overlapped by *darker* value or by harmonious or saturated color. Let the local color dry.

3. BUILDING COLOR SATURATION AND FORM SHADOW SHAPES

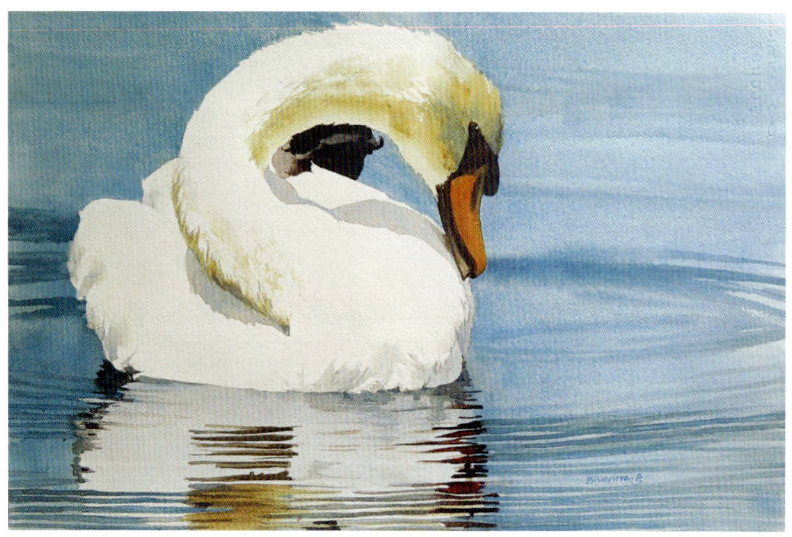

Peaceful Preening, 15" × 22"
Both the cast shadows on and under the neck and those at bottom suggest the bird's round form.

Silhouette and textural details look most interesting where shadow and light meet.

Form shadow is the shadow on a particular object that defines its three-dimensionality. Since they pick up color from neighboring hues, shadows are improved by occasionally dropping color temperature changes, dry-on-wet, into them.

After the local color is dry, add a colorful object's form shadow by first building color saturation and then warming or cooling its shadows. This maintains local color vibrancy. Keep value no darker at this point than midvalue 4 or 5 (see page 102 for tips to darken color).

For instance, on page 87, red develops the flower's form and enriches its orange (local and illuminated) color. A bit of blue (temperature change) cools some of the lower petals' shadows, adding more interest to the overall shadow color

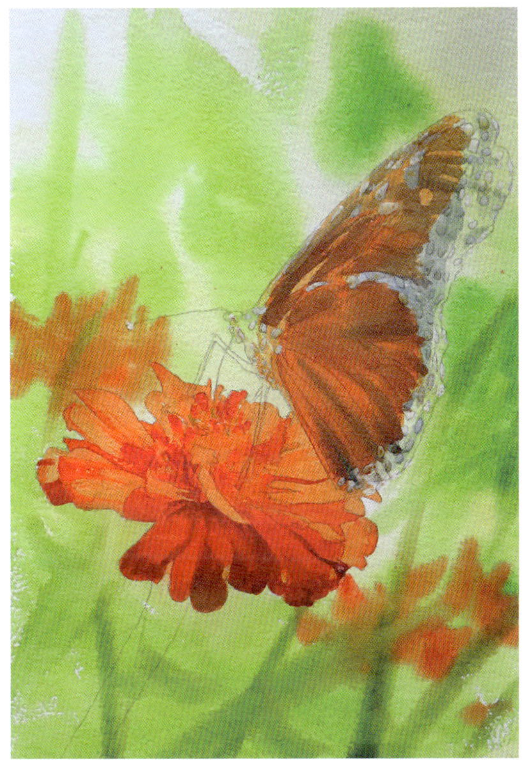

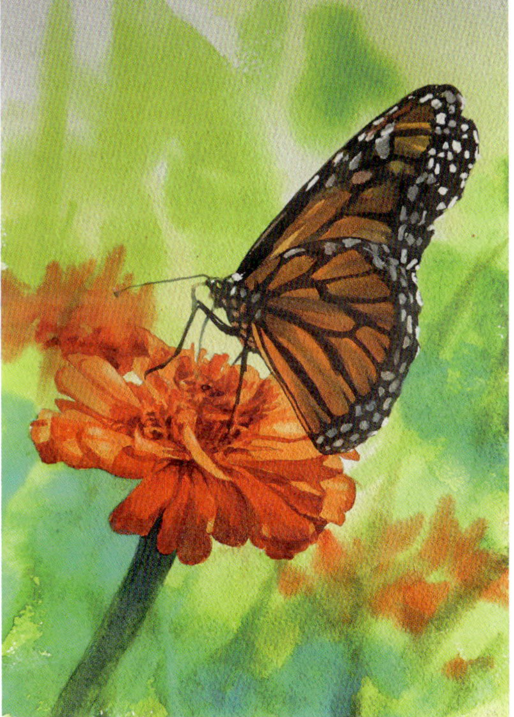

Welcome, Zinnia!, 12" × 16"

To optimize brightness, use vivid, clean, transparent paint in a coffee/cream consistency. Layer with the same or a harmonious hue. Don't change color temperature. Dry the paper between layers.

and form. In the butterfly, black markings appear gray through its diaphanous wings, suggested by Cobalt, an opposite hue to orange.

Like those of illumination, form shadows are also *shapes* and are best created both as simple and complex in a series of value or color saturation layers. The largest is often the palest and simplest, and the darkest (in recesses) is smaller and more complex. Do you see how the red form shadow shape is complex and wholly different from the illuminated petal shapes in *Welcome, Zinnia!*?

Though a glossy ibis is a dark subject, you can see that its palest value covers the entire shape (stage 1, page 75), followed by smaller, more complex, and slightly darker value, defining shadows underneath feathers (stage 2, page 75 and next page). The richest and most saturated color and value, added in stage 3, complete its form (page 104).

Use increasingly *more paint* and *less water* on *dry paper* (except for soft edges) in each successive saturation or value layer. Don't cover entire illumination shapes, use gray or go darker than value 5 or 6 for now.

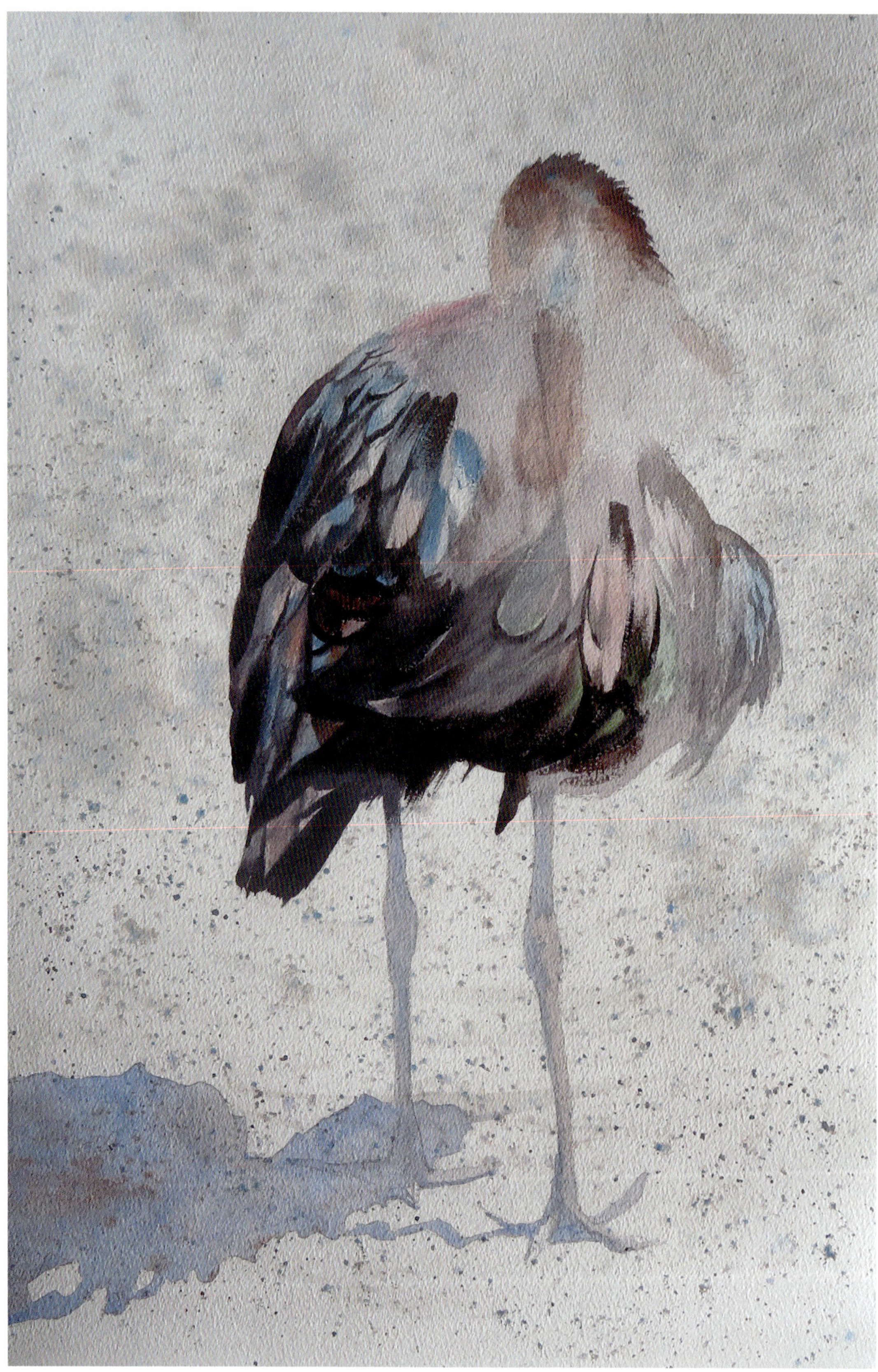

PAINTING FORM SHADOWS ON YELLOW OBJECTS

Shadow chroma affects the energy and vibrancy of a brightly colored object, particularly yellow. The more vivid and colorful its shadow, the brighter a yellow object will appear. Purple neutralizes yellow and causes even illuminated, high-chroma yellow shapes to appear dull.

Therefore, color *temperature* is critical.

Because yellow is a light-value hue, colors reflected onto yellow things are often evident, especially in shadows. Surrounding background and other object colors hint at shadow color temperature when unapparent.

For instance, a bright-yellow sunflower's petal shadows appear *cool* (yellow with hints of green) near its large green leaves. Green is yellow's darkest cool shadow, while shading near its reddish-brown center appears *warm*, as in *On Top of the World* (*above*). Red, sometimes brown, is yellow's darkest warm shadow. Keep both temperatures separate and darken shadows *gradually*. This is key because mixing the two will gray the shadow, or going from bright yellow straight to dark green or red will create too much contrast.

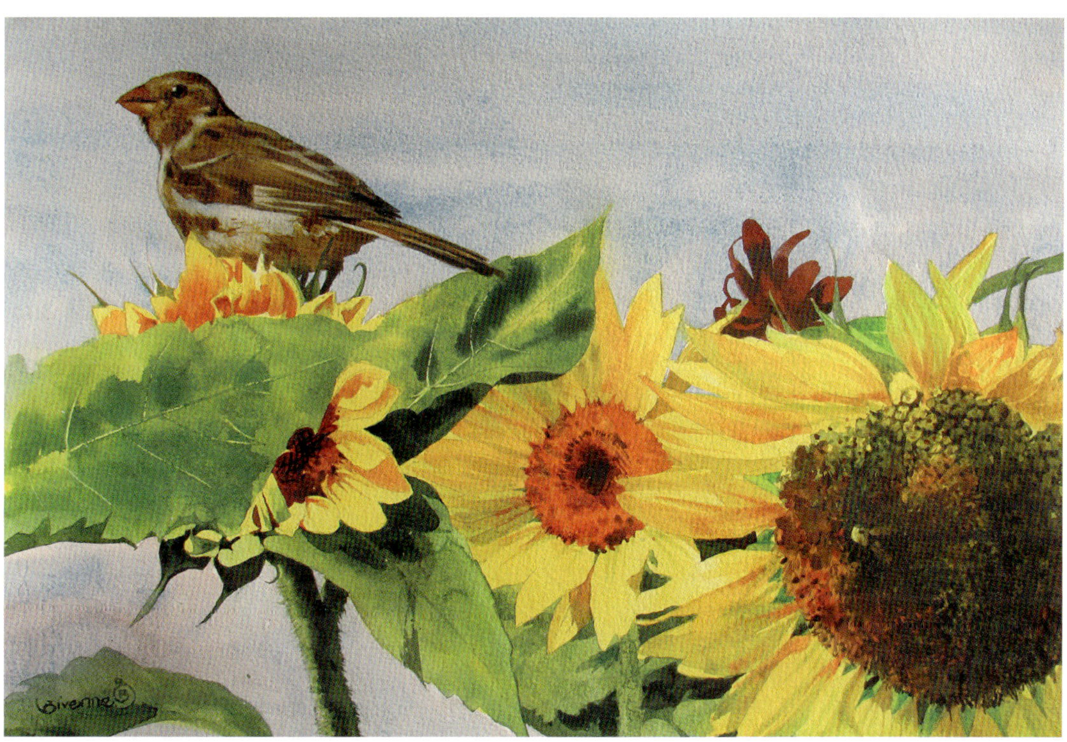

On Top of the World, 15" × 22"

Before painting, erase pencil marks or make them as light as possible, since they won't be removable. Paint the shape's local color and let it dry. Load the brush with very clean Aureolin in a creamy consistency, with hints of a particular temperature, and paint form shadow shapes around illumination shapes.

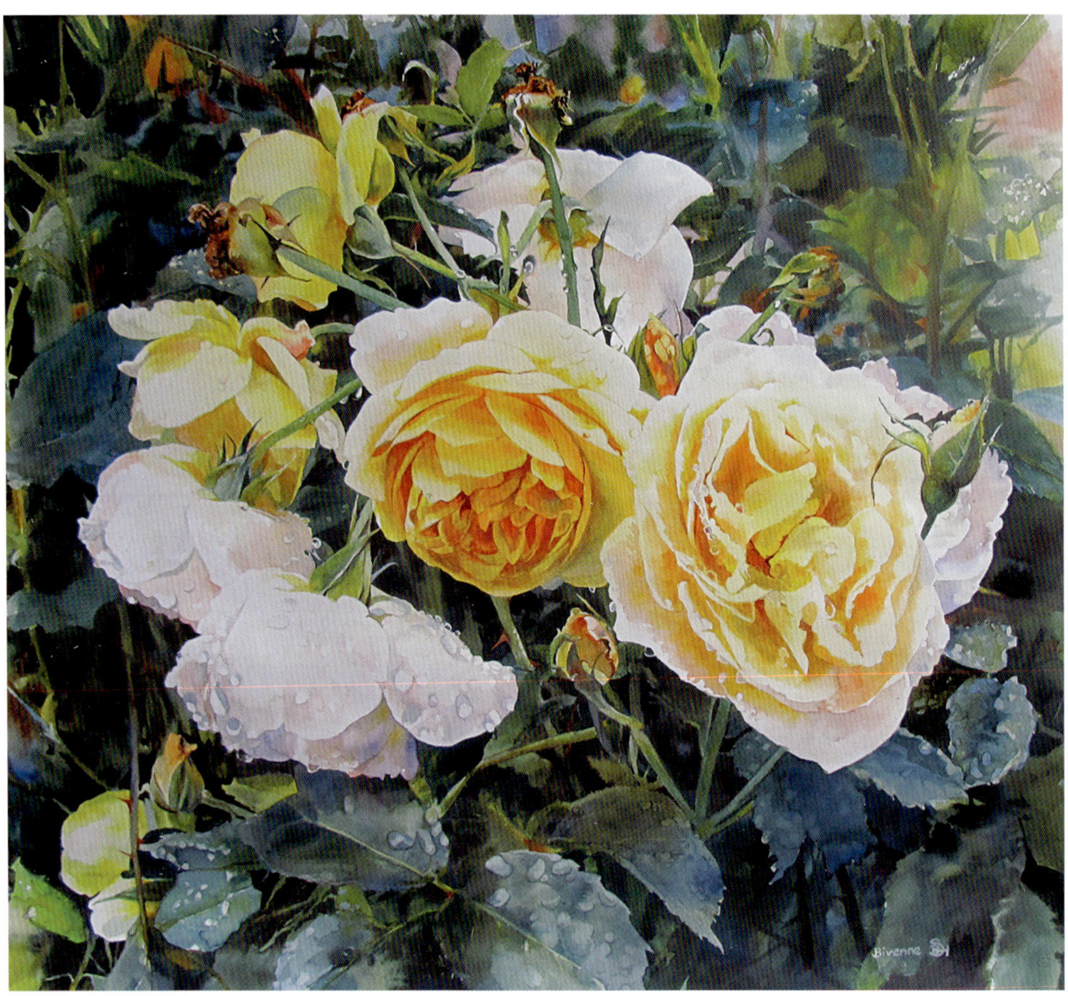

Liquids and Golds, 22" × 25"

WARM YELLOW FORM SHADOWS

To Aureolin, add a neighboring orange yellow such as Quinacridone Gold or *hints* of Quinacridone Red until you're satisfied with value and saturation. Use Brown Madder in the deepest, darkest shadow shape recesses.

COOL YELLOW FORM SHADOWS

To Aureolin, add *minimal hints* of Winsor Green. Add a bit more if the strength is too weak, but always keep yellow dominant and creamy as you add green.

Don't thoroughly mix green or blue into a warm shadow or red/orange into a cool shadow! However, *vary* the shadow's color temperature here and there to large shapes, such as cool at the bottom and warm at the top. Apply color temperature or value variation (or both) to all large shapes.

A warm *or* cool shadow temperature, not yellow's opposite (purple), keeps yellow shapes bright.

4. MIDVALUE BACKGROUND MASS

The easiest way to unify background elements (such as abundant foliage as a backdrop for flowers) is with one element: harmonious *color*. Think of all the background object shapes as a single, giant, local *color shape*. Usually done in stage 1 or 2, painting this at first as one major mass or underpainting actually makes the disparate shapes within the background easier to later define with negative space painting techniques (next item on this list).

Determine the dominant hue. Load a large brush and a script brush with paint in a coffee consistency. Apply clean water before painting wherever you want the value paler, but otherwise paint on *dry* paper behind light-value or bright subject shapes and *over* darker ones, which you'll paint later. Paint quickly, first with the large brush in open spaces, then with the script or small rounds to pull the paint bead into smaller peripheral subject shapes. Vary color temperature (cooler here, warmer there), possibly add texture (intentional blooms) while still damp, and let it dry.

Examples can be seen in the top image on page 60 and the images at right. Note that this mass clearly defines pale or white subject shapes in the first two but bleeds over the (darker) subject in the middle image. Each background mass suggests texture and has color and value variation. Gold, purple, and blue were dripped dry-on-wet into the dominant brown background mass of the bottom image.

Your carefully sketched background elements may seem lost underneath this large mass of color. If so, and once dry, resketch important obscured edges. Otherwise, negative space painting will bring them back and will establish a sense of depth by defining paler, individual background object shapes in front.

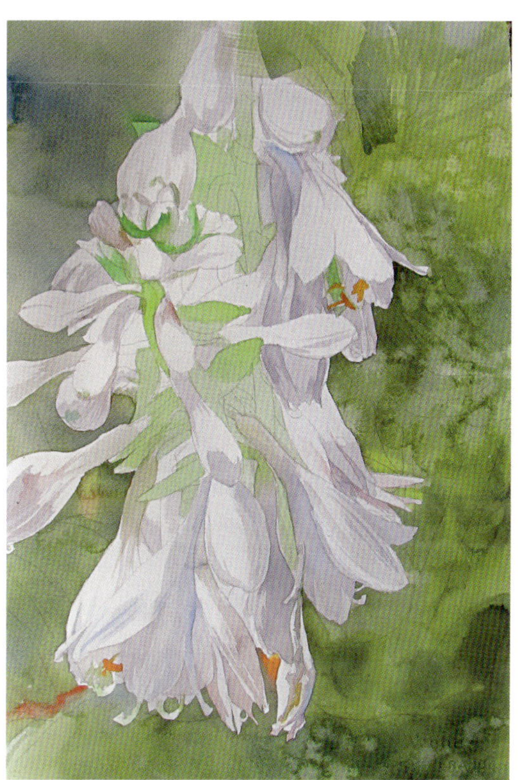

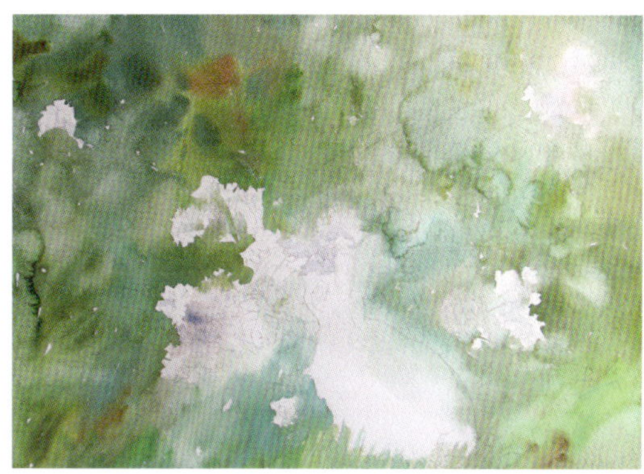

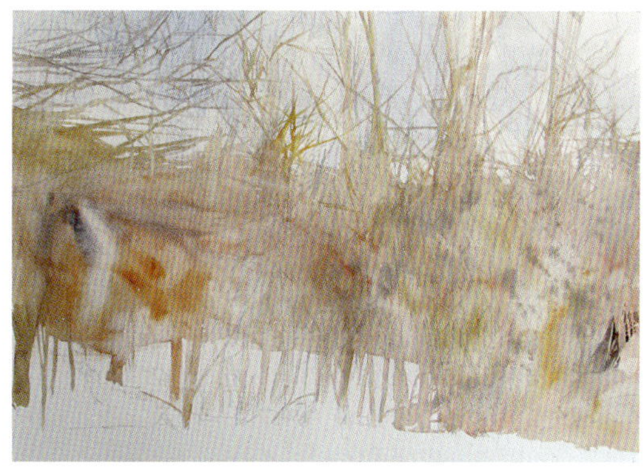

5. NEGATIVE SPACE

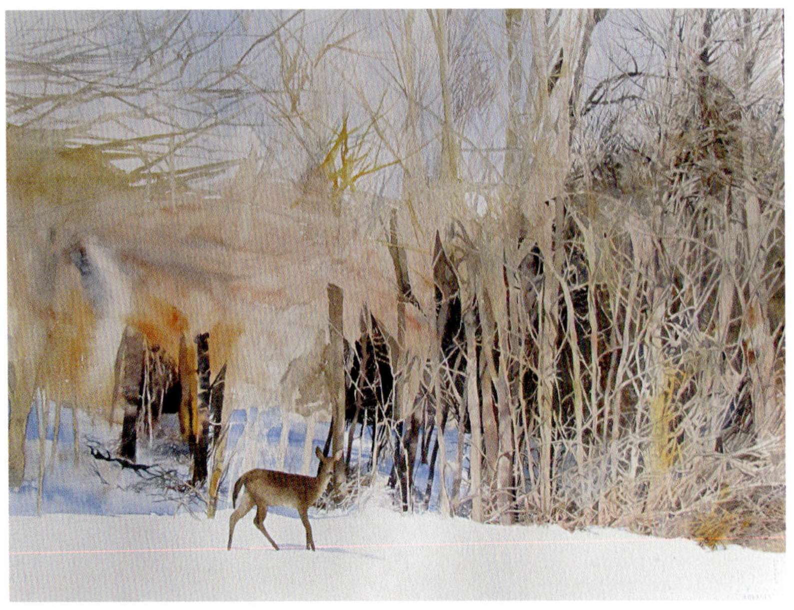

Here is an example of darker negative-space shapes beginning to clearly define front-lit trees.

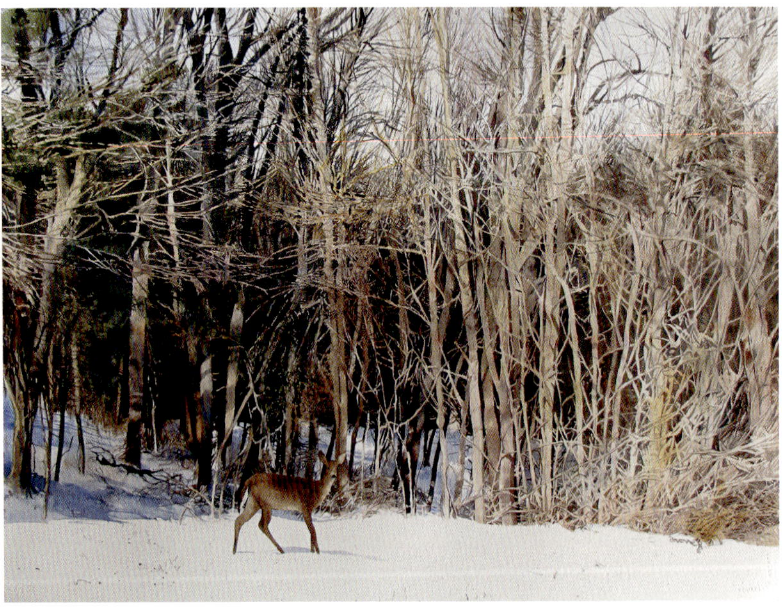

Oh, the Tangled Woods She Leaves!, 22" × 30"

While objects that compose the subject and its supporting shapes are considered *positive space* shapes when directly painted, there are always shapes behind, between, within, or around them that are either dark, midvalue, or light. These constitute *negative space*.

A background that is pale and bright (negative space to a darker subject) is usually painted in stage 1, across darker-space shapes. The value of one space is therefore relative to that of the other.

But since, just as often, objects are paler in value than the objects and background spaces behind them, watercolorists paint darker shapes in value stages from light to dark as negative spatial elements to define pale and midvalue shapes, because darker value covers paler more efficiently. Even an object's darker form shadow is a *negative* space to its illuminated shape!

Like form shadow shapes, the palest negative space shapes are often largest and cover most midvalue and dark negative spaces. Apply them layer by value layer, drying the paper between each. Darkest negative shapes are usually smallest.

Snowy Egret in the Reeds (here and on page 39) is another prime example of negative space painting. The green/gold background mass is the largest, palest negative space to the white subject. Beginning with a large and mostly pale shape, then smaller midvalue shapes, and finally smallest and darkest ones, negative space shapes add a sense of three-dimensionality to the background reeds. Note color and value variation. Do you see the progression of ever-darker value in these negative spaces?

Dark negative spaces are like pockets of shadowed depth behind light-value object shapes more forward in space. The smaller and darker shapes recede as in a cave, becoming increasingly cooler in color temperature too. Vary their sizes, value, shapes, and colors for interest.

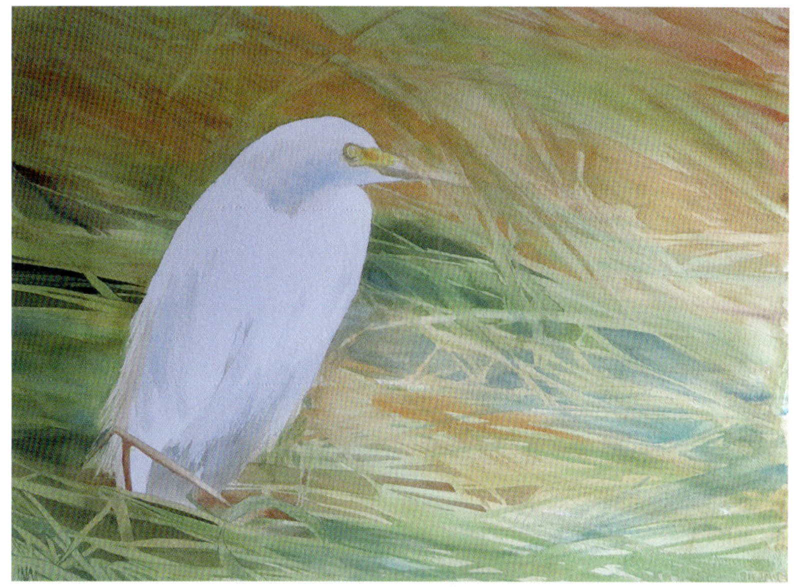

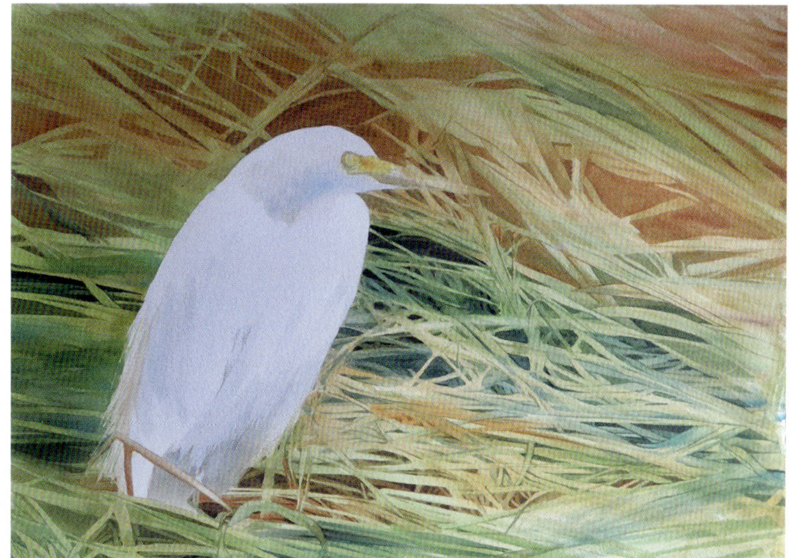

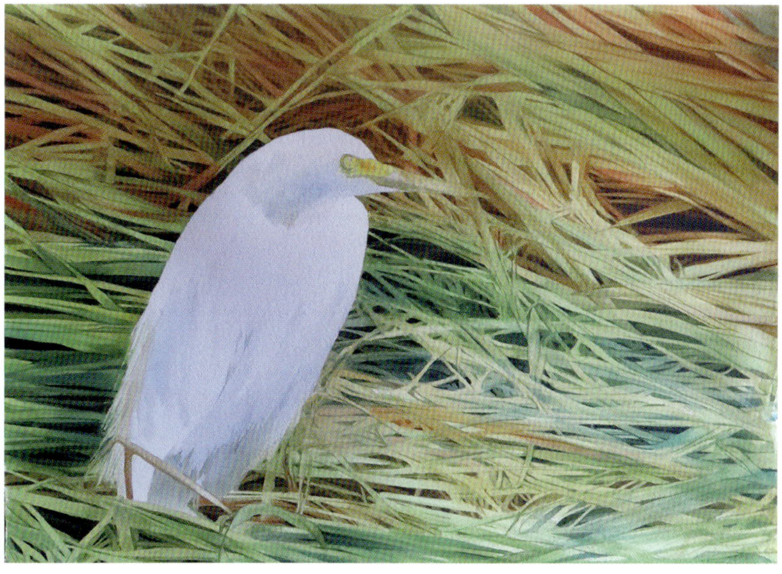

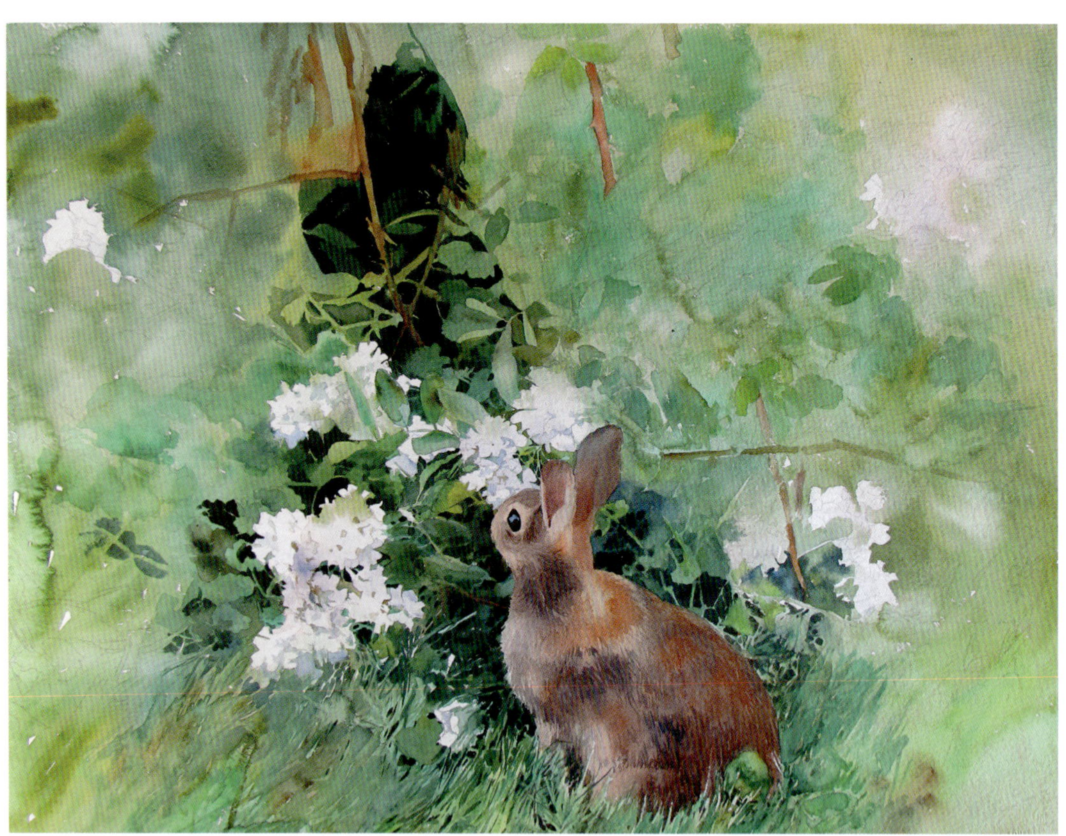

As the complicated background in this painting progressed, I found it easier at times to paint leaves and stems as midvalue positive shapes before adding their darker negative-space shapes. Completed painting is on page 108.

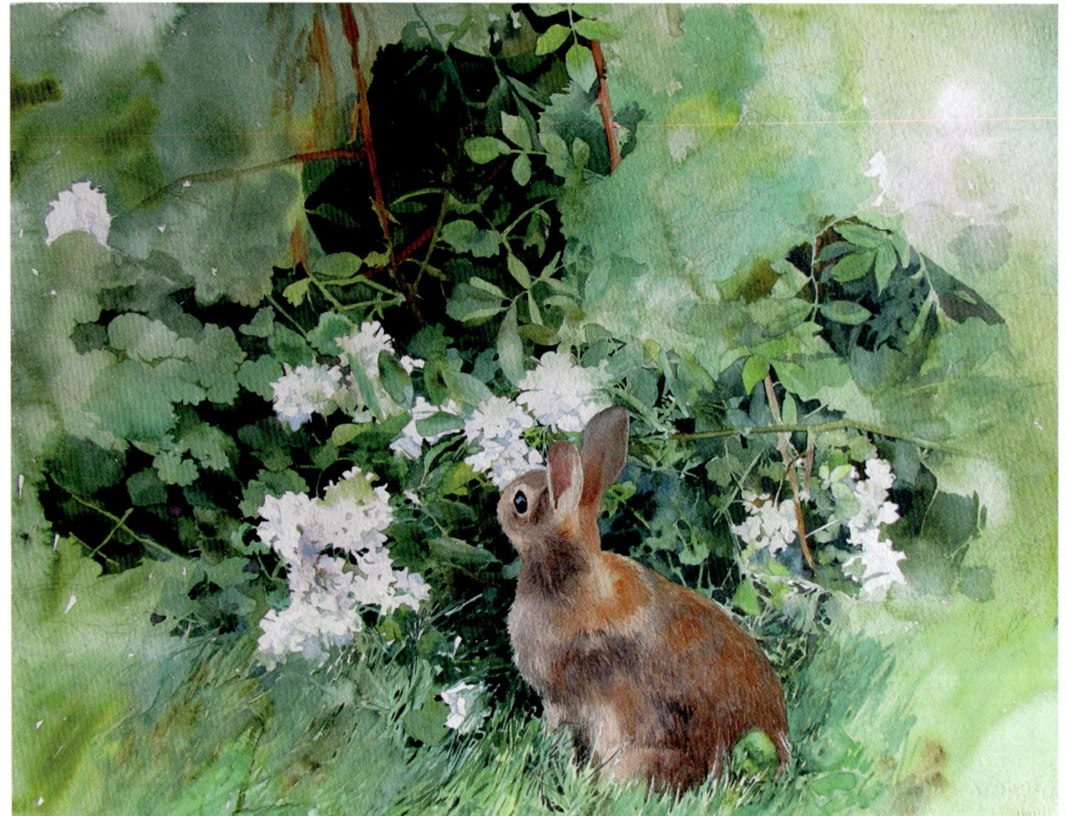

Negative space painting within a background color mass is the easiest, most efficient way to unify shapes related by color *without actually painting them* as individual positive space shapes!

Don't outline all paler-value shapes by entirely surrounding them with the same value, color, or shape, or make each element alike. Contrast some for interest and variation.

6. CAST SHADOWS

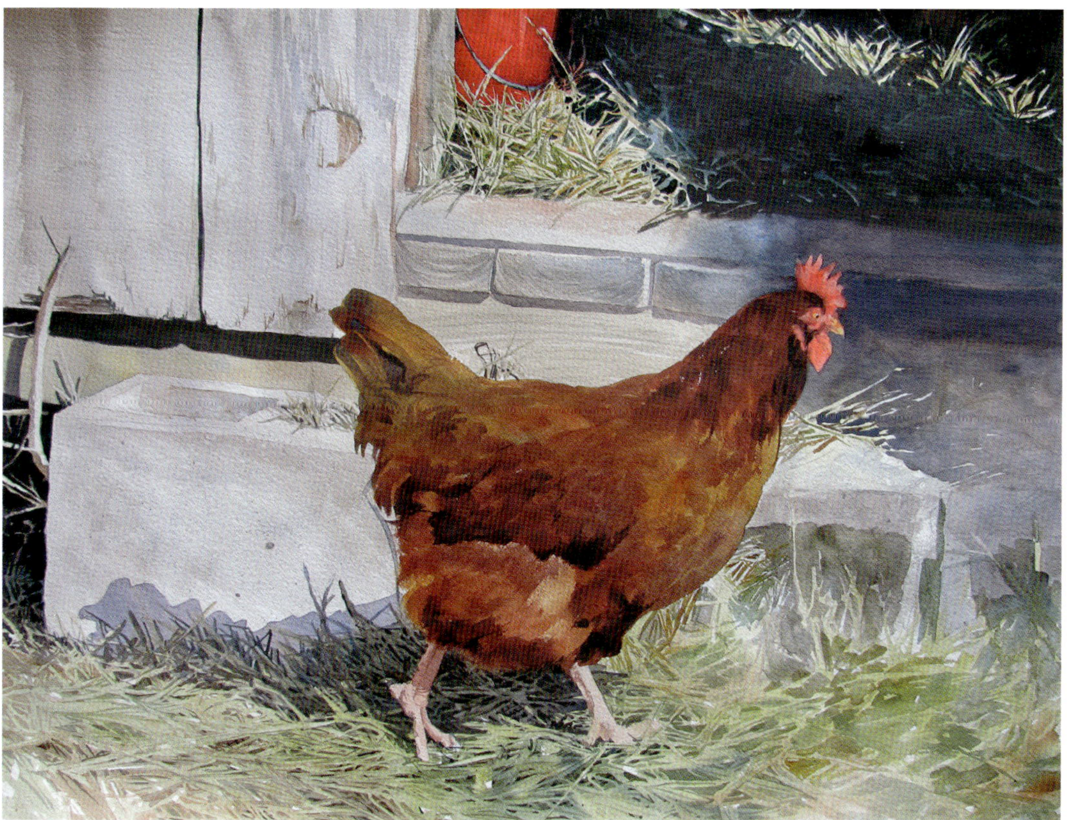

The hen's cast shadow painted as one solid mass and behind some illuminated hay stalks indicates a light source from above right. A softer shape behind her head implies shadow cast from a more distant object. The darker one above her head suggests depth in her shed.

A cast shadow is a shape on a surface created by a solid object blocking a source of light. Its specific shape is most distinct in direct lighting and closest to the object casting it.

The length of a cast shadow on the ground or on a flat horizontal surface is proportional to the angle of the light source's elevation. The higher the light source, the shorter the shadow. The sun casts the longest shadows when it's lowest in the sky. Many artists and photographers use long shadows to help visually connect disparate object shapes, creating paths for the

Shadows are not gray, though they are usually cool in color temperature. They pick up reflected color from nearby objects. If this is unapparent, use your intuition to vary cast shadow value and color temperature.

Paint all cast shadows in a coffee consistency at once with the same wash so they have the same value and color throughout the painting. Darken certain spaces within cast shadows to suggest depth in surfaces later, as in the shed of *Poultry in Motion* (page 21).

eye to follow around a composition. Shapes of light do the same thing.

All shadows are cast in the opposite direction from the source of light and follow the contour of objects that cross their paths. Vertical interruptions across a horizontal flat surface shorten their length. Once you're certain of the light source's position in your painting, don't change it or paint cast and form shadows in other directions.

Cast shadows follow rules of perspective, are lighter in value in the distance than close ones, and are less defined the farther away they are from their sources. Lit by the sun, a tall tree's cast shadow is darker and more defined close to its base and trunk than the shadow cast by the tips of its branches far from the ground.

Paint all cast shadows at once *after* local color(s) of all object shapes in the composition are dry—except where rounded shadow shapes require soft edges. Load the brush with a clean blue in a coffee consistency. Start the shadow on the object casting it, and paint in the direction opposite the light source, as seen in *East Haddam, CT* (page 97), in which the light source is at the right. *Never lose track of its position!* While it's wet, vary color here and there.

Allow adjacent shadow washes of the *same* or *similar value* but *differing colors* to occasionally bleed into each other for interest and to visually connect shapes. Paint quickly. Drop color in, but don't "help" it bleed. Don't cover *all* soft edges and bright, paler (illumination) shapes painted in stage 1, or you'll risk losing drama created earlier by light and by shadow later.

Vibrant, saturated color, made more dramatic by strong light and shadow, brings energy to paintings. Midvalues painted in stage 2 connect value extremes, softening their contrast. Use all three values in your work, and make one dominant.

A painting's two major values have now been established; let's paint the third!

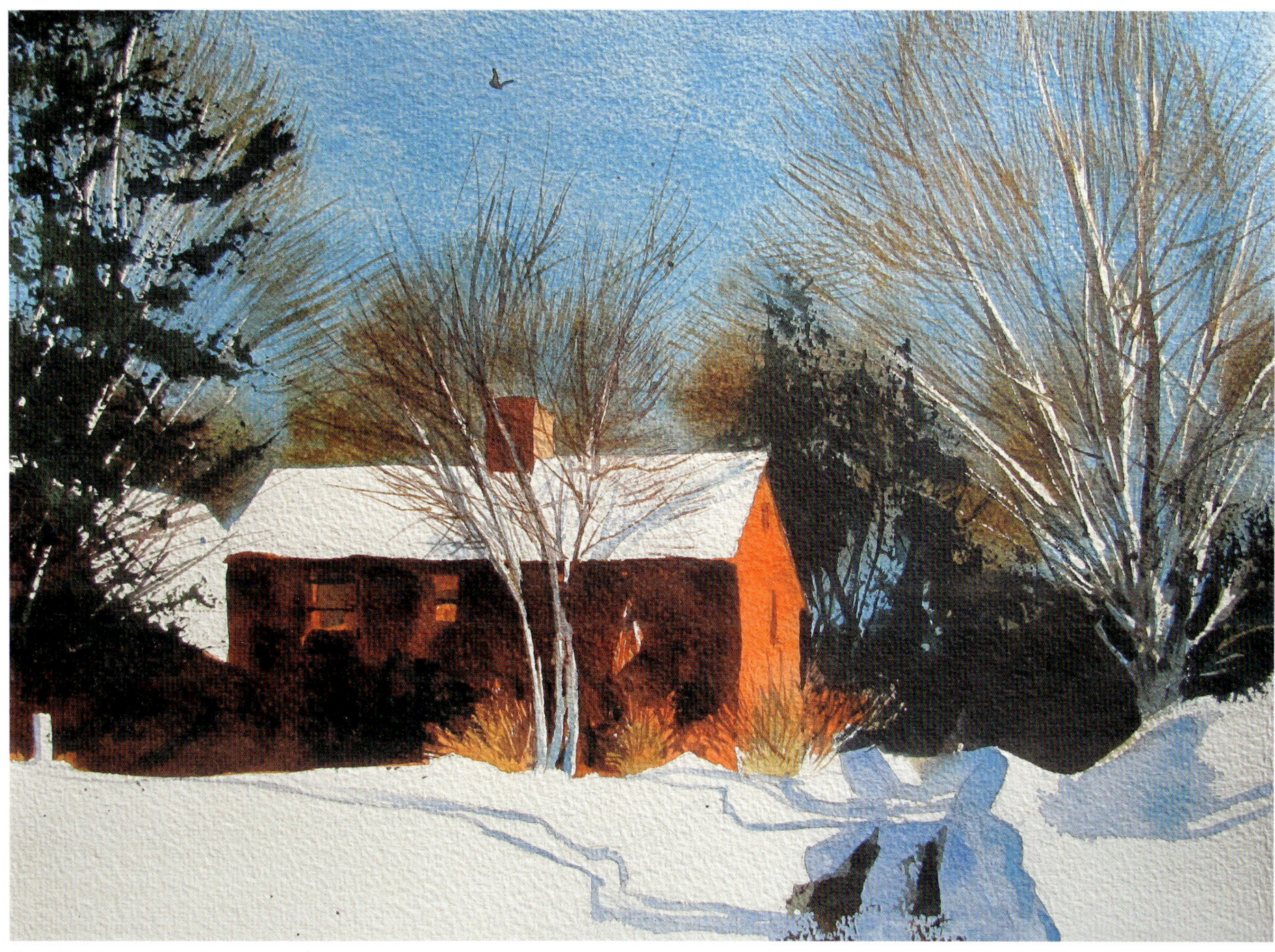

East Haddam, CT, 11" x 15"

Load paint with the brush you intend to use. Twirl it around in the well. Work the paint farther into the bristles on the palette. With dry or damp paint, this takes time and effort, but it's particularly necessary with fresh paint so that streaks are not left on the paper.

If more paint is needed or the brush feels too dry, dip the brush fully and quickly into the water (*don't* rinse the paint off!) and bring it directly back to the well. Repeat as often as necessary until the brush is loaded with paint and a large paint puddle like heavy cream or thin mud is on the palette.

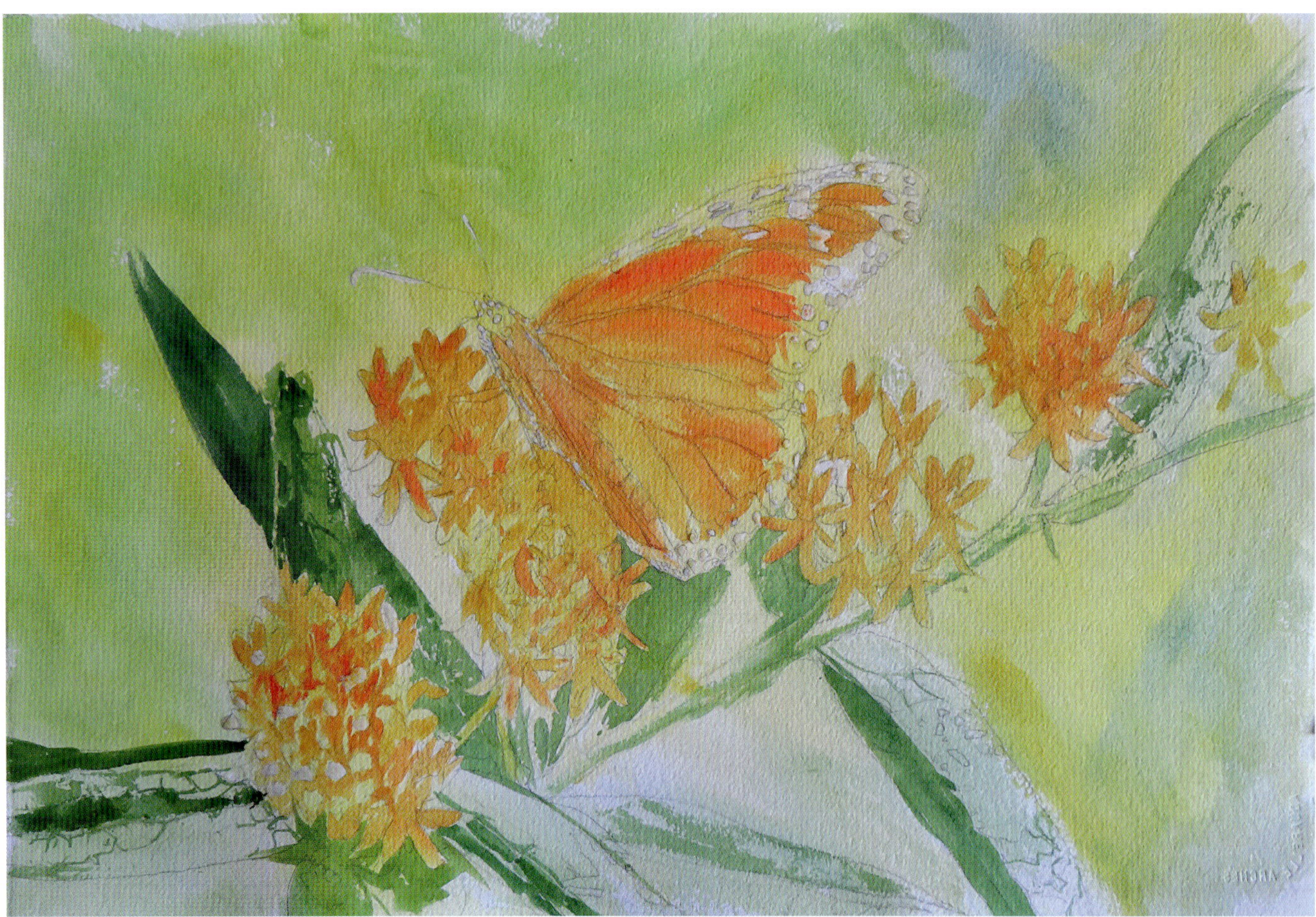

The local (orange) color of butterfly and flowers and critical green leaf shapes are painted in stage 2, with care taken to keep illuminated shapes white, pale, or bright.

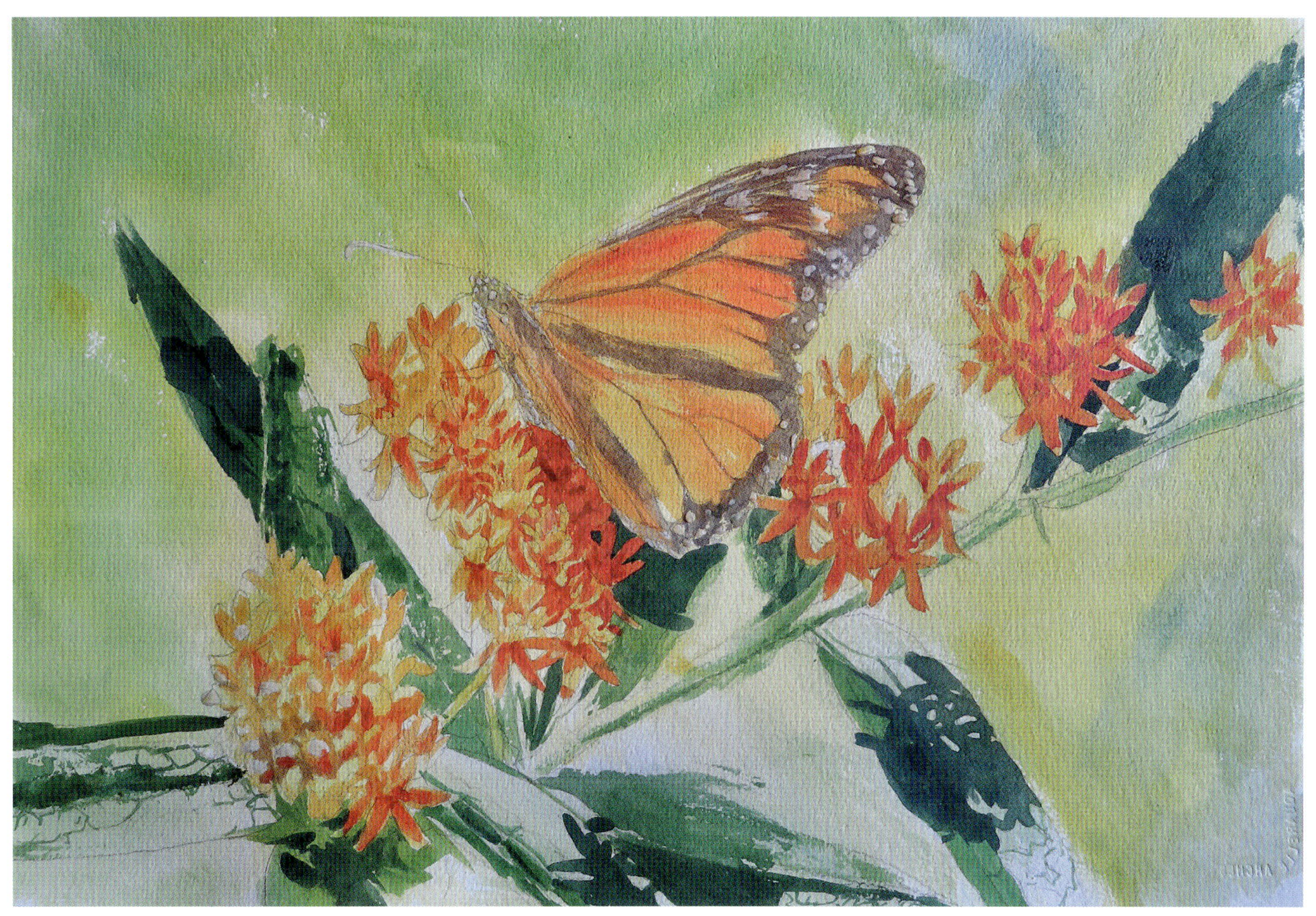

Both form and cast shadows are painted next, along with the palest local brown color of the butterfly wing pattern. Frisket still protects white spots.

Bottom Line:

After these spatial elements are added in stage 2, the bright, pale washes that obscured most sketched edges in stage 1 begin to suggest lighting, form, texture, shapes, and other painting details.

5 Stage 3—Building Darkest Shapes and Backgrounds

Adding saturated, rich darks to a painting is to me as exciting as applying the loose, drippy washes of bright color in stage 1 and defined shapes and shadows in stage 2. Juxtaposed strategically, dark value now not only accentuates shapes through contrast and hides others via harmony but also causes bright colors to throb with energy.

An Epiphyte, 15" × 22"

It can sometimes take resolve and patience to get through the previous stages without adding darkest value until now, but that effort is worthwhile. Darks visually wrap all the painting elements together, because they not only create new vibrancy and drama but also help establish a sense of the painting's completion.

Just as building shapes of light and color in the early stages requires advanced planning, the placement of dark shapes also requires a strategy. But why bring up planning again when most of the painting has been well established? Dark object and background spatial shapes carry more visual weight than pale or midvalue ones and instantly strengthen a light, bright, or midvalue subject. But sometimes their contrast and strength can create a visual imbalance, so adjustments in their placement and other elements may be necessary. Ill-placed dark shapes are difficult to remove, though not impossible.

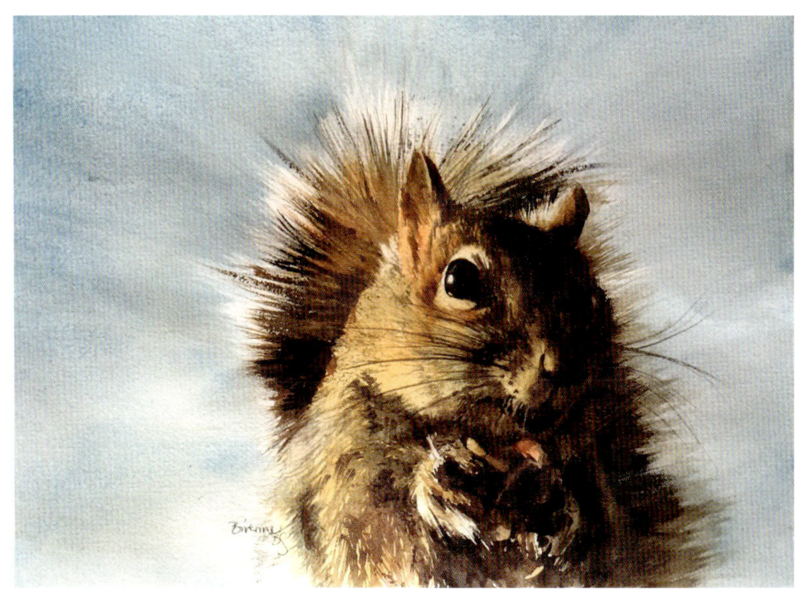

Mr. Squirrel, 11" × 15

Dark whiskers and eyes, silhouetted branches and leaves, inkiest shadows, and darkest backgrounds bring lifelike details to shapes.

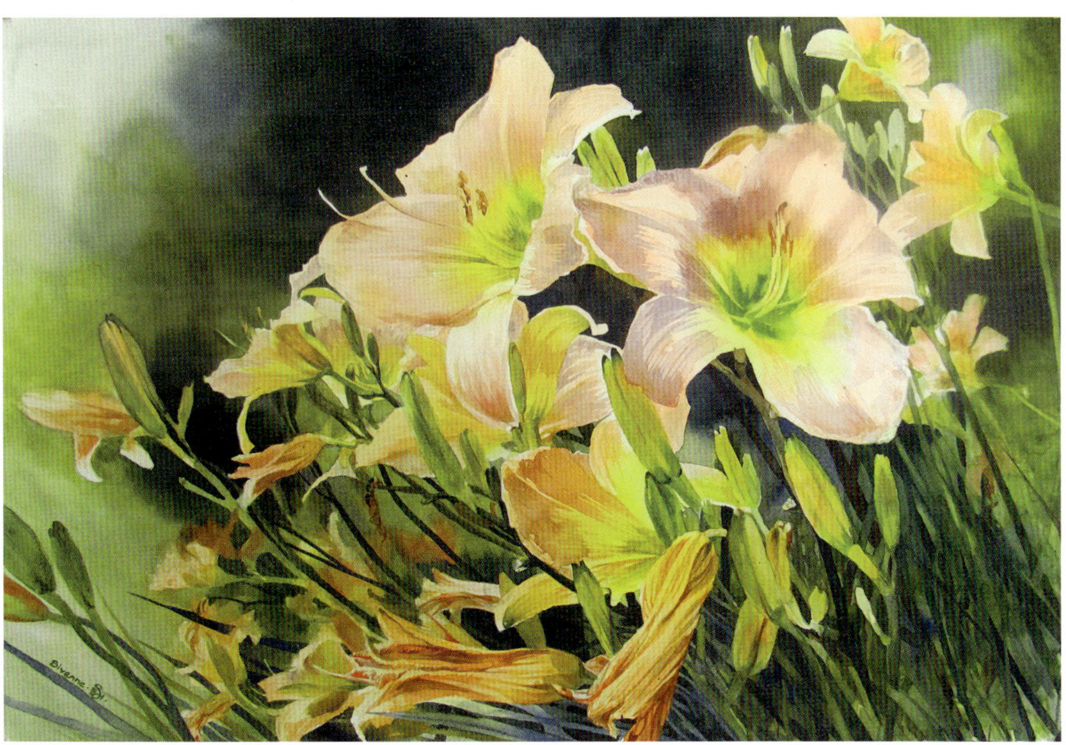

Lilies, Leaning, 15" × 22"

At this stage, care must be taken not to cover all passages of illuminated white, light-value, and midvalue color, because those overall *value shapes*, along now with those of darks, must each maintain interest and guide the eye around the painting from one element to the next.

If you haven't already determined by now where and how emphasis and contrast will occur and where and how insignificant elements can be toned down or obscured (for instance, by shadow), this is the last chance to do so using the dark value extreme.

From start to finish, especially now, ask yourself: Is value contrast the best way to highlight key subject details? Which element is most appropriate to obscure less important areas, such as background foliage or a figure's back and shoulder? Where, in particular, would dark value make a difference in highlighting or hiding elements?

The large, pale, unremarkably shaped flowers in *Lilies, Leaning* (page 101) contrast dramatically with the dark saturated background. Yet, the setting varies in color from warm yellows to cool blues, and in value from very pale to extremely dark. Open background space at the top left and large, dominant flower petals are visually balanced by a midvalue, complex leaf-and-stem pattern at the bottom and lower right. While color, shape, value, line, and direction harmony in the leaves and stems suggest their reduced significance, these same elements contrast the flowers, emphasizing and leading the eye toward them. Planning and a bit of intuition help properly place and unify disparate painting elements like these.

To achieve rich darks, use your darkest pigments (especially apparent when paint is dry) and less water. Prussian, Antwerp, Ultramarine, Winsor Violet, Burnt Sienna, Brown Madder, and Alizarin are excellent examples, especially when two or more are combined. Fill the wells to capacity—a pea-sized dollop will *never* do!

Use *color* to produce the darkest value extreme. Because black dulls color chroma, remove it (and white paint) from your palette. Vary value and color for interest.

ATTAINING DARKEST VALUE

Darkening value depends most critically on color temperature, cool or warm, no matter how dark you wish to go, and a paint consistency of heavy cream or thin mud. Use two or three very dark, harmonious, *related* colors in a particular temperature, which is particularly apparent where a shadow or value transition is soft. For instance, mix Green Gold with Ultramarine and Prussian for a cool dark green. The result is a richer, more interesting dark than black, which combines temperatures. If color temperature is unapparent, choose one, since integrating both warm and cool dulls chroma.

Finally, except where a soft transition in value or color is needed, paint on dry paper if possible, because the contrary will lighten dark paint.

Skipping midvalues as you go from pale to dark makes reintroducing highlights in dark painted spaces more difficult and less interesting. So take your time and add value layer by layer until you are ready to paint the darkest with less water. Remember, all washes dry lighter than they appear when wet.

The first hue in the following represents the local color, with which you should start. Consistency should be creamy. The more of the other colors and the less water used, the darker the value will be.

1. *Cool* ***Red***: quinacridone red + alizarin + a little Winsor violet
2. *Warm* ***Red***: quinacridone red + alizarin + brown madder and *hints* Winsor violet
3. *Cool* ***Orange***: aureolin + quinacridone red + raw umber + *hints* Winsor green
4. *Warm* ***Orange***: aureolin + quinacridone red + burnt sienna + brown madder
5. *Cool* ***Yellow***: aureolin + *hints* Winsor green
6. *Warm* ***Yellow***: aureolin + quinacridone gold + *hints* quinacridone red
7. *Cool* ***Green***: green gold + Prussian + ultramarine
8. *Warm* ***Green***: green gold + raw umber + brown madder + *hints* Prussian; *or* green gold + raw umber + burnt sienna + *hints* Prussian
9. *Cool* ***Blue***: cobalt + ultramarine + *hints* Prussian
10. *Warm* ***Blue***: cobalt + ultramarine + *hints* Winsor violet
11. *Cool* ***Violet***: quinacridone red + cobalt + ultramarine + *hints* Prussian; *or* Winsor violet + *hints* Prussian; *or* ultramarine + Winsor violet
12. *Warm* ***Violet***: quinacridone red + cobalt + Winsor violet; *or* Winsor violet + brown madder
13. *Cool* ***Pink***: opera + cobalt + *hints* Winsor violet
14. *Warm* ***Pink***: opera + alizarin + brown madder
15. *Cool* ***Brown***: burnt sienna + brown madder + ultramarine
16. *Warm* ***Brown***: burnt sienna + brown madder + *hints* Winsor violet
17. *(Neutral)* ***Black***: ratio of 51:49 – ultramarine: burnt sienna

Alternate neutral dark combinations:
alizarin + Prussian (both staining, strong colors)
Winsor violet + Prussian (both staining, strong colors)
brown madder + Prussian + Winsor violet

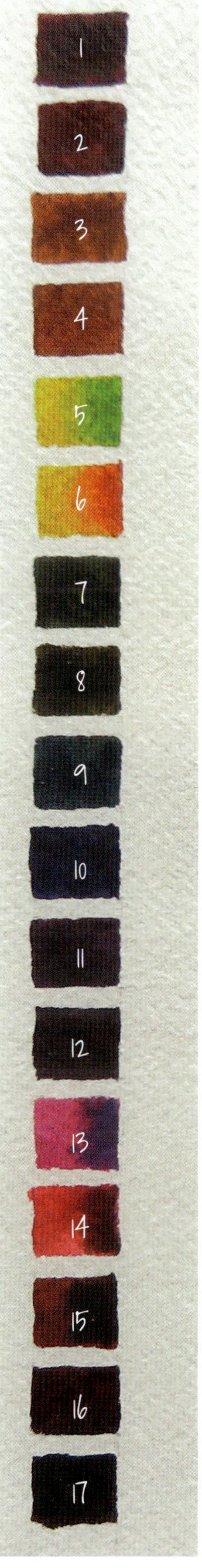

PAINTING A DARK SUBJECT

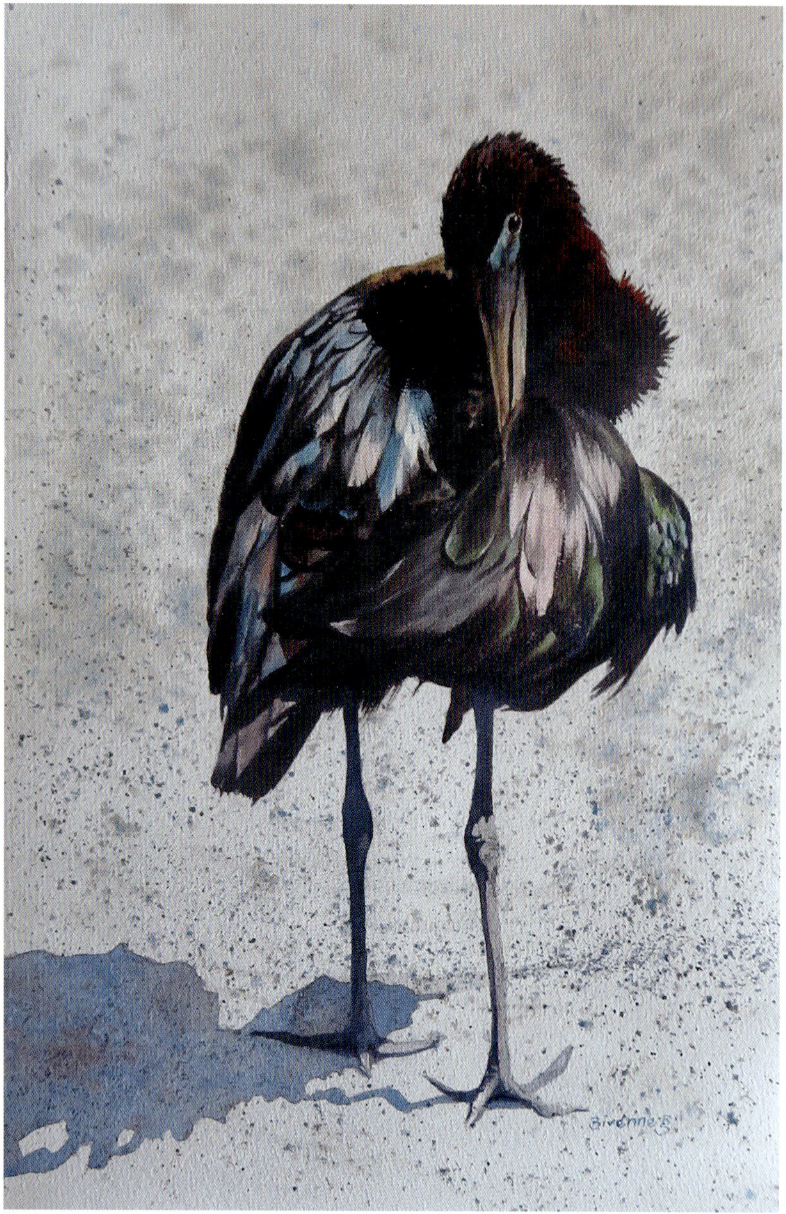

Glossy Ibis, 15" × 22"

Lighting, though sometimes challenging to convey on dark subjects, suggests a shape's three-dimensionality, or form. First paint the background paler or brighter than the subject. Then paint the subject's highlights with typically blue, purple, green, or brown, beginning with the palest so you don't lose any sketched illumination shapes.

As seen in on next page, the pink/blue background overlaps much of the subject's silhouette, stage 1. After a pink wash dried, I added Xs and dots with frisket, then blue from the background across cat highlights, including whiskers, and the first wash of his yellowish eyes.

Paint *dark subject* shapes after their bright or pale background is complete. Conversely, paint *dark backgrounds* last, as negative space shapes to paler subject shapes.

Next, a relatively pale, neutral wash of Burnt Sienna and Ultramarine (representing darkest value) was first added in the face around whiskers, eyes, nose, and shoulder as negative space to the (still pale) blue and brown highlights. This helped control form and texture development as shadows and darker value were built. Highlights of blue and brown and some shadowed areas were darkened next. Do you see how light and dark shapes further define surface texture and form within this subject, such as the head, chin, nose, claws, and legs?

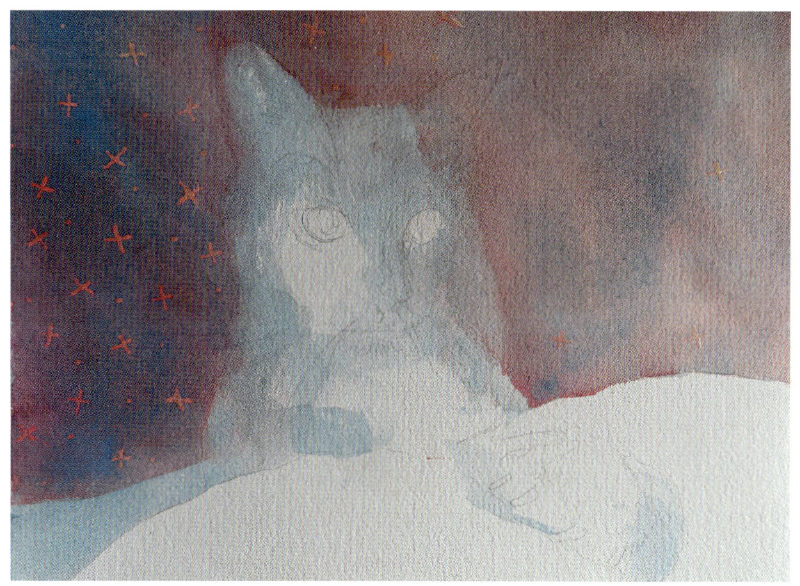

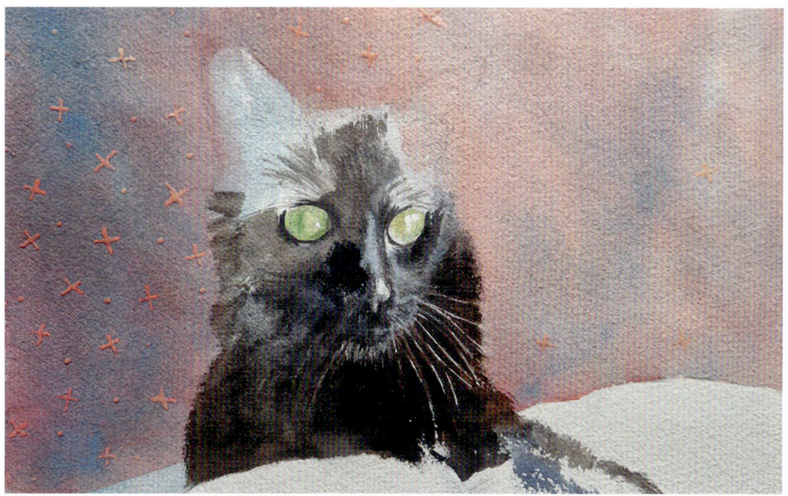

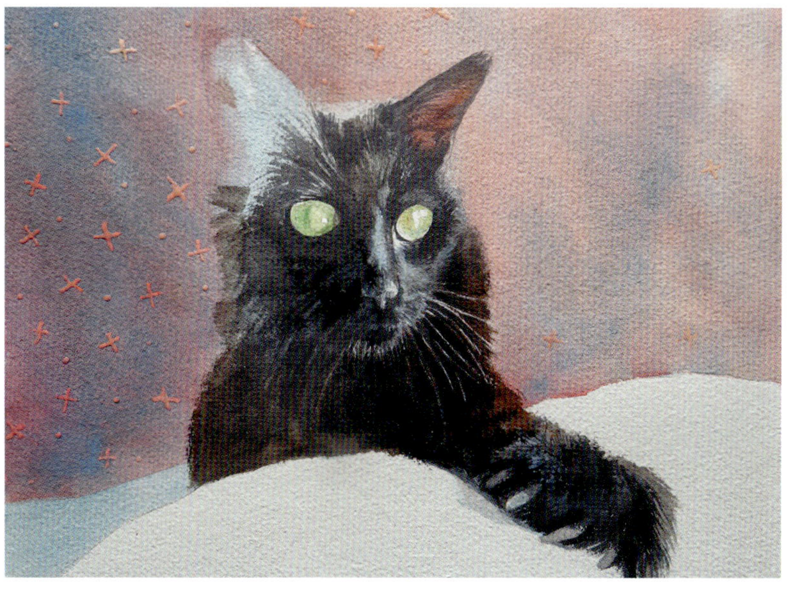

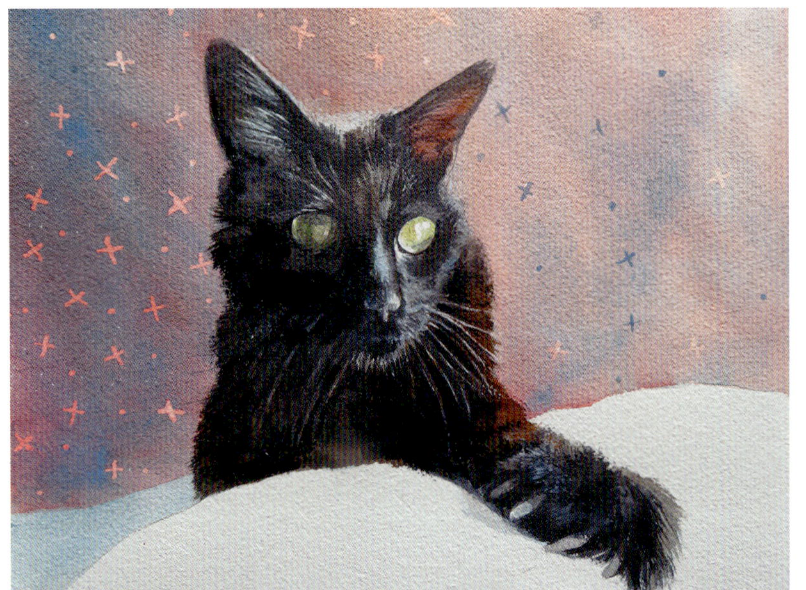

I removed frisket from the background design and added similar blue shapes at the right. The fur was further developed and darkened with negative space techniques behind whiskers, eyes, chin, and claws (*left*). Darkest washes, eye pupils, dark whiskers, and other dark silhouette hairs complete the painting. Notice that the whiskers and eye (*at right*) appear illuminated, and those at left shadowed (*below*).

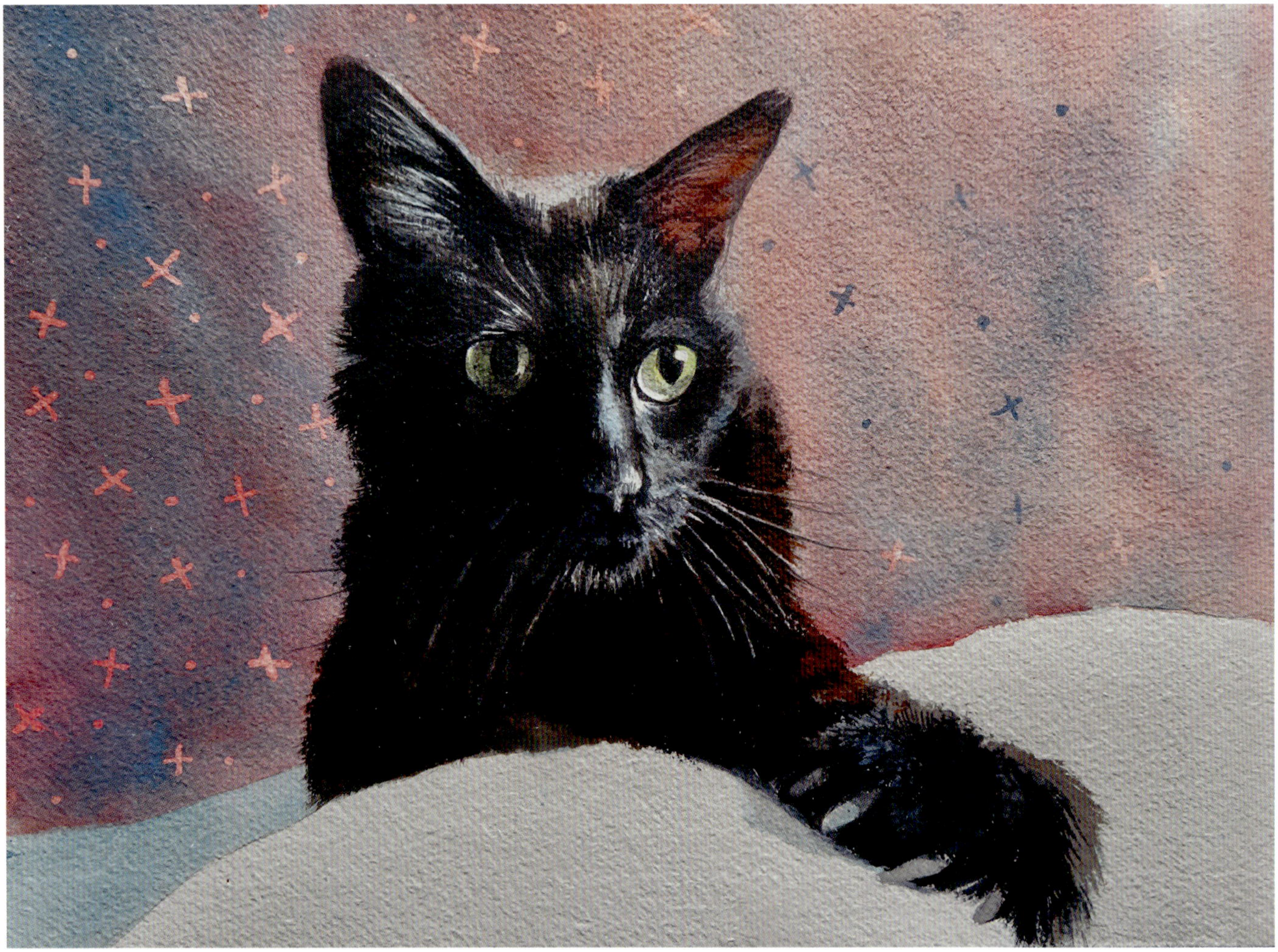

Being Pudge, 11" × 15"

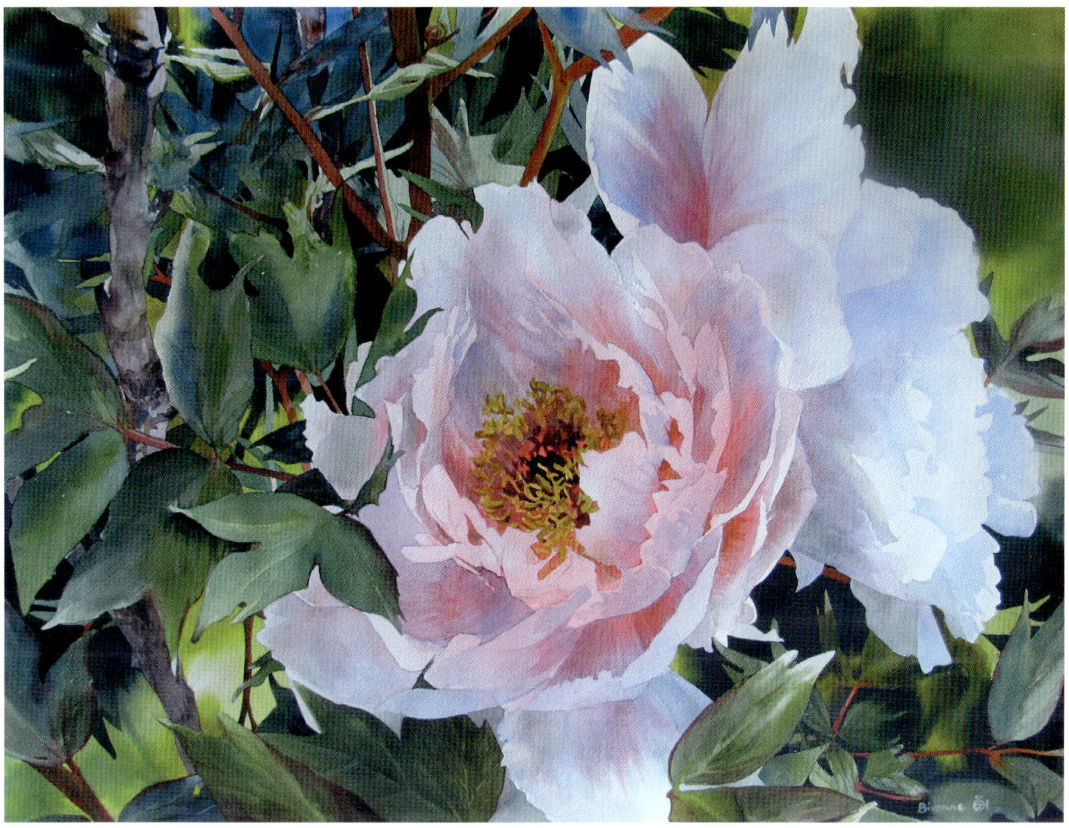

Pale open background space creates a diagonal from top right to bottom left, while midvalue and dark leaf shapes dominate from top left to bottom right.

Peony Scenery, 15" × 22"

PAINTING A DARK, COMPLEX BACKGROUND

As discussed in previous chapters, varying the many elements that compose a complex background requires planning and painting them according to the subject's key elements. The flower subject in *Peony Scenery* (*above*), for instance, has some large, simple petals surrounding complex interior elements. I decided some open background space would give visual relief to the elaborate leaf and stem shapes and balance the large petals. Varied open and complex background colors, value, and shapes add visual interest and support the flower.

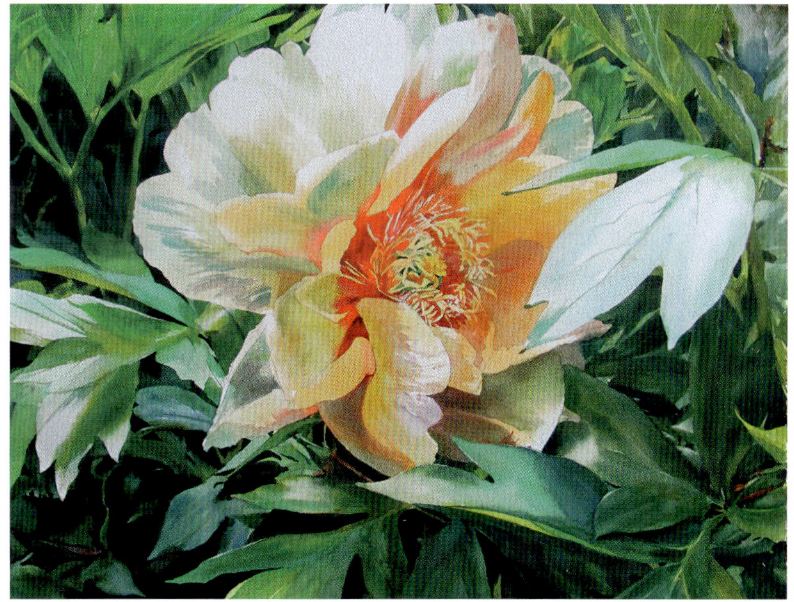

Peach Peony, 22" × 30"

Though value and color differences may seem imperceptible at times, negative and positive space shapes added gradually from palest to darkest yield depth and a beautiful value transition. Painting them takes patience and persistence. It's how the foliage was painted in, among others, *White Chrysanthemums* (page

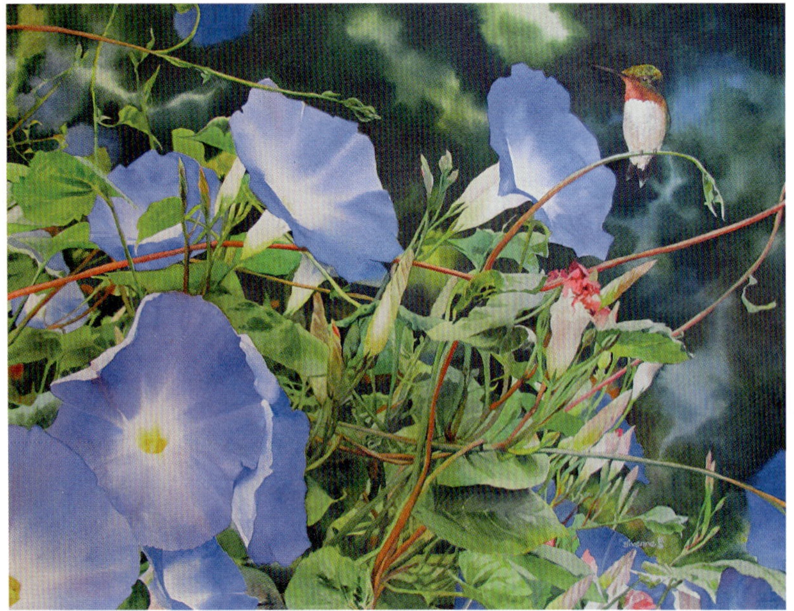

Brief Rest, 22" × 30"

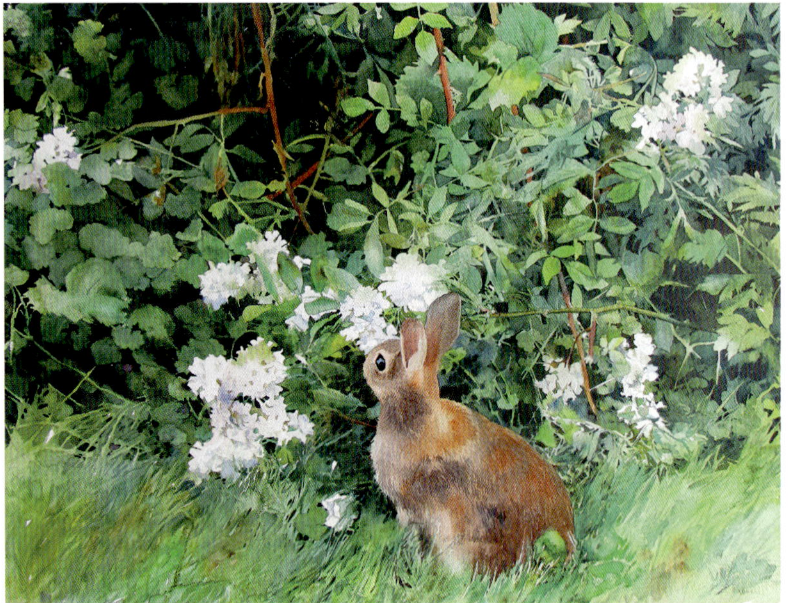

Happy Scamper, 22" × 30"

61), *Peach Peony* (page 107), *Brief Rest* (above), and *Happy Scamper* (above).

Slightly different negative space painting techniques were utilized to achieve the dominant dark background in *Egret in the Dark Lagoon* (page 109) and *Goldfinches in the Magnolia* (page 28).

Because the dark setting in both has less shape complexity within and is more uniform in value and color, their negative spaces are painted in several very dark layers rather than in multiple paler washes, as a more complex background requires. The thin, foreground supporting shapes of reeds and branches, respectively, also gave me ample opportunity to stop the background wash for rest. You can see samples of this technique in *Hidden in the Pine* (pages 110 through 113).

When *thin* paler object shapes like these break up dark background space, visualize both as distinct entities. Imagine the background without the subject and these shapes. How would it appear? Can you suggest an identifiable background object or shape to introduce a sensible radical color or value change relative to the subject?

In other words, don't drastically alter color or value in adjacent negative (background) spaces without making it clear why such a difference was necessary. Don't paint, for example, light green on one side and dark brown on the other of a thin stem unless the change represents an obvious background shape, such as a large green leaf or thick brown limb in this example. So the viewer does not wonder why the stem separated them, include more of the leaf or more of the limb on *both* sides.

Distinct value change behind the reeds at the bottom of *Egret in the Dark Lagoon* represents the bird's reflection. Very dark leaves punctuate the dark background in *Monarch*. Reflection and dark leaves benefit each subject. Such visual tricks drastically and successfully alter background value and support (thin) subject shapes because they make sense.

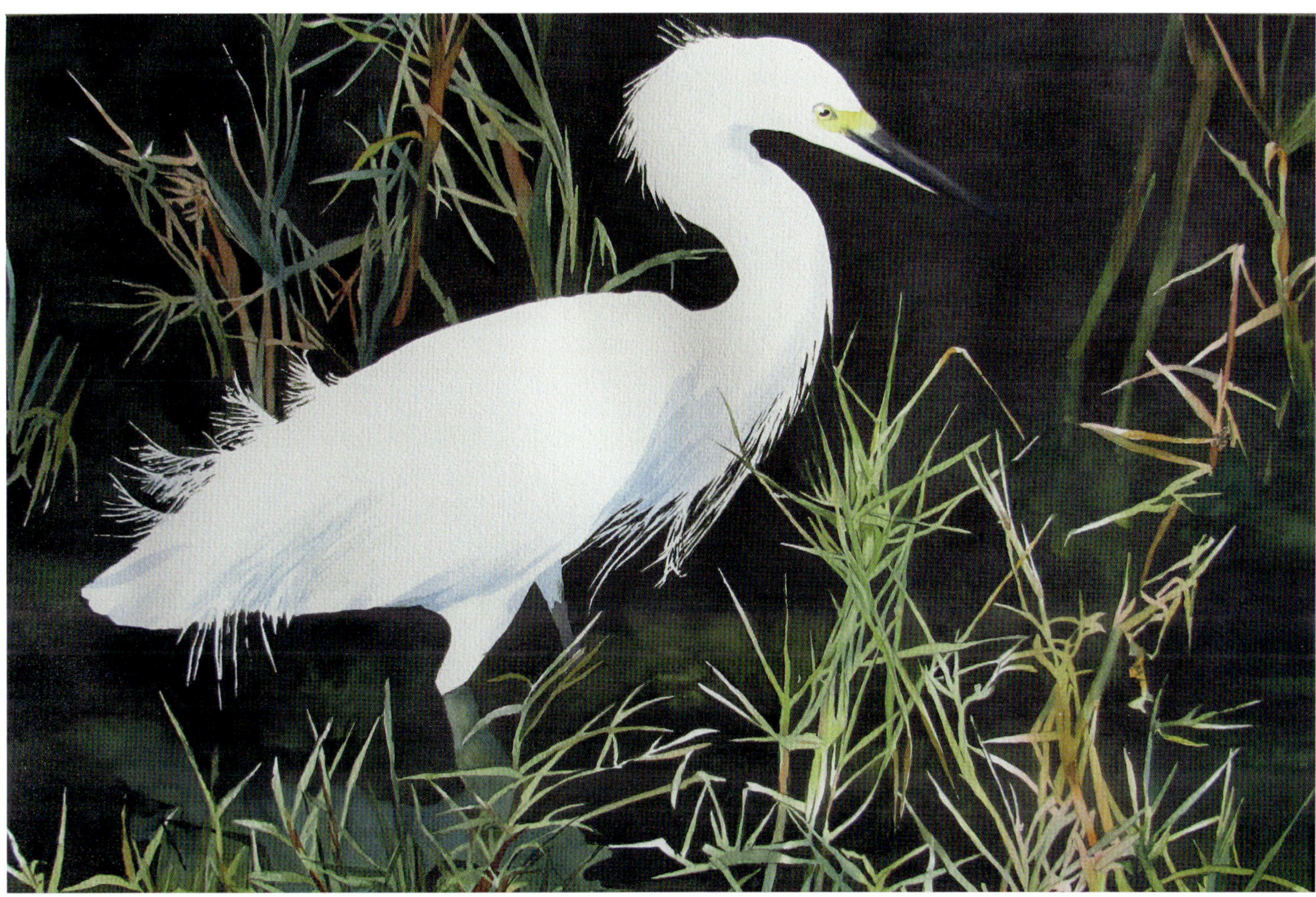

Egret in the Dark Lagoon, 15" × 22"

Keep or add only background object shapes, colors, or value that sensibly relate to or support the subject. Don't fill *all* empty background spaces with object shapes. Eliminate nonessential distractions. Less is more.

Here is an example of how a pale subject (the tree) is painted against a complex, dark background. In the first image (*below*), stage 1, a pale neutral covers most of the trunk and branches. Primary colors and purposeful blooms were loosely added, wet-on-damp. More saturated greens and warm browns varying in temperature came next (page 111). Note how shape edges are still undefined. Negative space painting techniques enable branches and foliage to become identifiable with extreme dark value (page 111). Unplanned until the painting was halfway complete, the owl shape was lifted out with a damp brush and then painted for a sense of scale (page 112). Note its position at a power point. Adjustments can be made at any stage!

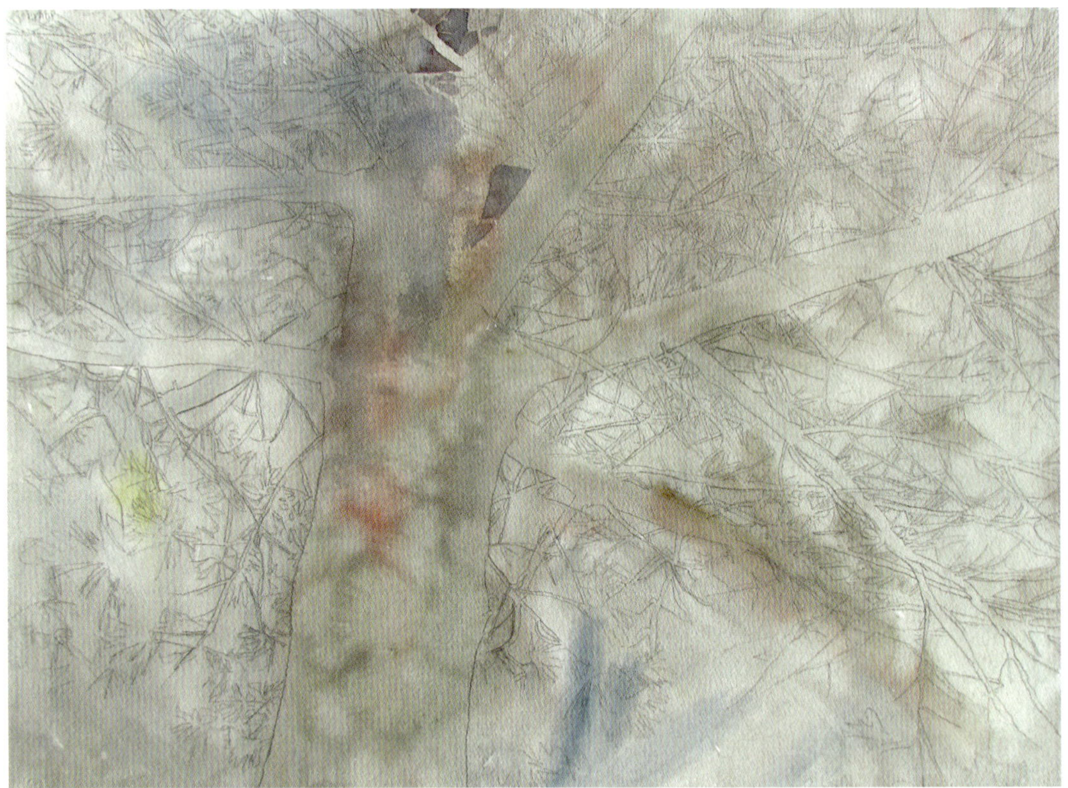

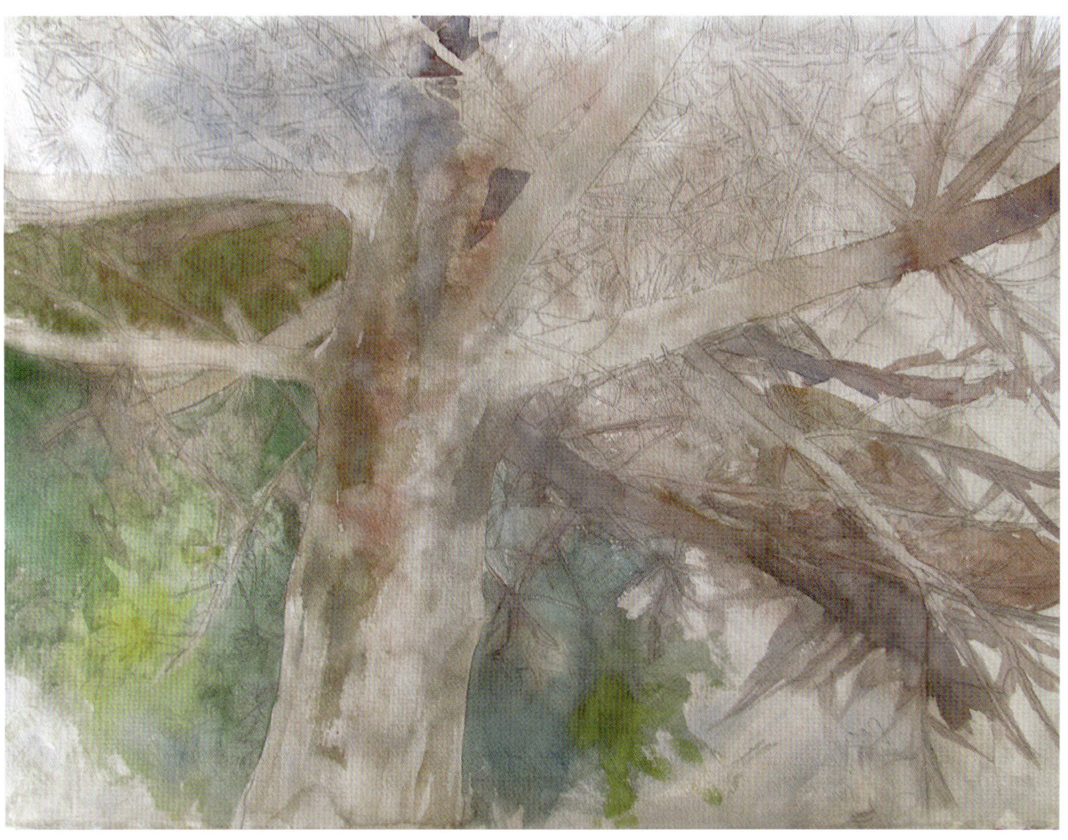

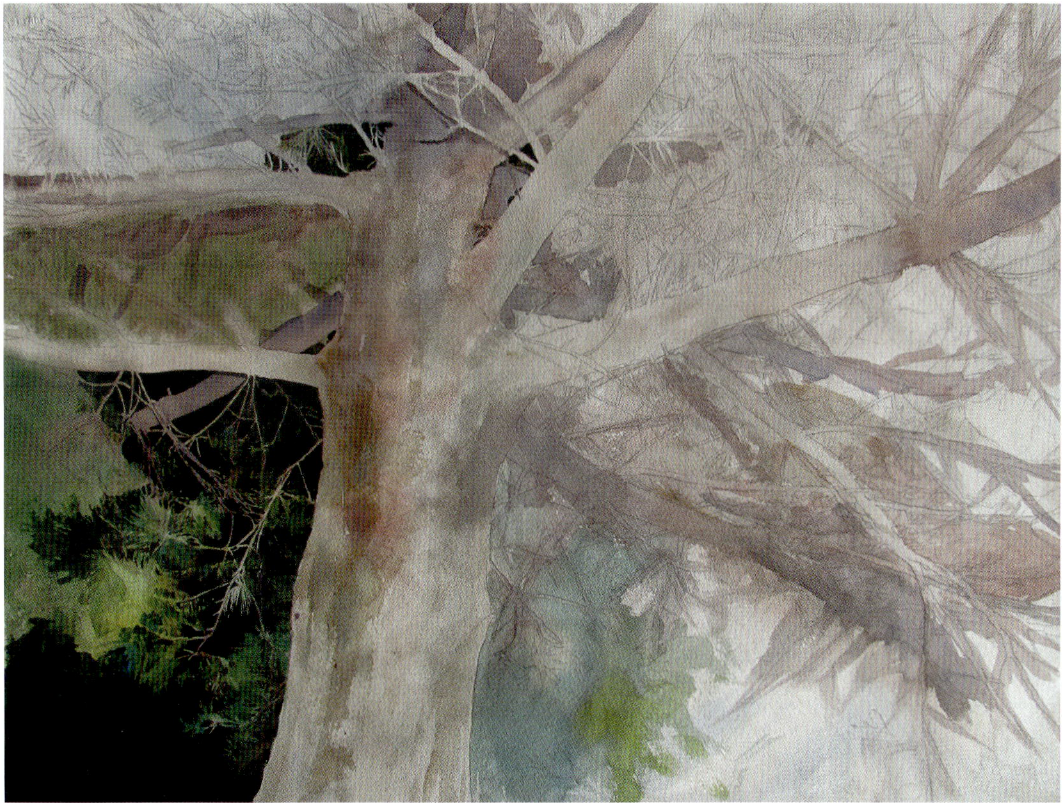

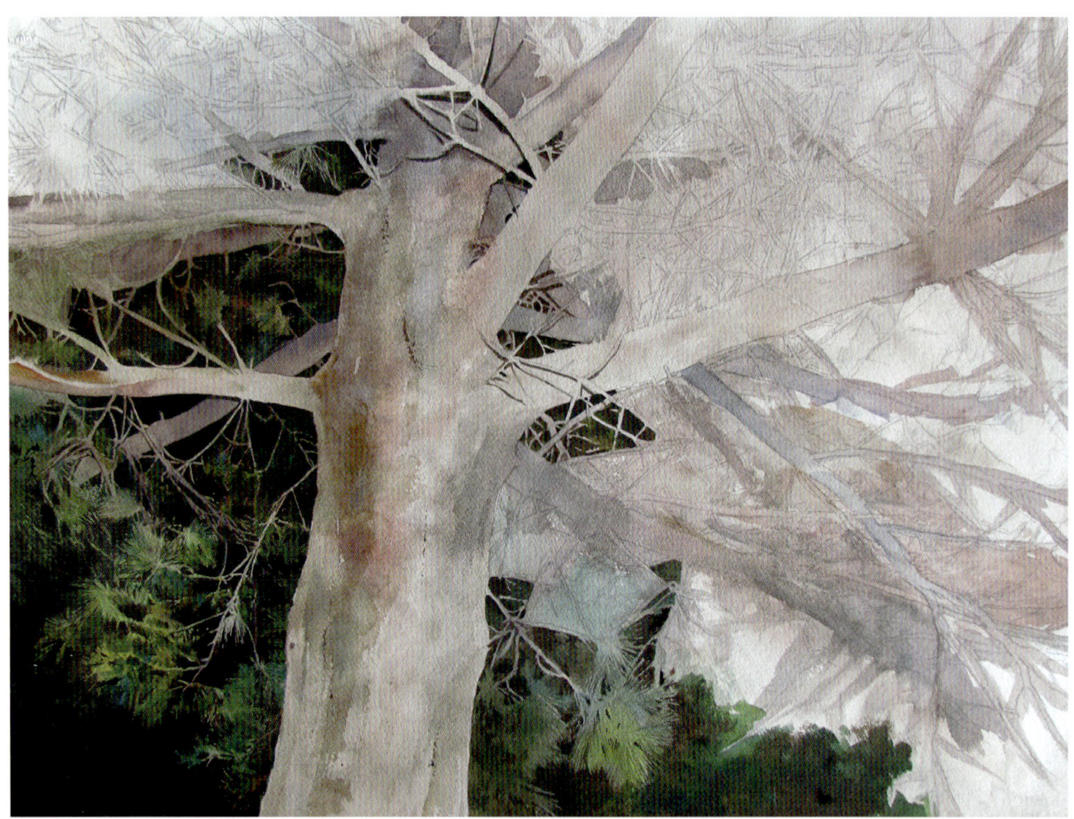

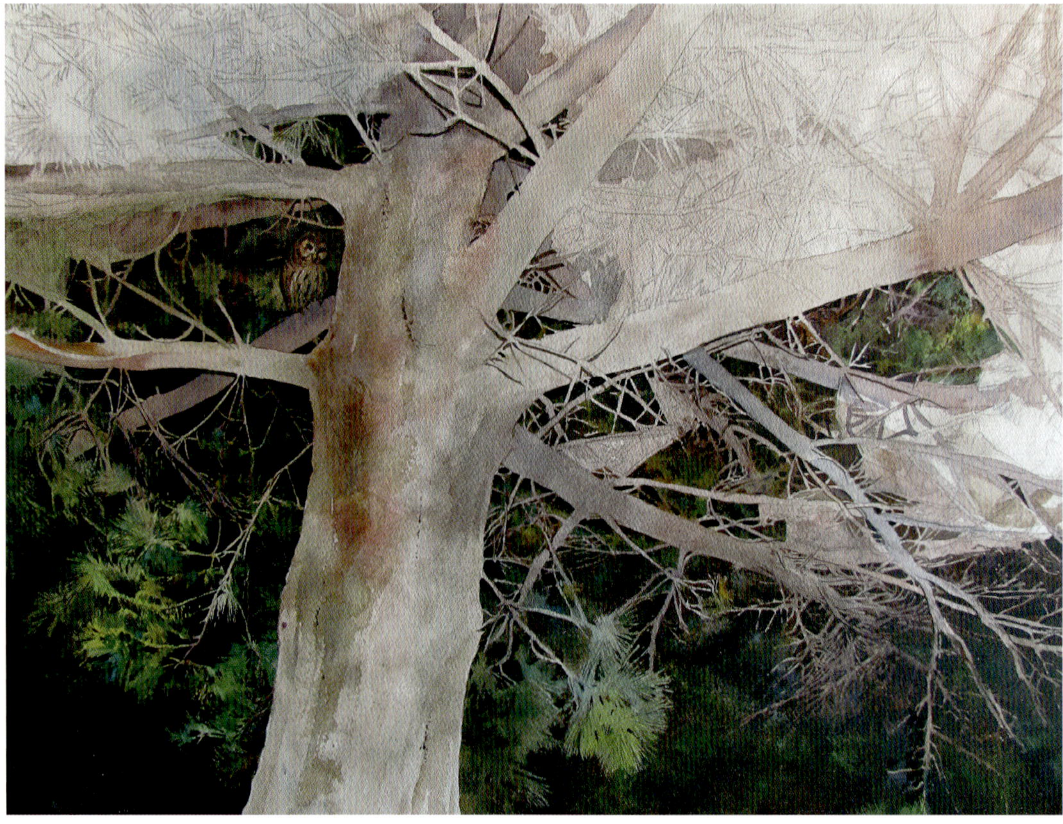

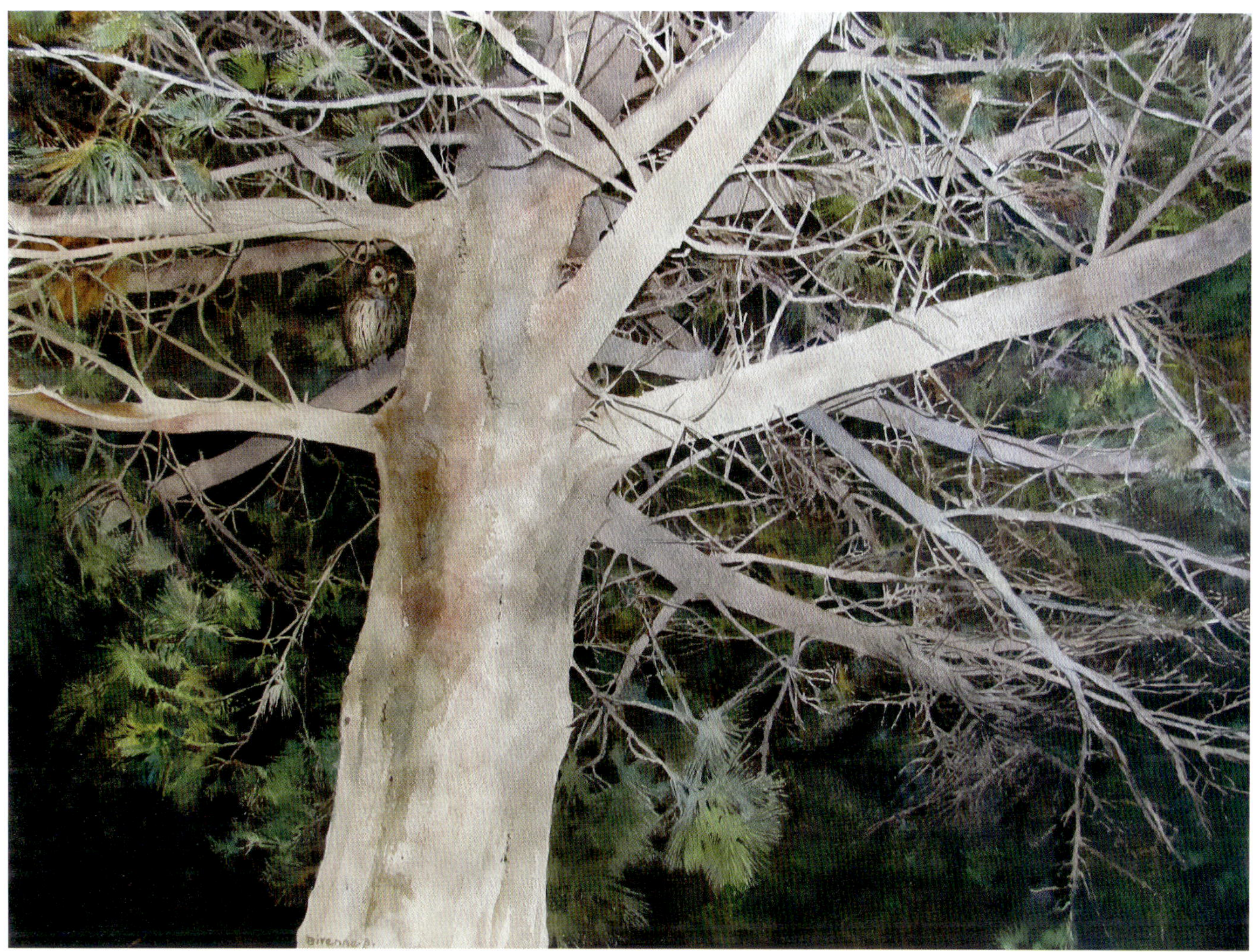

Hidden in the Pine, 22" × 30"

PAINTING AN OPEN DARK BACKGROUND

A rich, very saturated, open dark background emphasizes the color vibrancy and brightness of illuminated subject shapes. Like any other shape or element, such a background is painted in watercolor from light and bright to dark and saturated, and in this last stage.

Though this background benefits from color and value variation, sometimes an even, flat background of one color and value is perfectly suitable for certain subjects, in which case, paint each wash a value layer at a time, drying the paper between each until complete.

If this is not part of your plan, you'll have to make some decisions.

Ask yourself:

- Where and how can medium and light value morph into very dark?
- Where should color change? Can it both harmonize and contrast with the subject?
- Where and how should supporting subject and background shapes be minimized or softened for textural interest and depth suggestion?

The simplified background emphasizes the pale and somewhat complex composite flower subject shapes in *Hydrangea Shadows* (page 116) through extreme value contrast. Though value is not quite as dark as the inky setting, shadowed leaf and stem edges (*at left and top*) direct the

These flowers have dramatic, colorful centers; complex petal shapes; and simple silhouettes. I balanced these elements with a mostly plain dark background that varies in color and value.

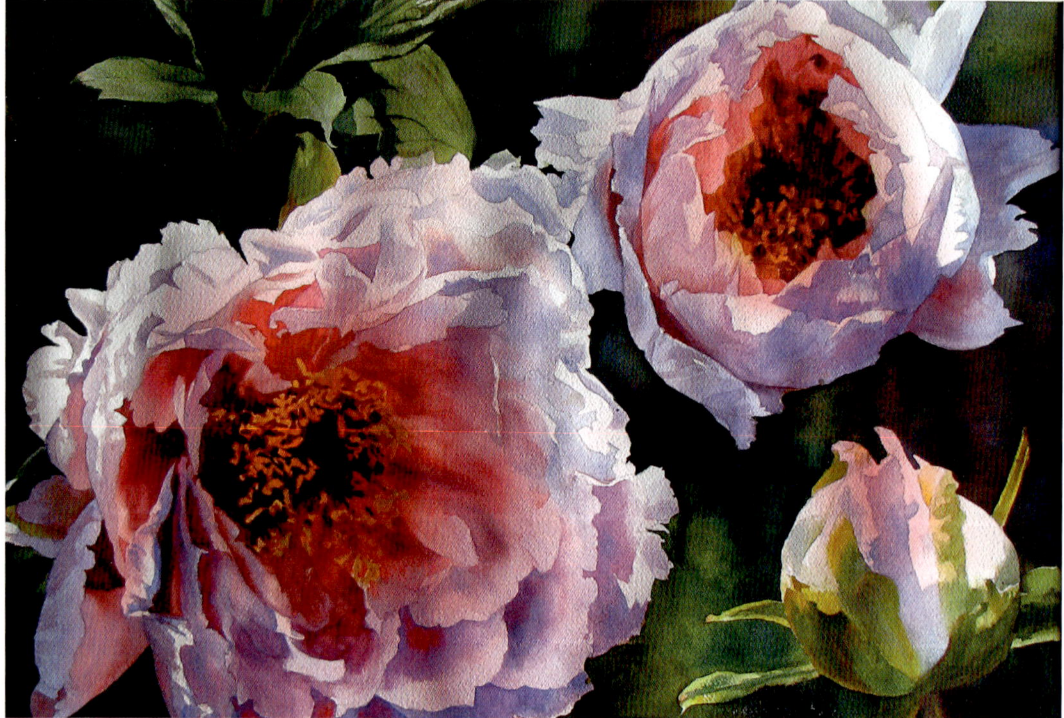

Peonies II, 15" × 22"

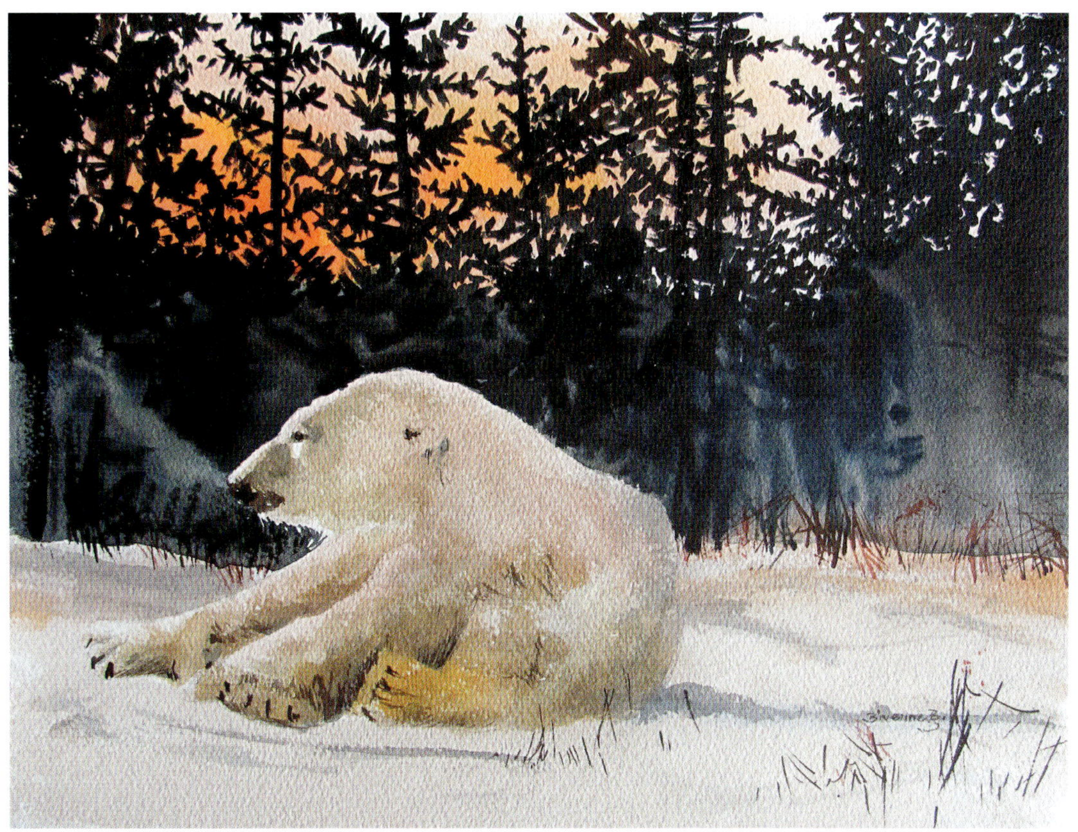

Taking It Easy, 11" × 15"

Because the bear's shape is simple and its value pale, the background's shape complexity, color, and value variation from pale to very dark contrast with and support the subject well.

eye to the flower subject. Other less critical, soft-edged, and more-muted yellow and white flower parts (*at bottom and right*) offer pattern and shape repetition. Meanwhile, the large, round leaf at the bottom left visually balances the dominant weight of the composite flower sphere through shape harmony. Such background tricks and secondary shapes successfully support the subject in different ways.

As you can see in the upper image on page 119, most of the upper background is very dark yet varies in color and value. Because the butterfly/flower subject pattern is quite busy, I originally intended an open-space setting, unadorned with many distracting shapes. But leaving it that way did not completely strengthen the subject. Very dark leaves and stems added in certain places (*bottom*, page 119) did the trick. They reduce distractions by contrasting minimally in value with the background yet support the subject through shape repetition. Even careful planning needs tweaking.

Thick creamy paint contributes to rich color saturation, but in large, open, darkest spaces, more than one layer is usually necessary. The open space in *Monarch*'s dark background required about five.

Because you'll also need courage, quick thinking, lots of paint, loaded brushes of various sizes, uninterrupted time for fast brushwork, and confidence, be sure that materials are handy and you can pinpoint places to stop the wash for rest or a phone call. You'll need:

- *Courage* . . . to paint quickly and to repeat washes if necessary (an initial dark wash is rarely as saturated as it could be).
- *Quick thinking* . . . to change value and color strategically, to leave soft and defined edges here and there, to use large brushes in big spaces and small brushes in tiny, and to wet the paper in certain areas with paint or clean water.

Simple, large, dark, cool, and soft-edged background forms help emphasize the intricate, small, pale, warm, and defined subject shapes.

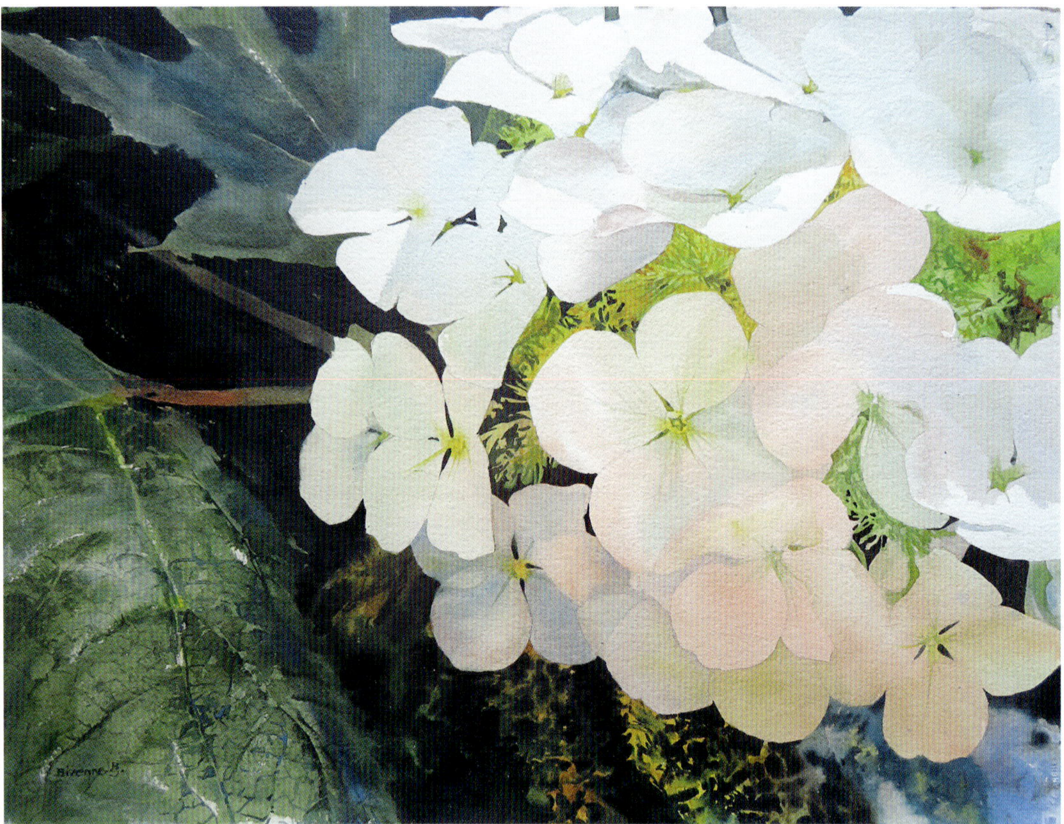

Hydrangea Shadows, 22" × 30"

- *Fast brushwork* . . . so that the bead (leading edge of wet paint) or certain parts of the paper do not dry before you can get back to them.
- *Lots of paint* . . . since there's no time to get more from the toolbox, and dark washes require copious paint.
- *Large, loaded brushes* . . . because the more that are available, the easier it is to paint quickly.
- *Uninterrupted time* . . . so that halting a large wash is ultimately unnecessary. *Any* interruption in a given layer before the entire wash is complete will hinder continuing the wash seamlessly in the same value and color (wet paint appears 30% darker than dry). *Speed is everything!*
- *Confidence* . . . in painting a large, dark space effectively.

To hide mismatched pigment at either side of a thin shape, apply new pigment in a harmonious hue to both sides, which will seem intentional.

Here are some tips:

(1) Prepare the brushes. Load at least two or more large *and* small brushes with cream-consistency paint. Make large puddles on the palette *with more paint than you think you possibly need* for each color you'll use, including combinations. Use midsized brushes to introduce new color. Set all brushes temporarily aside.

(2) Determine where you can rest. This can be at a defined shape edge or at an open area.

At a defined edge: Paint the wash (wet-on-dry) to a shape's defined edge. Carry the same color and value to the other side if the shape, such as a branch or stem, is thin. Don't let paint collect or bead up at long shape edges, or it will dry as a darker outline.

In an open area: After loading the brush, spritz

water on the paper in the "rest area" ahead or with another (clean) brush. Let the dark paint bleed into it, fading to white or very pale. Do not allow the bead to collect at the far edge of the wet area, since it will leave a defined edge there. When it's dry, paint over this lost edge with a new wash, dark enough to hide any hint of where you had stopped.

(3) Prepare the paper:

For a value change: Apply clean water with spritzer or brush where the dark wash will be paler, then immediately add paint. Don't spread the clean water too minimally or its effect on value will be imperceptible, or too far because it will pale the dark wash too much (though you can always darken more), or too soon (before brushes are loaded), since paint on damp paper might cause a bloom.

Let dark paint bleed into a soft transition on its own. This may appear just as dark or darker while wet because wet paint appears darker than dry. But the drier and more loaded the brush is, the less likely that paint will spread far on wet paper.

For a color change: It's easier to transition color from light to dark value than the reverse. For instance, apply (paler) yellow first, then very dark green. Load, then set the dark brush aside. Paint the bright, paler, or contrasting color first on dry paper with a separate brush in a *larger* space than you'll need and beyond the area you'll darken. Immediately drop the dark paint gently into the wet area's peripheral edges, using the dry-on-wet application. Don't push the dark paint too much. Letting the paint bleed into the wet (paler/brighter) color on its own prevents the first wash from disappearing and the second from appearing streaky. Don't cover the first entirely or touch the bleed further.

Both dark background value and color changes in *Hosta Bells* (*right*) and *Goldfinches in the Magnolia* (page 28) were achieved this way.

Gently soften an undesired hard edge with a damp brush and blot with a tissue.

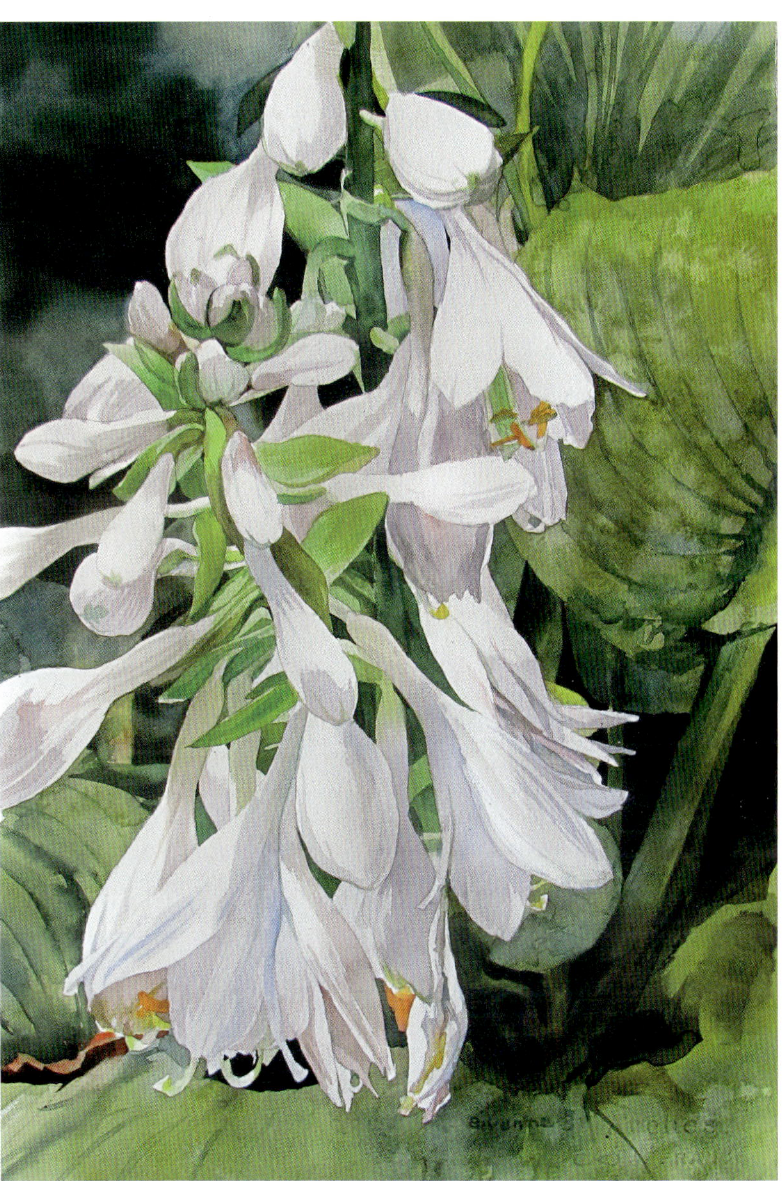

Hosta Bells, 15" × 22"

(4) Paint quickly! Start with the largest brushes in the open space. Pull the paint quickly with small brushes from open background space (where a heavy bead should be) to the smaller negative spaces around the defined subject and other object shapes. Apply paint as quickly as possible. Although accuracy is important, neatness is a little less critical than *speed* to complete the entire wash before the bead dries, and to maximize a smooth appearance. A hard edge in open space could result where none is desired.

Use brushstrokes perpendicular to long shape edges wherever and as often as possible, and carefully sop up any bead collecting there with a thirsty brush. This prevents outlines from forming around defined shapes.

Since initial dark washes often require a second or even multiple layers for full saturation and richness, imperfections such as streaks, blooms, or a value too pale at first are not a problem. In fact the first layer is rarely as dark and as smooth as it could be, though this should always be the goal. Adjust later, but *never* while the paper is damp or cool to the touch! Likewise, don't use tissue to lift troublesome spots in open spaces. Let it dry, then protect satisfactory soft-edged areas with a spritz of clean water or the same color, and simply paint another layer just as before.

Use large brushes for large shapes and small brushes for small spaces. Go back and forth quickly from heavy bead in open space to small, tighter, peripheral spaces, changing brushes according to the size of the shape being painted.

Drips, splotches, and "happy accidents" happen easily as large open spaces are painted quickly. Don't worry about them. Let the paint move on wet paper without interference wherever possible, and control it at critical defined edges on dry.

Once you're finished adding the dark-value shapes to your painting, you'll notice, I hope, that all elements now convey a strong design that's balanced, emphasizes the subject well, guides the eye around the piece via an interesting path, and sustains attention. If so, you have successfully incorporated the composition principle of unity. Tiniest details known as the artist's calligraphy often complete the painting,

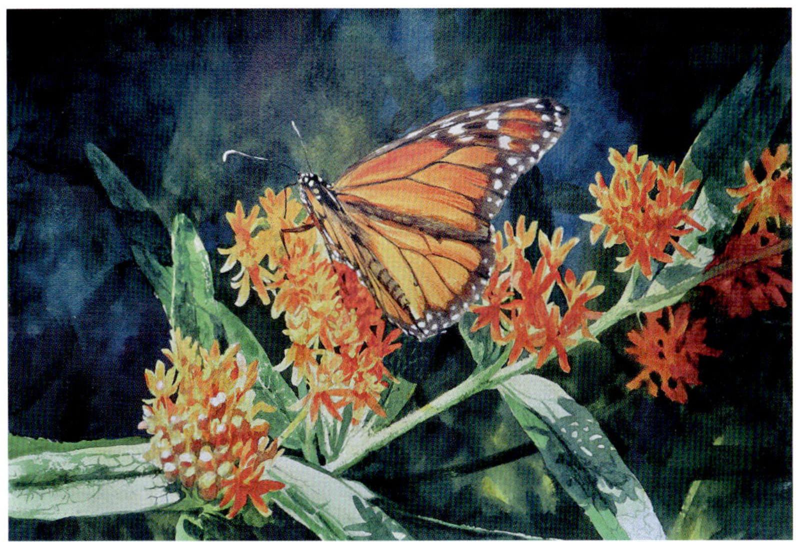

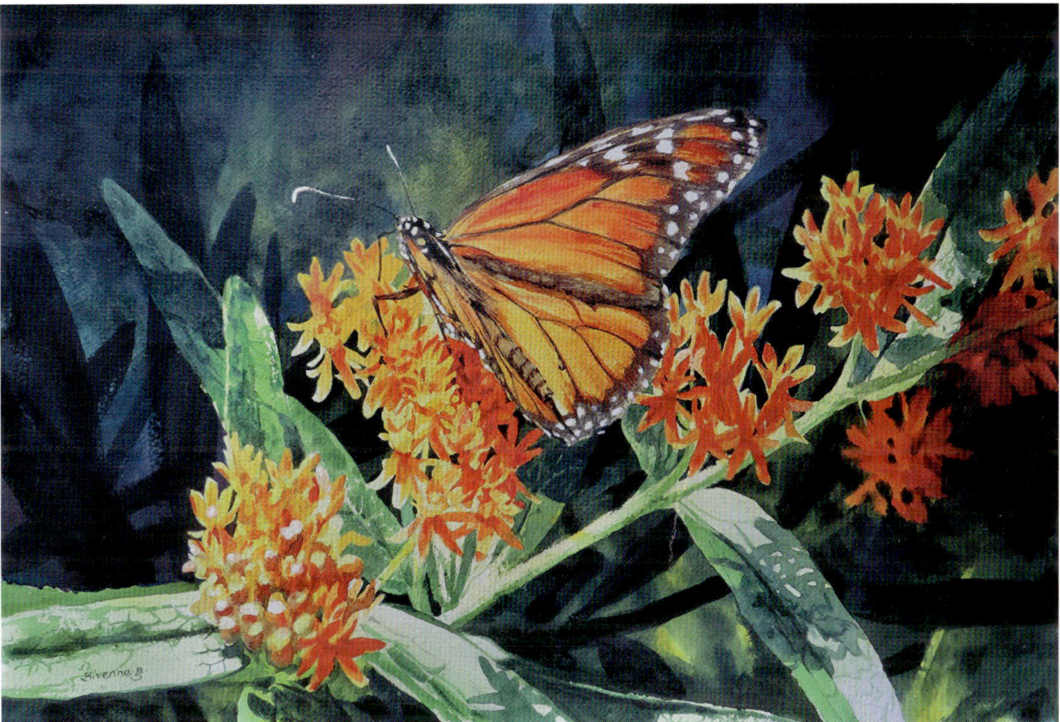

Monarch, 15" × 22"

Bottom Line:

Planning and preparation, and then building dark value gradually, using color in one temperature with increasingly more paint and less water, produce the inkiest, richest value in watercolor. Juxtaposing this extreme with brightly lit white and colorfully saturated shapes delivers strikingly dramatic results.

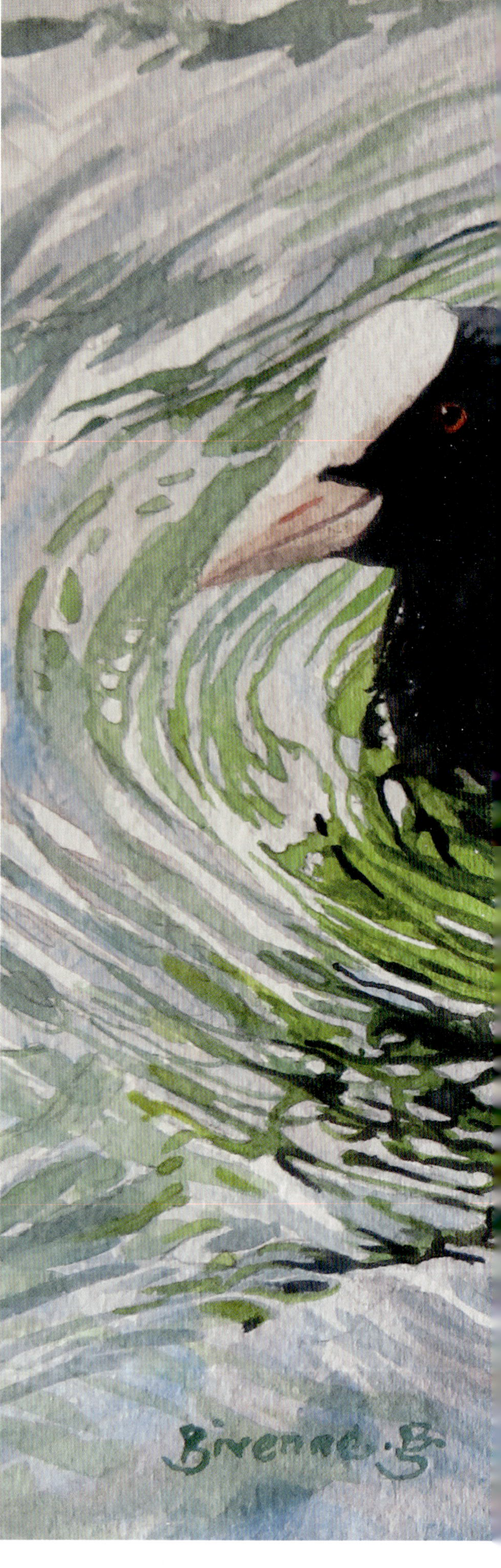

Concluding Points

The planning guidelines incorporating design principles laid out in Part 1 and the three value stages for applying watercolor paint described in Part 2 apply to almost any motif, including still life and portraiture. They also apply to landscapes, seascapes, and cityscapes, though those often have a variety of added subject options and involve incorporating additional factors such as perspective principles and tricks for conveying spatial distance and atmosphere. It is hoped that these techniques therefore open up many more painting possibilities for you.

Essentially though, whatever your motif, all paintings benefit from following composition principles and from a good drawing that assimilates both key subject and supporting background shapes and spaces. One area can't exist without the other. Each painting element separately and together affects all others in any one representation.

And for watercolor paintings, though some purists don't bother, taking time to draw the motif in proper proportion, with emphasis on some vital details and a few reinforcing shapes, is worth every effort. Remember to save illuminated white and brightly colored shapes as you

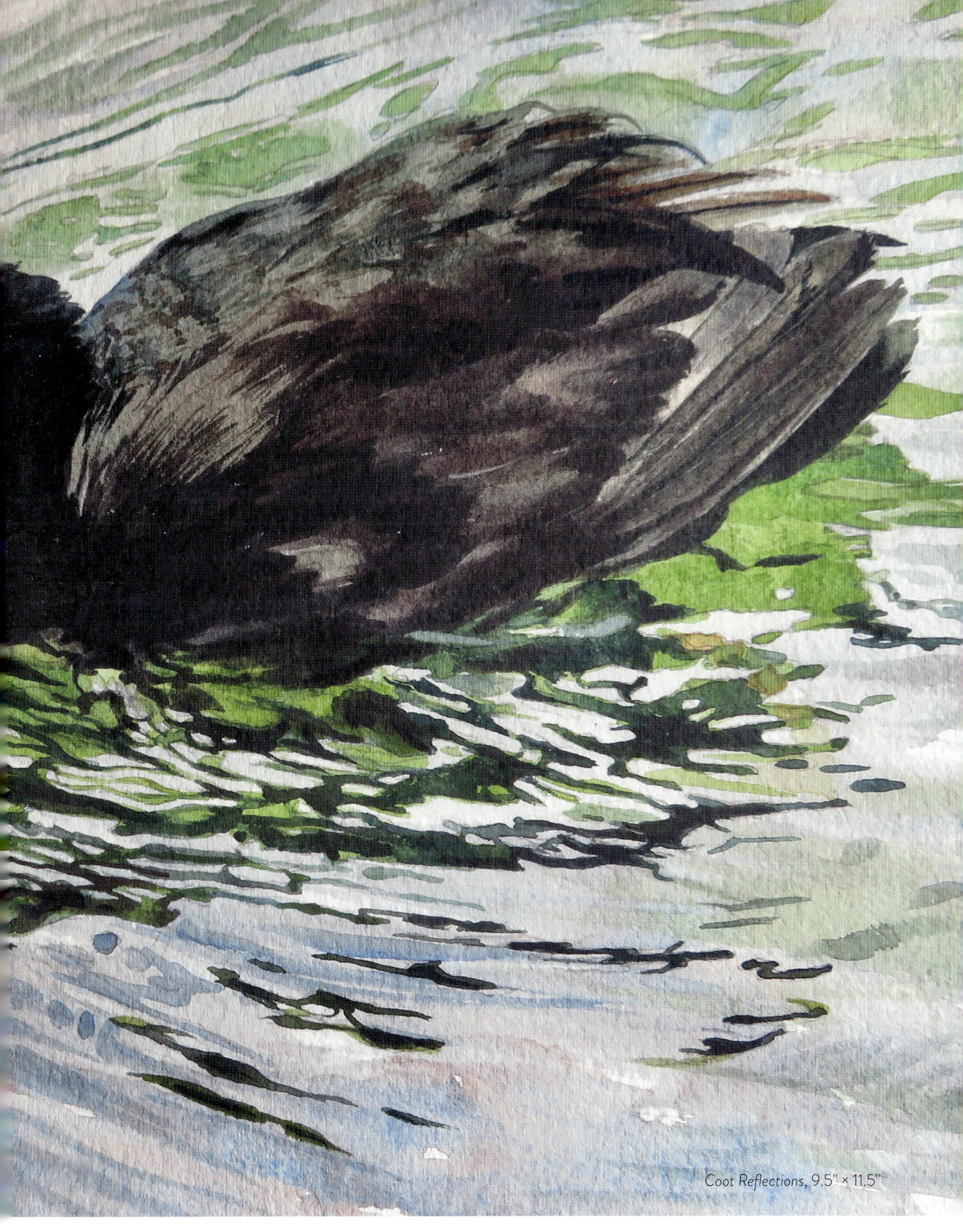

Coot Reflections, 9.5" × 11.5"

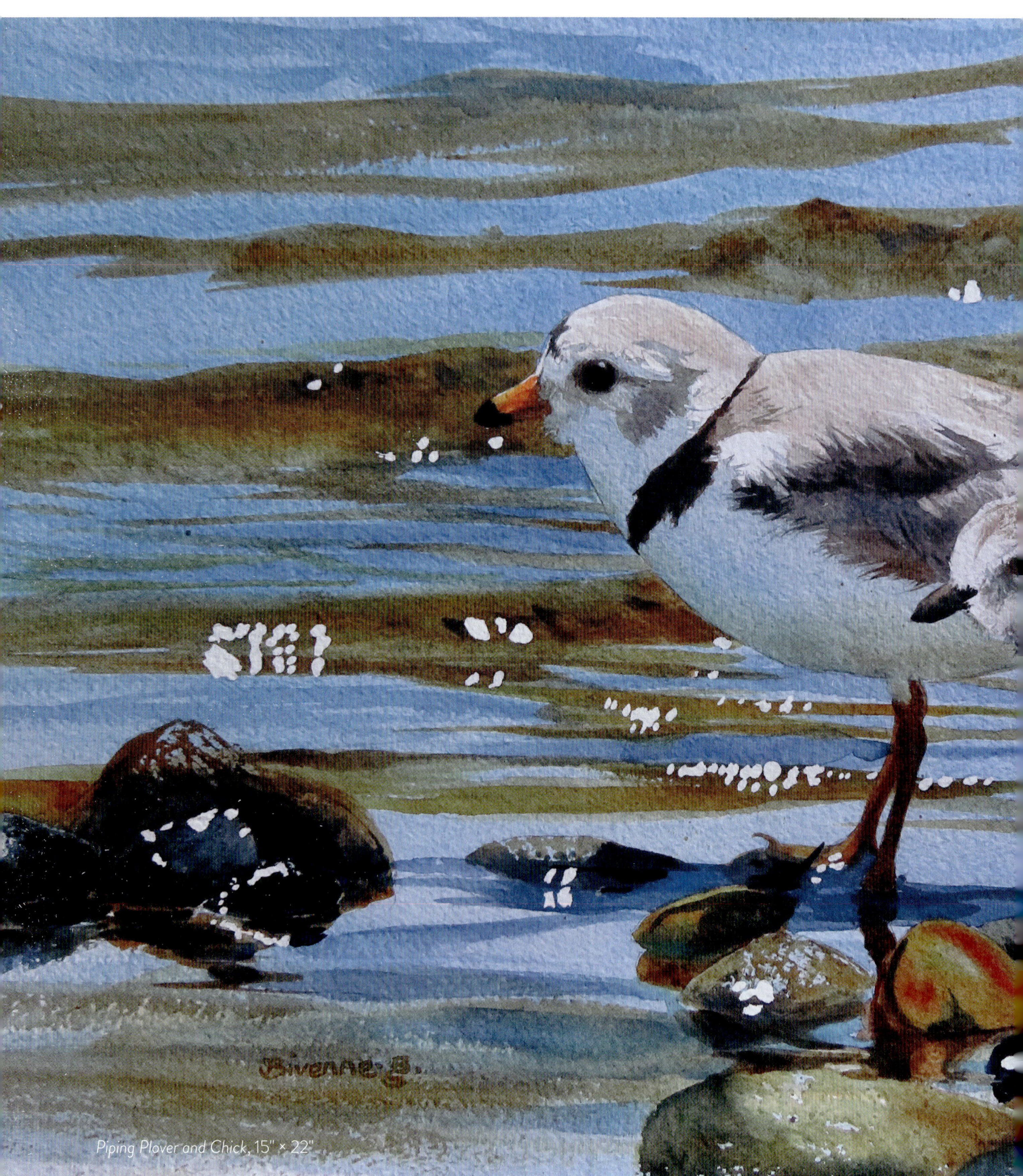
Piping Plover and Chick, 15" × 22"

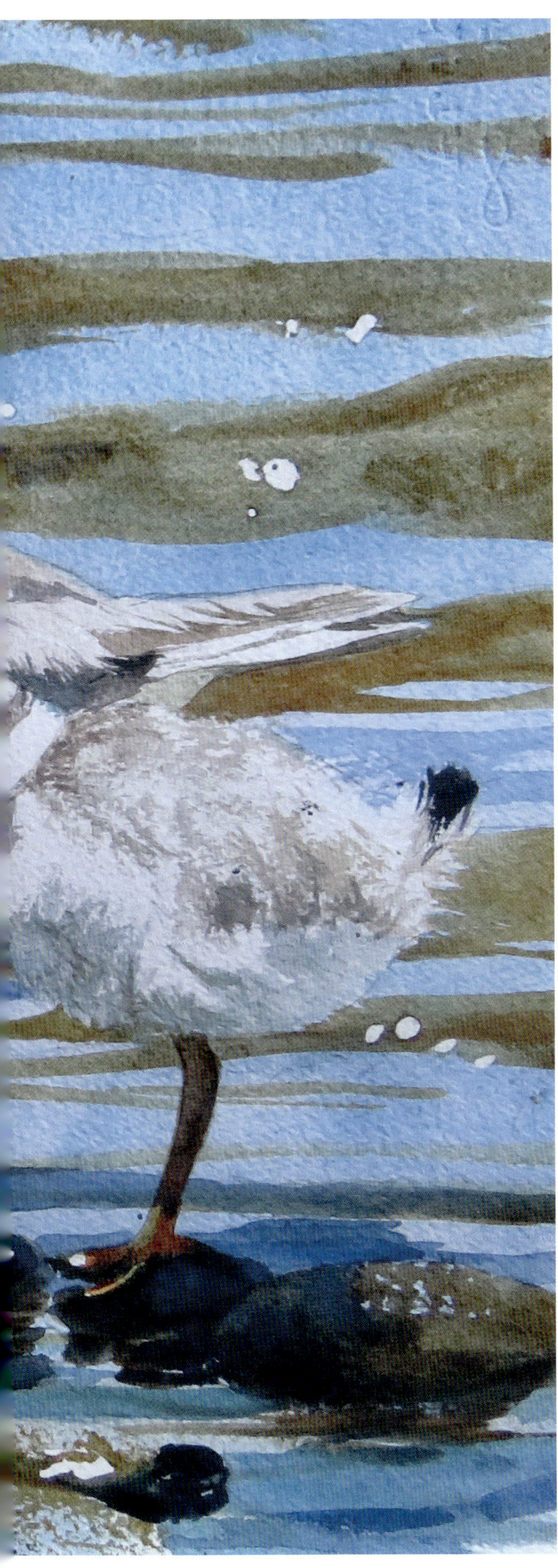

paint because they suggest lighting, which, together with shadows and extreme darks, conveys form and enhances color.

Don't forget to paint pale washes in bright, harmonious color across shape edges of both subject and background early and wherever possible, and, since this is unique to watercolor, frequently let paint seep across shape edges and commingle with other colors on wet paper. Leave some soft edges visible for some mystery and intrigue.

These fundamental guidelines make it possible to paint almost anything successfully in watercolor. It is a medium so wonderful, versatile, forgiving, and fun, and I hope that it will bring you, as it does me, endless joy.

Addendum

Fixing Painting Problems

While mistakes in *composition* are difficult if not impossible to fix once painted, almost all *painting* errors can be overcome! Imperfections are common, so expect and accept them, but sometimes they're distracting and thus undesirable. Since wet or damp paint is easier than dry to lift, pick it up with tissue or a thirsty brush as you work. Use more pressure on dry paper, then blot with tissue. Repeat as often as necessary.

Soften or pick up small amounts of paint with a finger, brush, or Q-tip. A wet sponge removes huge swaths.

Lift paint from bone-dry paper with sandpaper or a knife's sharp blade, but only when the painting is otherwise complete, since both mar the paper's surface.

As a last resort, hold the painting under running water and scrub gently, or paint over it with opaque acrylic or gouache.

All of this is very freeing.

Removing blooms: Known as watermarks and caused by water or paint dripped on *damp painted paper* that's lost its sheen, blooms create pale splotches with darker outlines, more apparent as they dry. Try to accept and love them! If these are unintended as texture, here are some removal options:

(1) After drying, hide with darker paint.

(2) Remove immediately if possible: *Quickly* cover the entire wet, painted space beyond it with lots of water and a large brush. Add a bit more pressure to lift the bloom's ring as you cover the space. This lightens the value, but let it dry, and paint again. If the paper is already *damp*, STOP. Let it dry completely and try the next option.

(3) This is a tricky repair. Lift the bloom and ring; let the paper dry. The area will be paler. Load a brush with a *slightly darker* value of the same wash and set it aside. *Carefully* add clean water about an inch or more beyond the now-paler, dry bloom (like a donut) covering the surrounding (dry) paint. Leave the blotted bloom dry for the moment. Now apply the darker "fix-it" wash only to the dry bloom area, just enough so wet paint bleeds into the clean wet wash. *Don't let the dark "fix-it" paint reach the outside edge of clean "donut" water surrounding it!* It will appear darker than the surrounding until dry. Hope for the best; it should dry equal in value to the original wash.

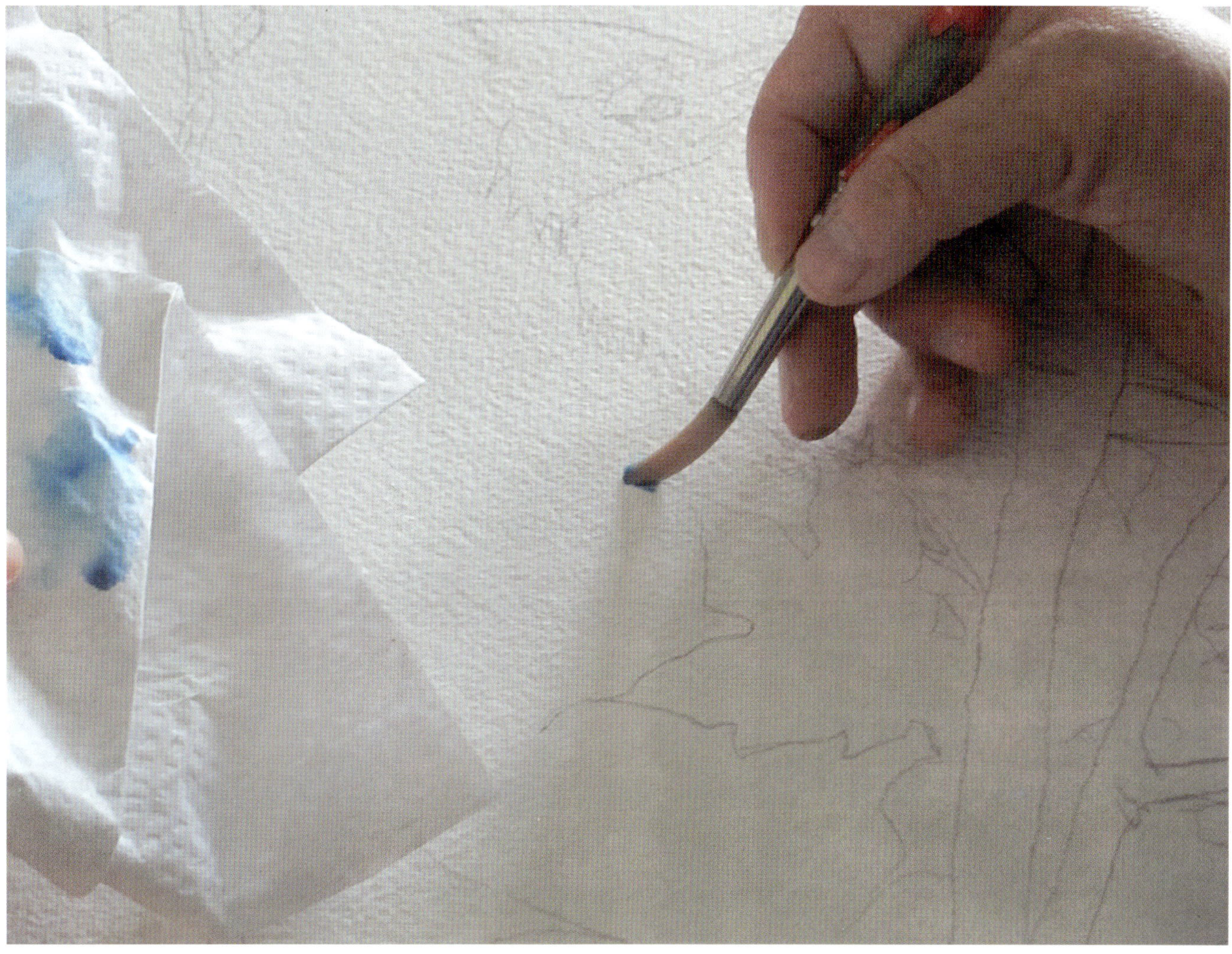

(4) Also tricky, this repair requires maintenance. While the paper is drying, absorb only the bloom's excess water *carefully and gently* with a bit of tissue. Meanwhile, carefully lift its dark edge with a damp/dry brush. The objective is to equalize the amount of water in the bloom with its surrounding wash while also removing the ring. Don't apply excess pressure. Keep a sharp eye on it so that surrounding paint doesn't creep back. Sometimes this is all you need to do; other times, this makes matters worse, creating new streaks on damp paper or lightening the spot's value too much. If this doesn't work or you've made it worse, go back to options 1, 2, or 3.

(5) Lift just the thin line of dark paint at the dry bloom's edge with a damp tool, as suggested above, gently blotting only that thin ring. A staining color will require more lifting or scrubbing. Again, the interior may be paler than the surrounding wash, so refer to options 1, 2, or 3 for different ways to reapply paint.

"My painting is too muddy!" A grayed painting is easier to avoid than fix: Drop clean, bright color dry-on-wet onto the paper, maintain shapes of value extremes, and do not thoroughly mix two or more bright harmonious or opposite colors into homogenous puddles. While paint dries, don't help it along. All cause the problem.

Start rescuing the entire painting by lifting any painted *illuminated* shapes and let them dry. Either leave them white or repaint them with high-chroma transparent color in a paler wash. Add more high-chroma color to midvalue sections. Then repaint sections that should be darker. Or start over, using techniques described in this book.

"My painting is too streaky and overworked." Caused by painting too slowly, with brushes too small or too dry over large expanses of dry paper, or with a flat brush's thin (not widest) edge, this is easier to avoid than fix, so:

Prepare ahead with plenty of paint in the wells and loaded large (and small) brushes. Use the widest part of largest brushes for large shapes and small brushes for smallest shapes. If you lack large brushes, use a sponge loaded with paint, squeezing the paint as you pull it across. Paint very fast!

If streakiness happens despite all, *stop* the wash where it is, and fade it out by blending with clean water. Let it dry completely. Then start properly again by painting over the streaks with wetter brushes, more paint, perhaps wet paper, and more brush pressure at the streaks. Fading the wash out first makes these later adjustments easier.

"There's an outline around shape edges." Lift the outlines. Don't paint the negative space of another shape's edges entirely with the same color and value. Instead, employ perpendicular strokes and change color and value here and there ever so slightly. Don't allow paint to bead up at the edges.

"My greens seem artificial." Unfortunately, there is little that can be done except to wash them out and then repaint with better choices. See page 53, "Mixing Greens."

"My painting doesn't flow." Likely from too many defined edges and not allowing paint to bleed on wet paper, more soft edges will fix the problem. Bravely cover at least half of *un*important defined edges with a large brush, sponge, or a spritzer and clean water. Gently lift irrelevant edges. Some dry paint will bleed. Quickly cover with another wash of cream-consistency paint, *wet-on-wet* or *dry-on-wet*, if too much paint has been lifted away. Let the paper dry. This remedy might also appear to have ruined your painting. Don't worry: Anything of *key* interest that lost its edge contrast in this fix can be repainted when the paper is again dry. Be sure to save white and new soft-edged areas!

"My paper is warped!" Using thin, low-quality paper, letting water puddle up on it, and not drying both sides of the paper are usually the cause. Heavier-weight paper makes a difference, but don't tack it to a board or table. Bend the paper gently in the opposite direction as needed, or iron the back with care when it's completely dry.

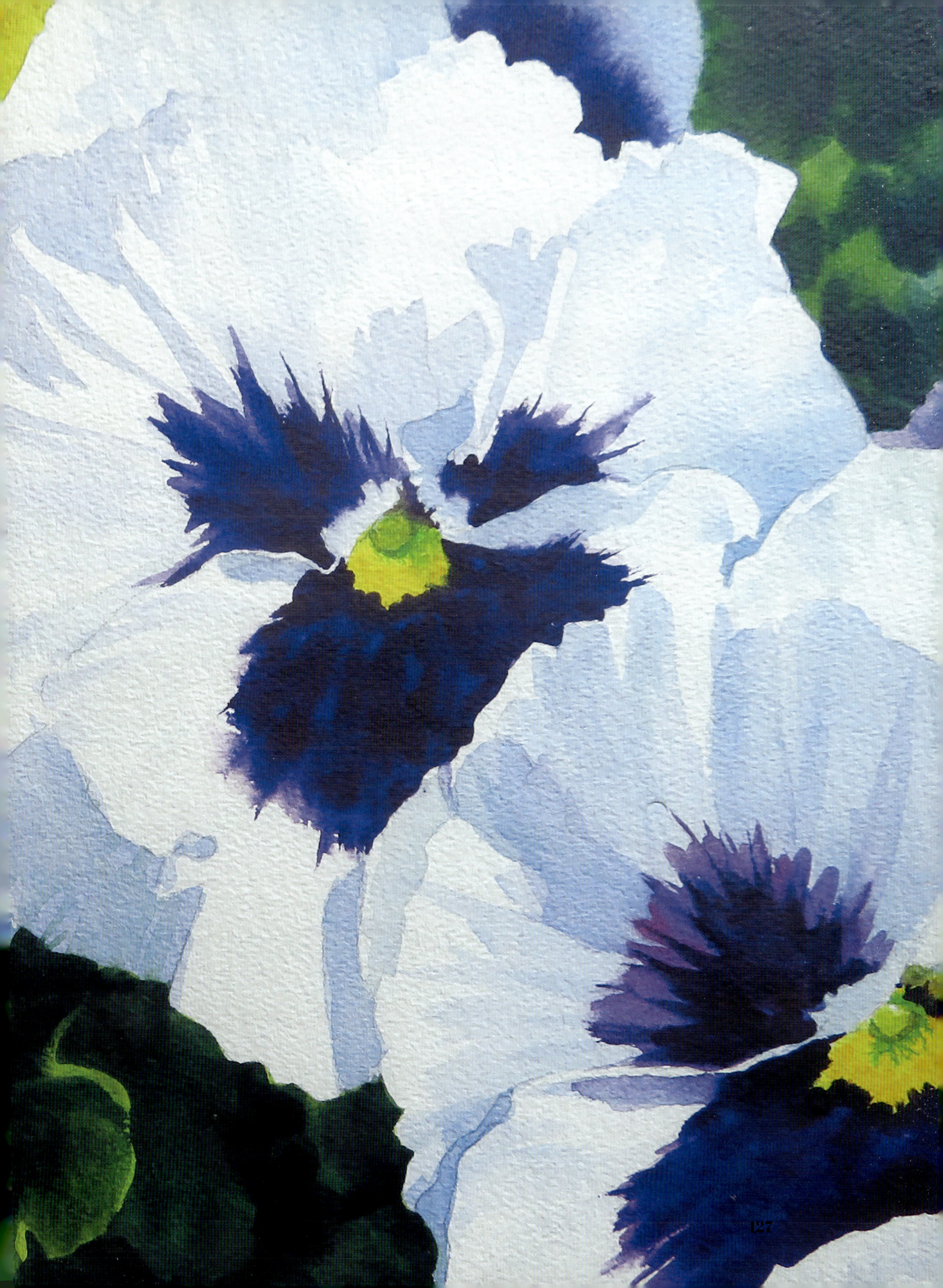

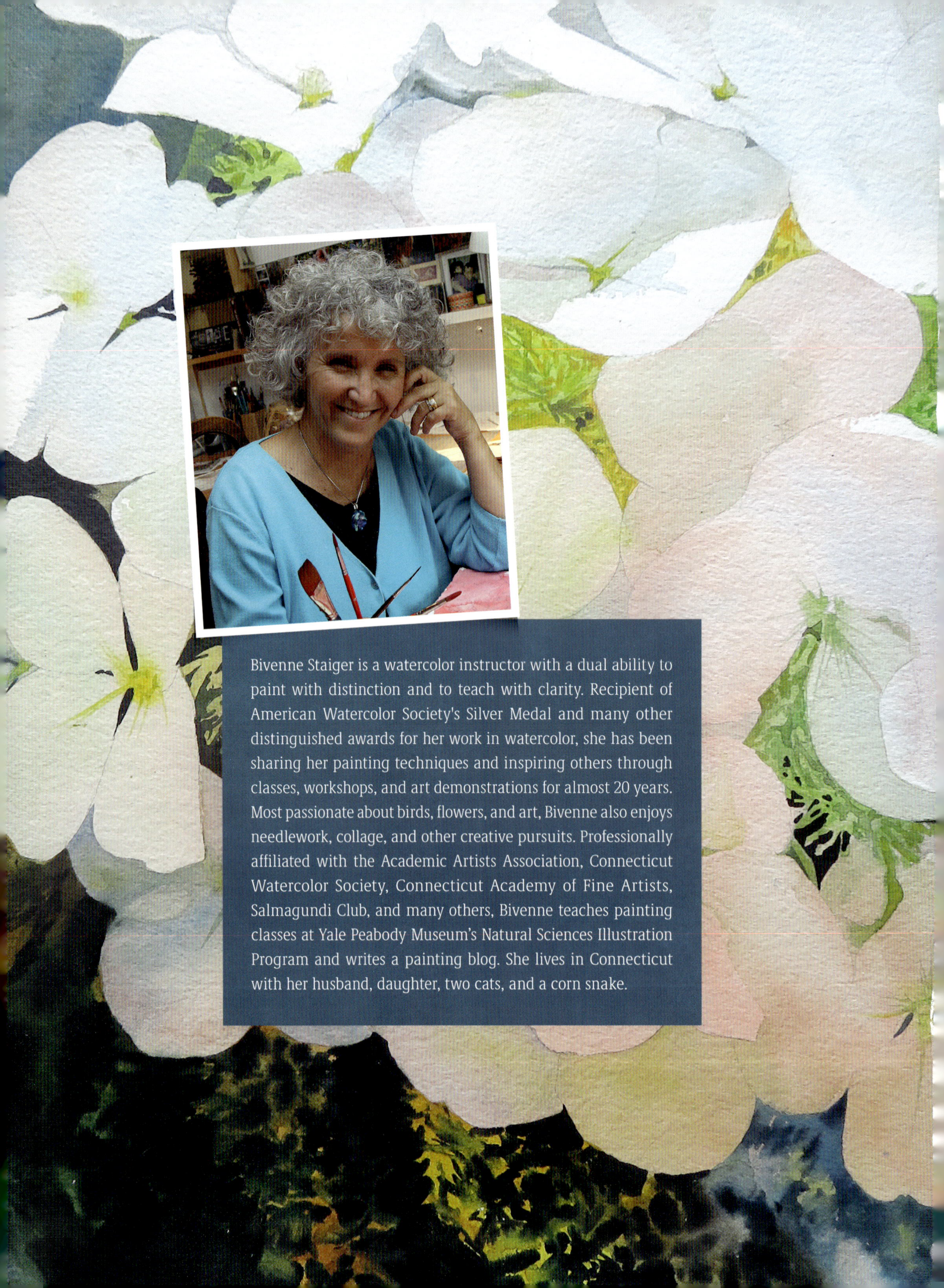

Bivenne Staiger is a watercolor instructor with a dual ability to paint with distinction and to teach with clarity. Recipient of American Watercolor Society's Silver Medal and many other distinguished awards for her work in watercolor, she has been sharing her painting techniques and inspiring others through classes, workshops, and art demonstrations for almost 20 years. Most passionate about birds, flowers, and art, Bivenne also enjoys needlework, collage, and other creative pursuits. Professionally affiliated with the Academic Artists Association, Connecticut Watercolor Society, Connecticut Academy of Fine Artists, Salmagundi Club, and many others, Bivenne teaches painting classes at Yale Peabody Museum's Natural Sciences Illustration Program and writes a painting blog. She lives in Connecticut with her husband, daughter, two cats, and a corn snake.